ALSO BY THOMAS H. TAYLOR

NONFICTION

RANGERS, LEAD THE WAY

LIGHTNING IN THE STORM

WHERE THE ORANGE BLOOMS

FICTION

A-18

A PIECE OF THIS COUNTRY

BORN OF WAR

THE SIMPLE SOUNDS OF FREEDOM

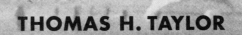

THOMAS H. TAYLOR

RANDOM HOUSE NEW YORK

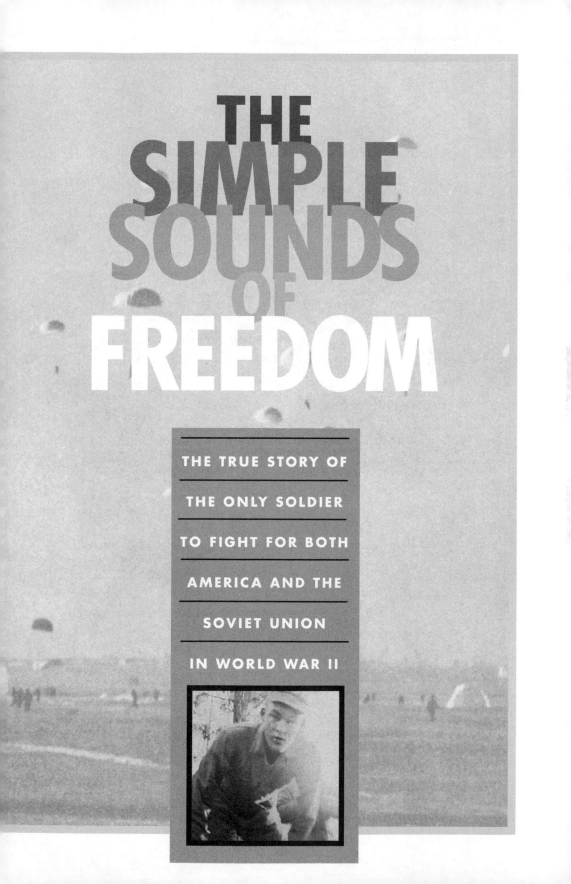

THE SIMPLE SOUNDS OF FREEDOM

THE TRUE STORY OF

THE ONLY SOLDIER

TO FIGHT FOR BOTH

AMERICA AND THE

SOVIET UNION

IN WORLD WAR II

All rights reserved under International and Pan-American Copyright
Conventions. Published in the United States by Random House, Inc.,
New York, and simultaneously in Canada by Random House of
Canada Limited, Toronto.

Random House and colophon are registered trademarks
of Random House, Inc.

Grateful acknowledgment is made to Harcourt, Inc., for permission
to reprint excerpts from "Hatred" from *View with a Grain of Sand,*
copyright © 1993 by Wisława Szymborska, English translation by
Stanisław Barańczak and Clare Cavanagh copyright © 1995 by Harcourt, Inc.
Reprinted by permission of the publisher.

Library of Congress Cataloging-in-Publication Data is available.

Printed in the United States of America on acid-free paper
Random House website address: www.atrandom.com

2   4   6   8   9   7   5   3

FIRST EDITION

Book design by Barbara M. Bachman

In June 1994, on the fiftieth anniversary of D Day,

President Clinton looked out on the American Cemetery

at Colleville-sur-Mer in Normandy and

spoke these dedicatory words:

THESE ARE THE MEN WHO GAVE US OUR WORLD.

THE SIMPLE SOUNDS OF FREEDOM WE HEAR TODAY

ARE THEIR VOICES SPEAKING TO US

ACROSS THE YEARS.

ACKNOWLEDGMENTS

FOR CHAPTERS DESCRIBING COMBAT IN WHICH JOE WAS NOT IN-volved, I'm indebted to Ed Albers and Mark Bando, the latter author of *The 101st Airborne from Holland to Hitler's Eagle's Nest* (Motorbooks International), from which the stories about Charles Eckman and Ross Goethe were derived. For maps I've relied on *Rendezvous with Destiny,* an eight-hundred-page hardback published by the 101st Airborne Division Association.

Phil Wallace published his pre–D Night letter to his wife through the association's quarterly, *The Screaming Eagle,* from which Dutchman Robert Postman's remembrance of September 17 was also taken. The most senior 101st officers of World War II, still living, are Harry Kinnard and Julian Ewell, both retired lieutenant generals, lieutenant colonels at Bastogne. They graciously provided me elucidating insights about the realities during that epic siege.

Then of course there was my father, whom I plied for 101st lore when I became a Screaming Eagle veteran after Vietnam. He died in 1987. For the many honors and titles he received, including command of all United Nations forces in Korea and the chairmanship of the Joint Chiefs of Staff, the only emblem he directed to be engraved on his headstone was the Screaming Eagle.

Good fortune for me was doubled when Owen Laster of the William Morris Agency offered this manuscript to Bob Loomis of Random House. Their combined appreciation of Joe's singular place in the American experience of World War II was invaluable.

Any author's spouse must be gratefully acknowledged for patience, support, and understanding. No less so for me, as I grappled to put in words what was sometimes too much for words. So, as is her due, I give the last word to Pam. Joe, in turn, is indebted to his wife, JoAnne, and I am too for her unique ability to decipher and transcribe Joe's handwriting.

CONTENTS

Joe Beyrle's War, 1943–45

1 *Liverpool*—Arrives on September 17, 1943. Trains with Third Battalion around Ramsbury through the spring of 1944.

2 *Alençon*—Two solo parachute jumps to support French resistance forces near Alençon in April and May 1944.

3 *St. Côme-du-Mont*—Captured, escapes, recaptured in June north of Carentan.

4 *Paris*—As a POW, paraded by the Nazis in August, then shipped by rail to Stalag *XII-A.* His train is strafed enroute with great loss of life among the POWs.

5 Sent to Stalag *IV-B,* then on September 17, 1944, to *III-C,* in what was formerly Poland.

6 In October, escapes from III-C but is recaptured in *Berlin,* where the Wehrmacht saves him from the Gestapo.

7 In January 1945, escapes east and joins a Soviet armor force that liberates III-C.

8 Badly wounded near the Oder River; evacuated by the Soviets to *Landsberg,* where he goes AWOL from Soviet hospital.

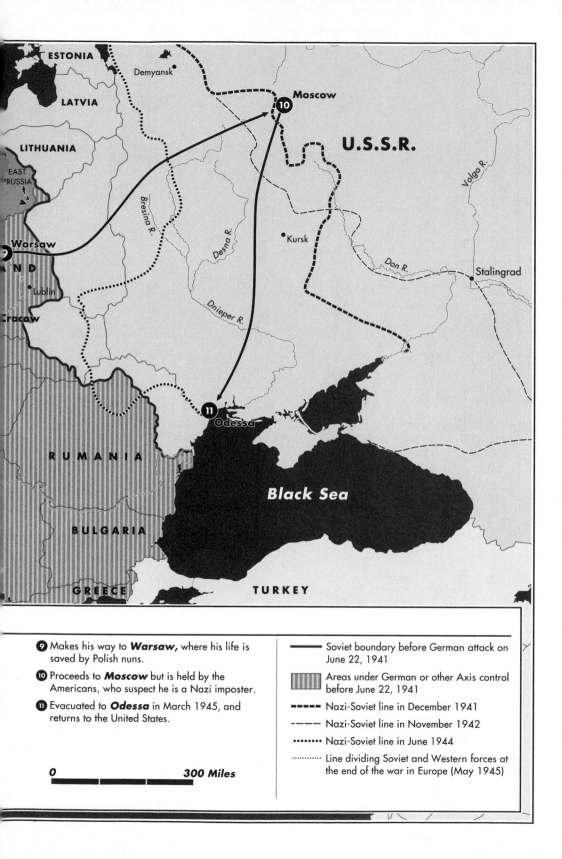

ESTONIA

Demyansk

LATVIA

LITHUANIA

EAST
PRUSSIA

U.S.S.R.

Volga R.

Bresina R.

Desna R.

Kursk

Don R.

Stalingrad

Warsaw

Lublin

Cracow

Dnieper R.

Odessa

RUMANIA

Black Sea

BULGARIA

GREECE

TURKEY

9 Makes his way to **Warsaw,** where his life is saved by Polish nuns.

10 Proceeds to **Moscow** but is held by the Americans, who suspect he is a Nazi imposter.

11 Evacuated to **Odessa** in March 1945, and returns to the United States.

———— Soviet boundary before German attack on June 22, 1941

▨ Areas under German or other Axis control before June 22, 1941

------ Nazi-Soviet line in December 1941

– – – Nazi-Soviet line in November 1942

•••••••• Nazi-Soviet line in June 1944

············ Line dividing Soviet and Western forces at the end of the war in Europe (May 1945)

0   300 Miles

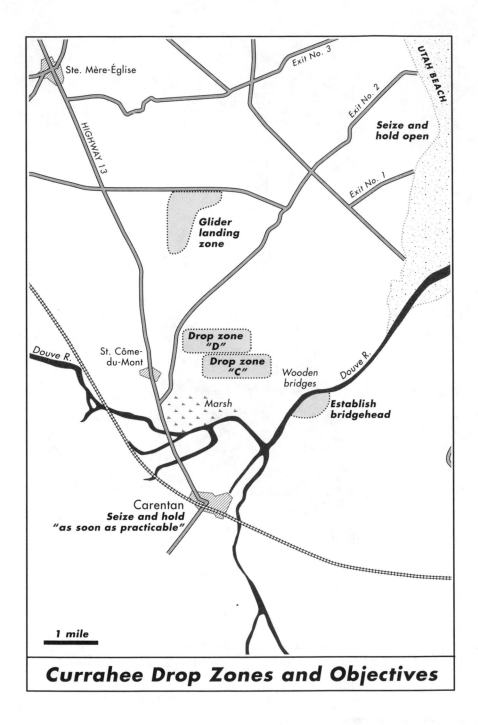

Currahee Drop Zones and Objectives

WORLD WAR II REUNIONS ARE SMALLER, THE VETERANS ALARM-
ingly fewer as actuarial predictions become morbidity statistics. The
101st Airborne Division holds its reunions at different locations each
year in August, the month of the division's birth in 1942. These veterans are the Screaming Eagles, and their casualties to age are said to have
"soared." I'm a second-generation Screaming Eagle—my father commanded the division during World War II and I fought with it during
Vietnam—so naturally my interest in the 101st is intense, so much so
that I wrote a history of its campaigns in the Gulf War and a biography
of the longest-serving Screaming Eagle in Vietnam.

I continued to browse reunions in search of a remarkable war story,
especially from the Big One: "Let me hear from you old guys before you
soar!" I'd say. Despite this urging the response most often was bemusement from a septuagenarian as he studied his shoes. He wasn't ready
to relive that war and never would be; or he deflected the thought with
an increasingly popular laugh line: "The older we get the better we
were!"

Eventually the vets began mentioning Joe Beyrle (pronounced "buy
early"). Did I know he had fought longer with the Soviet army than with
the American? No one, to my knowledge, had even fought with both.
We were introduced at a snowbird reunion in Kissimmee, Florida.

It didn't take a long interview with Joe to realize that his is one of the
most extraordinary American adventures of World War II. A true story,
beyond doubt in all matters of importance, with only small indulgence
needed for accuracy of times and places. There is corroborating evidence
from other POWs; where there is not, Joe's modesty speaks for his ve-
racity. Diaries and journals in POW camps were of course forbidden by
the Germans, and any attempts to keep such records were punished and
noted in a prisoner's file. Ironically, Joe was able to capture those records
from his former captors.

In relating his story my most difficult contemplation was perspective. What was predominant, what was key in his experience? Luck and its fickleness seemed the theme. Was Joe's luck ultimately good or bad?

Good! He is not just alive—after his burial—but leading a satisfying life. His health concerns are more reminders of that than pain from the past, even though they carry dire medical labels like beriberi, amoebic dysentery, frostbite, skull fracture, and multiple wounds. Survivor's guilt, usually a major ingredient in the psyche of ex-POWs, is no evident part of Joe.

In Normandy on the fiftieth anniversary of D Day, Jack Smith of ABC asked Joe why he allowed himself to be captured. A flicker of reflection revealed a half century of mulling that question. "Preservation" was his answer. Preserving life, at least temporarily, made better odds than dodging submachine-gun bullets fired from six feet away. So stark a choice cannot be second-guessed even in light of its consequences.

From that inevitable choice concatenated unimagined misery. A fellow POW said that those who saved their lives lost their ego—a salutary exchange if ego is the root of all evil. But ego is also the stem of individuality. Joe survived as an individual, with an individual outlook, individual obstinacy, individual daring, and individual faith. That personality, plus inordinate luck he pushed beyond reasonable limits, got him through situations that killed all of his closest buddies.

He is an exemplar of what Tom Brokaw has called the Greatest Generation. Joe's thoughts of that generation are not his focus today; instead it is his family, the rising generation, his children, their families. He would not dedicate this book to anyone in particular but approved the dedication in the World War II yearbook of the 101st Airborne: "To the memory of our buddies, living and dead, the many rich and varied experiences we shared; and to hope that we may, in some measure, abide by and help to preserve the way of life for which we went to war."

No veteran more deserves the way of life Joe now enjoys. This book is a way of paying last respects to him and those like him who gave us our world.

Thomas H. Taylor

A NOTE ON MILITARY ORGANIZATIONS

AT THE BEGINNING OF JUNE 1944, THE 101ST AIRBORNE DIVIsion numbered about 14,000 soldiers. As one of four infantry regiments in the 101st, the 506th Parachute Infantry Regiment had an initial strength of about 2,500 paratroopers, divided into three battalions of equal size, each with three rifle companies of about 200 men.

German divisional strength varied widely throughout the war. In Normandy the Screaming Eagles were opposed by the big 709th Division (14,000 coastal defense troops) and the 243rd Division, which was half that size. Dreaded panzer divisions rarely fought with their full complement of 160 tanks.

Russian divisions were even smaller than German, and were replaced by whole new divisions when they took heavy casualties. Joe guesses that the Russian tank battalion he fought with numbered about 400 men and women, not quite twice the number of his American company.

THE SIMPLE SOUNDS OF FREEDOM

CHAPTER ONE

THE EUROPEAN THEATER OF OPERATIONS

IN THE SUMMER OF 1943 U-BOATS TOOK A HEAVY TOLL OF ALLIED shipping, so the 101st Airborne Division would be in peril and out of their element while crossing the Atlantic, but at least the enlisted men now knew their destination: northern Europe, to open a second front against Nazi Germany. That basic mission had been concealed till they reached Camp Shanks, thirty miles upriver from New York City, the division's staging area for embarkation. They'd had to remove the Screaming Eagle shoulder patch and wear regular GI shoes instead of the distinctive paratrooper jump boots, their pride and talisman. An officer tried to explain the reason: "The Axis has to be kept guessing."

German spies were thought to have infested New York City, and it was a strategic secret that the 101st would be committed against Hitler rather than Hirohito. Initial betting had been otherwise. It had been the Japanese who attacked Pearl Harbor; Germany declared war on the United States four days later, the only time in World War II they bothered with such a formality.

The stay at Camp Shanks was only long enough for inoculations and inspections before it was time to go, time for "the arsenal of democracy," as Churchill called America, to push another seven thousand soldiers across the sea to join the Allied counteroffensive that had already reconquered North Africa and knocked Mussolini's Italy out of the war. Feeling like lemmings, Screaming Eagles jammed onto Hudson River ferries, which converged on a pair of troopships at Manhattan's piers. At one was the great French liner the *Normandie,* gutted and blackened by fire. The name meant nothing to most paratroopers, for they'd yet to learn where Normandy was.

Awaiting Joe Beyrle was the HMS *Samaria*, decrepit and sooty, hardly resembling the cruise ship she had been for the Cunard line. His squad, within an endless walking serpentine, shouldered ponderous duffel bags as they staggered up the gangplank, then descended to search for space below the waterline. They would sleep there in eight-hour, "hot hammock" shifts, as the number of soldiers embarking was more than twice the capacity of the ship. They were accustomed to the tubular constriction of an airplane, but the *Samaria*'s massive gray perpendiculars were alien and intimidating. Soon they returned to deck, uncharacteristically subdued, some mumbling about the previous night's send-off by New York girls when they had been allowed a last pass to the city, but for most it was time to just lean on the rail, look down on dockside, take it all in, and think.

Joe thought mostly about the last year, how he had come so far from Muskegon, the pleasant town of his childhood on the east shore of Lake Michigan. From Kalamazoo's induction center the army had swept Joe away to Georgia, eventually to march him across the state like one of General Sherman's infantrymen. He was an infantryman, a bullet launcher, but also trained as a radio operator with a subspecialty in demolitions. He spent a few weeks in Panama, then moved on to North Carolina, Tennessee, and Kentucky for large-scale maneuvers, then back to North Carolina again and finally to bleak Camp Shanks. There had been so much travel and training, so much of the school of the soldier, that homesickness had become a memory like an adolescent disease.

With straining hawsers, a cluster of small tugs gathered around the *Samaria* to tow her from the pier. On the waterfront men in suits stopped to watch a ritual that over the previous year had been so often repeated but was never routine, that of soldiers crammed afloat setting off to war, an army going to sea. Some civilians waved slowly with their hats, igniting a response on board. Under steam, the *Samaria* made way by the Statue of Liberty, passing a ferry whose deck began to undulate with waving passengers, a further sign that the USA was behind them in support, as it soon would be in distance.

With Sandy Hook still abeam, the troopers were issued life vests to be worn at all times except in hammocks. It was also time to go below; no cigarettes were allowed on deck as a total blackout went into effect while the ship's engines slowly thumped en route to join a convoy forming off Long Island. Dusk settled into a darkly rising mist as if America were receding into the past.

The past was the civilian world, what it had been for soldiers who were wrested from it, what it had made of them. In June 1942 Joe graduated from Saint Joseph High School with twelve other seniors, who voted him Best Informed, Most Obvious Temper, Class Shark, and Best Dressed. That last title may have been awarded by sarcasm because he owned but one threadbare suit and was color-blind, likely to wear mismatched socks unless his mother noticed. Fortunately she did before the graduation prom held at the Muskegon Women's Club, chaperoned by nuns. Music was on records, nothing but waltzes and two-steps—jitterbugging was considered too controversial for a Catholic-school dance.

A shark meant an opportunist, and Joe was that. In the Depression, opportunity for him included sweeping out a barbershop for pocket change or fighting for choice discards from a grocery store. Such rummaging became his talent after "standing in line with my brothers, for nine family members, waiting to receive surplus government handouts. At the age of twelve that hit me like a blacksmith's hammer."

From then on opportunity meant an escape from ignominy. That's what the army provided him more than anything else.

As smokers left the *Samaria*'s decks there was enough room for Joe and his two best buddies, Jack Bray and Orv Vanderpool, to wedge together on the rail, their life vests pressing one another like adjoining cocoons. No doubt there was something Sergeant Duber wanted them to do, but he would have to find them in the darkness among unidentifiable pods of whispering troopers. Vanderpool, a laconic Californian, kept glancing over his shoulder, while Bray had to be muted lest Duber detect his Cajun accent. He was nostalgic, most immediately for last night in New York, secondly for his hometown of New Orleans. It seemed probable now that the 101st would be visiting France, where Bray looked forward to using his French connection.

Soon troopers from the "first seating"—a euphemism from the

Samaria's cruise-ship history—surged on deck grumbling and still hungry after their first meal of fish that tasted like it had been pickled during World War I. What went with the fish smelled worse; the oily stench so pervaded the ship's interior that the first seating brought their blankets on deck. Advice for the second seating was break out your K rations, as those tasteless bricks would be the best food for the next couple of weeks.

The first week at sea was one of sullen nervousness, with officers seething against the inability to exercise, except for calisthenics, and train, except for target practice at crates thrown overboard. They saw their men as Olympic athletes at the peak of fitness, losing their edge during the listless transit to venue. Preparation for combat had emphasized how scattered they would be after their parachutes drifted apart; now the troopers were suffocatingly crammed together. There had been a cadence chant when they'd run in formation back at Fort Bragg: "GI beans and GI gravy. Gee, I wish I'd joined the navy." No such envy anymore.

Nevertheless, the 101st was in the war now while not yet into it. U-boat alerts put the convoy into zigzagging maneuvers. Day and night, like overworked sheepdogs, destroyers wove between the lumbering transports. One of them developed engine trouble and turned back for Newfoundland with a regiment of paratroopers aboard. Watching ships change position was one of the few things for men to do, but the main relief from idleness was interminable gambling as the weather cooled over iron-gray seas that rocked so slightly that dice rolled true when bouncing off bulkheads. As constant as the thumping of the ship's engines was the clickety-clack of crapshooters wherever three or more could huddle.

They themselves were chips in the greatest gamble taken by the U.S. Army to date, that of creating airborne forces made up of paratroopers and glider riders. In 1940 General George C. Marshall had been stunned by the success of German paratroopers in capturing the island of Crete from a larger force of first-rate Commonwealth troops. German losses were so high that Hitler, hardly the type to count his dead, never again attempted a large-scale airborne operation. Nor did Stalin, for whom loss of life meant even less, though he produced more such units.

While the dictators saw only prospects of airborne disasters, Marshall would not let fear distract him from high hopes. During construction of the Pentagon he sent his planning staff a quote from prescient Benjamin Franklin: "Where is the prince who could so afford to cover his country with troops for its defense as that 10,000 men descending from the clouds might not in many places do an infinite deal of mischief?"

Marshall was a man of great humanity—author of the postwar plan that saved Western Europe—and the army's all-time greatest chief of staff. He was also godfather of the American Airborne, convinced like Franklin that "vertical invasion," as the press would call it, offered too much potential to be rejected because of anticipated casualties. Marshall set the minds of two of his best and brightest generals, Omar Bradley and Matthew Ridgway, to the task of creating a satisfactory trade-off between losing soldiers and taking the enemy's from the rear.

The result was that in 1942 the 82nd ("All-American") Infantry Division, with battle streamers from World War I, was split in half to form two small airborne divisions, the 82nd and the 101st ("the Screaming Eagles"). To bring the 101st up to strength, a glider regiment was attached, along with what was to be Joe's parachute regiment, the 506th, whose cadre gathered at Toccoa, a remote National Guard camp in the mountains of northeast Georgia.

When told he would be sent to Toccoa, Joe had asked, "To what?" It is a Cherokee word, as is Currahee, name of the mountain overlooking Toccoa. *Currahee* means "stand alone." Till it was attached to the 101st, the 506th would indeed stand alone, so "Currahee" became their motto, shouted when they jumped from airplanes. The second parachute regiment to form at Toccoa, the 501st, coined the famous jump cry "Geronimo."

At Camp Custer, Michigan, with twelve other recruits ordered to report to the 506th, Joe was the alphabetically ranking man and so was given a big official envelope addressed to the regimental commander, Colonel Robert F. Sink, their first and only wartime commander. He had a tabula rasa to create his outfit, to test organization and practices with minimal oversight, to help write the U.S. Airborne manual as he went along. Sink had plenty of officers to help. An initial expectation was that Airborne fatalities would be so high that each platoon was assigned two lieutenants, not just one as in the rest of the army.

Facing the draft that swept up every teenager in Muskegon, Joe volunteered for the Airborne, inspired by its recruiting poster of a tommy-gunner dangling from a parachute over the slogan JUMP INTO THE FIGHT! But he had to tell the recruiter of his disqualifying color blindness. The sergeant nodded, affirming that troopers jump when a light in the fuselage flashed from red to green. Had Joe ever gotten a traffic ticket for running a light? No? "Then don't worry, Beyrle," he said, stamping "Approved" on Joe's application. "A dozen guys will push you out when the light changes."

Joe and his cohort from Camp Custer were the last passengers at the last stop of a mile-long steam train, earlier full of GIs bound for other destinations, arriving at the Toccoa rail spur after three days of stops and switches. They were met by a sergeant from the 506th, who took Joe's envelope, then trucked the Currahee candidates up Georgia Highway 13.

He was unexpectedly friendly, pointing out a casket factory off the road and noting that the 506th's camp had originally been named for a Confederate general, Augustus Toombs. Caskets and a name homonymous with *tombs* were not good morale builders, so Sink had revived the name Toccoa. Besides, the sergeant said, Toombs had been just a so-so general and Sink didn't want anyone's name connected with the camp unless he was a great soldier. Whatever the symbolism of its name, Toccoa was in the hills of nowhere. There Joe was housed in tar-paper barracks that had been hastily constructed by the Civilian Conservation Corps.

The CCC had been one of President Franklin Roosevelt's anti-Depressants. Joe's older brothers, Bill and John, had gone off to Michigan's Upper Peninsula to plant and cut trees for the CCC. Meals and bunks were free, so the boys were able to send home half their meager pay. That hadn't been enough to prevent foreclosure on the Beyrles' house. The family was evicted, their mortgage money lost. If it hadn't been for Granma Smith, they would have gone on the dole. Her side of the family had been Schmidts, changed to Smith when they emigrated in the early nineteenth century to escape Germany's wars. By way of Canada, the paternal side had come from Bavaria—Bayern in German—deriving into Beyrle.

Joe was the middle of William and Elizabeth Beyrle's many children, all of whom attended public school through second grade, then went on to Saint Joseph's. Joe was held back his first year because of language confusion from hearing and learning as much German as English at home. Home was next door to Granma Smith. Most family time was there, as she, a widow, had four bedrooms while the Beyrles shared three among nine members. Mrs. Smith was considered well-to-do for another reason: she drove a 1926 Oldsmobile. Selling it helped her ride out the Depression.

Joe's parents had no such asset in reserve. His older siblings dropped out of school into menial jobs necessary to keep the family together. Joe, in the seventh grade, barely made the cut, and only because his dad would not give up the graillike goal of having one of his children graduate from high school. One daughter had died in quarantine from scarlet fever. It was for Joe to take up a humble mantle.

It did not fit well. He was a multisport star, a big frog in a small pond. Ignoring academics, he reveled in athletics. He could run a mile in under five minutes, an accomplishment noticeable enough to the University of Notre Dame that they offered him a scholarship to enroll in September 1942. It was probably a hedge: Notre Dame knew that its wartime classes would be culled by the draft.

Athleticism was also Joe's entrée into the esprit of the 506th. More than any war up to that time, World War II required physical, that is, aerobic training. Though a heavy smoker and drinker himself, Sink was one of the first regimental commanders to appreciate this requirement, as well as the fact that close-order drill and rifle-range marksmanship—not that the Currahees didn't do plenty of both—were largely relics of the First World War.

With very few vehicles, and those subject to loss because they were landed in gliders, his men would have to backpack all their wherewithal into battle. Hence endurance marches under crushing loads were the hallmark of Toccoa training. Paradoxically, paratroopers were designed to be shock troops striking the enemy rear, the military equivalent of sprinters in contrast to distance runners. Therefore speed and bursts of violence were what Sink sought in tactical exercises.

Additionally, the unexpected had to be exploited by instantaneous initiative. Unlike the 1st Infantry Division (now veterans of North Africa), Currahees would not be attacking from friendly lines against well-located enemy positions. Instead the paratroopers were to land on the enemy's heads and make sudden chaos their ally. This situation was the most difficult to simulate in training. Sink's attempts produced the cruelest memories from Toccoa.

Joe's included an unusually arduous day when the training cadre came around all smiles to announce that dinner would be spaghetti, meatballs, and Parmesan. This was a feast for these teenagers of the Depression, who cheered before chowing down, feeling good about themselves, encouraged by a cadre strolling around delivering pats on the back for exceptional performances that day. Then the executive officer appeared, smiling as he rarely did. That, Joe learned, was a tip-off. The XO instructed the cooks to bring on strawberry shortcake, a favorite dessert. It was nearly devoured when the CO banged open the mess-hall door. "Hit it!" he yelled. "Fall out on the double, company formation. Last ones to the top pull KP."

It was another run up thousand-foot Currahee Mountain, three miles on a winding trail, a routine ascent for them but not with a full stomach and as a complete surprise. Troopers staggered, farted, puked, and swore in anger at the malicious timing of the run. They did everything but quit because buddies grabbed them and kept them going, mostly by curses and kicks. These unannounced fire drills were hated and dreaded like nothing else. Sink's lesson was to always be ready for anything even when relaxed. Sudden combat could come at any time, when least expected.

Such initiations arc-welded camaraderie. Like Euripidean characters, each young man had at least one strength and one weakness to emerge situationally. Joe, strong from the best and most plentiful food in his life, was one who could support the stumblers up Currahee Mountain. And he had a strong stomach. His uncle had been a butcher, so crawling through pig entrails strewn under barbed wire—another Sink training innovation—bothered him little. But at gambling (with its GI gold medal for craps) Joe's luck was less than average. Compensating for that deficiency there was Shorty, son of a Chicago gambler-mobster and next-door neighbor of Al Capone, whom Joe met when detailed to pick him up from jail.

Shorty owed Joe for not handcuffing him as required, so on the train back to Fort Bragg he demonstrated how to roll dice: lightly on three fingertips and the thumb of the nondominant hand, limp-wristed with double sixes up. This worked best in GI games where the dice didn't bounce off anything except a blanket.

"Don't *shoot* dice, Joe—you don't want to kill 'em. Imagine them bouncing like bingo balls, with your number coming up. And only bet when the shooter is coming out. Those are your best odds in a casino or anywhere else. Watch the shooters. Follow your instinct, and don't be impressed by the ones always yelling 'seven-eleven' or 'eighter from Decatur,' stuff like that. I don't yell numbers, I *think* them."

Shorty's fate had raised more than average interest in I Company. He had gone AWOL shortly before embarkation. His punishment was expected to begin by being drummed out of the Currahees, his jump wings and shoulder patch torn off, his paratrooper boots removed forever. This was the fate of those who were late returning from their first furlough, the humiliation inflicted in regimental formation reminiscent of the Civil War, complete with muffled drums as the disgraced were marched out as if for execution. That was the way Sink made his point that no one could be late in combat.

But Shorty had not been drummed out, only consigned to the *Samaria*'s brig. Barron Duber, I Company's communications sergeant, speculated that it was Shorty's Mafia connections that saved him. Others felt, more logically, that paratroopers were now so valuable that none could be spared even for deserved punishment. Few would dispute that they were Eisenhower's elite, Hitler's dread, far above "straight-leg" GIs in the rest of the army. Paratroopers kept their knees bent to absorb the shock of a parachute landing, approximately the same impact as dropping off the tailgate of a truck going fifteen miles per hour. "Legs" was their derisive term for everyone else in the world. A favorite paratrooper chant on training runs was "There're just two things that we can't stand—a bowlegged woman and a straight-leg man!"

Such pride and prejudice had been thoroughly inculcated by the time the Currahees put to sea, but they deteriorated from pilferage on the *Samaria*. Troopers would give one another their lives but also take from one another, as if nothing was individual, so anything left unsecured was communal and its "requisition" tolerable. The most frequently requisitioned item was the aluminum mess kit, prized for resisting the corrosiveness of seawater, which was all there was to clean anything or anyone. Fresh water was available only for drinking and only fifteen minutes per man per day. Seawater soap produced slime rather than lather, so Currahee officers looked at the sea as beards grew during the passage to England.

It wasn't a difficult passage by Atlantic standards. Though there was little seasickness, appetites even as robust as Joe's weakened to the point of voluntary fasting. All K rations had been consumed till they became gambling chips, and it took a stronger stomach than Joe's to think of food while swishing his mess kit in a wash pail teeming with flotsam of bread crusts, fish heads, and cornflakes.

Time on deck to see the sea was rationed like fresh water and hammocks. Sometimes the convoy closed up so tightly that troopers on one ship could yell to those on another. Once the *Samaria* was nearly rammed. More frequently the convoy spread out almost to the horizon. All the while the Atlantic continued an undisturbed tempo. It was for those who traversed it, unconsciously influenced by it, to adjust. Most did so by projecting rather than reflecting. For none of them was the past as significant as the future. Unless they did their job—unless that job was doable as General Marshall had gambled—home, in the medium future, would be ruled by monsters who did not speak English. In mid-1943 it was that simple, that evident, that true.

True because European civilization had submerged like Atlantis into the darkest depths and clutch of fascism or communism. Their exemplars, Hitler and Stalin, were now tearing at each other like tyrannosaurs. It was a time for democracy to make a statement, albeit compromising as Churchill had, that he would find cause with the devil to send Hitler to hell. That holy endeavor produced America's most inspired and titanic mission of the twentieth century. Colonel Sink rarely addressed his regiment as a whole, so Joe remembered a sentence: "The U.S. spells *us*!" Sink had shouted at the formation where the AWOLs were drummed out.

During his own furlough Joe confirmed what Sink had averred. In Muskegon Dad had plunged into seventy-hour workweeks at Continental Motors, turning out aircraft and jeep engines. His personal and the national depression were over. The war effort was unified, universal.

For Joe that furlough was like a return from space or some exotic expedition. Everyone wanted to know what jumping was like, what else he had been doing, but their unasked question was how he'd changed. His folks met him at the bus station, and Mom cried a little, saying that he looked different in a way she didn't expect and couldn't explain. Dad said that was good—Joe was just growing up fast—no need to talk about it. Off they went to the 539 Grill, passing a popular poster:

USE IT UP,

WEAR IT OUT,

MAKE IT DO,

OR DO WITHOUT.

That would not apply to Joe as he sat down to a meal of prewar viands: veal Parmesan, buttered noodles, and asparagus, topped off by Black Forest cake made with a pound of rationed sugar. The owner of the grill announced that the feast was on her, and that Joe should come back anytime. He, a private in the army, was a privileged celebrity in a way he'd never imagined.

That was confirmed when Sister Angelique, Saint Joseph's principal, summoned him—her authority over Joe, an alumnus, never questioned— to address the student body and guests. The school was too small to hold everyone, so he would speak next door in the church. His mother mildly protested that she'd heard only religious teachings at church. True, Sister Angelique agreed, but in wartime everything can change—as just about everything already had.

Joe remembers his speech as corny by current standards, but at the time everyone took it very kindly. Outside the church he was obliged to sign autographs like some big-league ballplayer. This embarrassed him because he'd done nothing in the war yet; but then came a public relations task he enjoyed—a visit to Continental Motors, where he had worked before induction and where his father was now a supervisor. The vice president of Continental had met Joe and escorted him down the assembly line of a plant roaring as never before, working around the clock, running off military engines by the thousands. With mutual pleasure Joe shook hands with a hundred workers.

Those days at home sped by in a dazzle. Joe had resolved to treat the furlough as just a break, a break so short it would not leave him longing for civilian comforts. Only sheets were such a smooth luxury that Joe would miss them. Currahee training had shown him a second self, that of a soldier related to his civilian persona but qualitatively different. He felt there would be another similarity, though with much more overlap, when he jumped into battle. He looked forward to the progression. He had, by this point, defined himself as a soldier, with a soldier's standards of success or failure. The feast at the 539 Grill, the speech at Saint Joseph's, the handshakes on Continental's assembly line—he could not fail those who so esteemed him.

Preparing to resume his second identity, Joe packed up in his bedroom. Like typical parents, Mom and Dad had left the room just the way it was when he'd gone off to Camp Custer—the high school pennant, souvenirs from places he'd visited, the Chicago Cubs banner, a picture of Notre Dame's golden dome. Joe wrote something on a scratch pad as he left the room, his shoulder bent by an army duffel bag, something left undisturbed till he returned:

> Will I ever go to N.D.? How long will the war last? This room will look different when I see it again . . . different like a fairyland.

Even with Bray and Vanderpool such ruminations were not much discussed on the rail of the *Samaria*. Recalling their initiation as parachutists was more topical for soldiers steeling themselves to jump on the side of good in its stark fight against evil. Their big day, remembered more vividly than first sex, was their "cherry" jump.

Wearing football helmets with numbers chalked on them, the fledgling parachutists had marched out onto the Fort Benning airfield to be briefed on wind conditions and where to assemble after the drop. This was their reminder to consider a jump, even the first, as no more than the means of delivery from here to there—quite like the train to Toccoa. Don't do anything significantly wrong, and you'll arrive at the designated destination.

With that attitude the prejump briefing included nothing about parachute malfunctions. If one did occur, there would be no one to blame except the rookie himself, for he had packed his own chute, the ultimate designation of personal responsibility for a teenager to contemplate as he accelerated toward the ground.

Twenty-four cherry jumpers loaded into each C-47, the transport later said (with the jeep) to have won the war, moving men and matériel over the oceans and the Himalayas. The weather was cold in December 1942, but the rookies were sweating. A "stick" is the basic jumping unit, six to sixteen paratroopers, their leader jumping first. Joe was second. While the C-47 climbed slowly to fifteen hundred feet, Joe peeked outside. This was discouraged; they'd been told not to look down, to keep their eyes on the horizon, but he watched Georgia and Alabama spread out below. The control tower had loomed tall while they were on the ground but now became smaller and smaller.

"Stand up! Hook up!" shouted the jump master.

All Joe remembers was shoving up tight to the big parachute pack of the stick leader, who disappeared like a leaf in a gale. Joe took a step to follow, was sucked out into the engines' roar and the wind blast, then felt a blow to the chest before realizing he was hanging in space. He'd jumped! It was an act of faith and a result of training that defied every natural instinct. What must be done could be done and would be done. That became a premise of the Airborne. It was said in a speech on its fiftieth anniversary: "We took our name from the air but gained our fame on the ground." Nonetheless, hurling oneself into the air had a lot to do with what one did on the ground.

That evening Joe's stick celebrated their cherry jump with beer. The army had delivered on its implied promise throughout parachute training: "Do what you're told, as you've been trained, and you'll get to the ground in one piece." That pledge had been fulfilled, and Joe's faith was reinforced immeasurably.

For officers there was a ceremony called a prop blast, where each cherry downed an eye-watering potion from the hub of a C-47 propeller. The celebrant was to gulp fully while his fellows counted to four, the tensest interval before the chute opened with what was called "opening shock." If, after four seconds, those watching felt he was insufficiently blasted, he had to "pull the rip cord" of his imaginary reserve parachute and drink all the way to the floor (about a minute).

An elderly lady in Muskegon who saw Joe during furlough noticed his gleaming jump wings and thought he was in the air corps. "How many flights have you made?" she asked. "Eleven takeoffs, ma'am, but no landings," was his answer. That cherry jump was Joe's first ride in an airplane. There were thirty-five more before he landed in one.

THE SECOND WEEK AT sea was trying and wearying enough to nearly dissolve the Airborne spirit. Scabies broke out, cultivated in fatigue uniforms that could only be washed with seawater, which left a starchy irritant causing crotch rot. For this the medics had only gentian violet, which became compulsory whether infection was evident or not. Applied to body parts, gentian violet fluorescently stained underwear, olive-drab shorts, and T-shirts, which were as scarce as aluminum mess kits. Joe, Jack, and Orv began to ask one another if their battalion commander had anything to restore morale for crusaders who were feeling like convicts.

Colonel Sink had labeled the battalions of his regiment Red, White, and Blue. Commanding the Blues of Third Battalion was Lieutenant Colonel Robert Wolverton, a West Pointer from West Virginia, hardly in the mold of Sink (that mold was broken after the original). Sink was to say that Wolverton helped develop "a spirit unsurpassed among fighting men, not one of stupid following but rather of initiative and bold aggressiveness." That was Sink's recollection of how Wolverton trained the Blues. To Joe he was a demigod in a hierarchy beginning with Captain Shettle, his company commander. Their inspiration faded like old letters from home while the Currahees were stifled and impotent at sea.

So no less exhilarating than a prop blast was the cry "Land ho!" from *Samaria*'s bullhorn. Paratroopers rushed starboard, nearly tilting the ship. The land, the island, was Ireland, but it didn't look emerald, not even green. Nevertheless the loud talk on deck was about Irish origins; it seemed some Currahees could trace their ancestors by apocrypha and what they remembered from grandparents.

Landfall marked the end of sleeping in passageways, the ship resembling a Bowery flophouse and almost as lawless. At the sight of Ireland the chain of command sprang into life. "Reread your *Guide to En-*

gland," officers ordered. "Hand-press your fatigues. Fall out on deck for calisthenics. You troopers are in worse shape than a regiment of WACs." Blues believed in their officers but not everything they said. Just get us off this tub, Joe and his cohort grumbled; we'll show you what kind of shape we're in.

More than the New Yorkers who had seen them off, the Liverpudlians who received them looked wan and worn by the impositions of war. The Salvation Army was at dockside with tea, biscuits, and a few faint horns, which expressed an attitude less stimulating than sympathetic. Longshoremen tending the *Samaria* were listless relics from World War I. Lieutenant Colonel Wolverton saw how this initial impression of the ETO bemused his Blues. Before they debarked he counseled that the British had been holding off the Nazis for four years. "We're their reinforcements, the force to drive a stake in the heart of Hitler's Reich. What we have in common is a language and V for Victory."

That was signaled by upraised fingers, the symbol on every wartime matchbook. As the Blues rode their train to Hungerford, natives flashed a V the way they used to tip their hats.

Grateful to march once more, to have escaped the *Samaria*'s rancid bowels, Blues lugged weapons and duffel bags from Hungerford station five miles to the village of Ramsbury, population 350. Third Battalion numbered a hundred more than that and dispersed like some oversized tourist group that couldn't be put up in a single hotel. Part of I Company went into a livery stable, a sister company went behind an inn, another ended up out on a farm two miles from town. Joe was billeted by a manor house.

Home for the next nine months would be this residence in Wiltshire County where water was drawn from a well, where there was a once-a-week shower at a drayman's garage if the Blues were not out on a maneuver when their allotted day came up. If so, shower day was postponed till next week. At least this preserved soap, a commodity rationed like cigarettes and sugar.

Wiltshiremen were as hospitable as if they had every amenity to share, though they had hardly any at all. Grubby from extended training, Joe's squad would amble into a favorite pub, down pints with World War I veterans, and frequently be invited to their homes. Colonel Sink's policy, however, was that all such invitations were to be gratefully but politely refused. He did not want young Americans drawing on their allies' scant resources and telling them how much better things were back home.

Midwesterners like Joe, accustomed to the extravagant spaces of rural America, blinked at the compact quaintness of English farmsteads and the reticulation of the landscape by mile after mile of neat stone walls. Everything, even the trees and streams, seemed older, more in order. Everything, including rabbits and deer, belonged to someone here; there were no vast tracts of federal land like Toccoa and Fort Benning. Bemused, the troopers debated whether it was preferable to have their parachute dragged by wind into a high wooden fence back home or a low stone wall in the Midlands.

"Hey, Joe," Orv once asked, looking up from a letter he was writing, "is Wiltshire a county or a state?"

"It's called a county, but it's like a state back in the States."

"Oh."

CHAPTER TWO

JUMPIN' JOE

SERGEANT DUBER APPROACHED HIM SLYLY. HOW WOULD JOE like some brandy—*really* good brandy? The offer didn't appeal. A couple of pints of bitter at village pubs like the Bleeding Horse or the Bell, Crown & Anchor were enough alcohol for Joe after training six days a week, and some nights, in Wiltshire County and beyond. Nonetheless he was interested because of previous collaborations with Duber to improve I Company's chow, especially in the field.

Duber was a crack marksman, able to drill some lord's hare with a single shot from his carbine fitted with a silencer he'd obtained from no one knew where. For further fare he had called on Joe, trained in demolitions at Fort Benning, to help him fish the streams as I Company marched and countermarched through battalion maneuvers. Duber gauged the depth of dark eddies, then stated an amount of explosive. It was for Joe to prime and toss it into the stream with a waterproof fuse.

The detonation was like a depth charge and usually produced a shell-shocked trout, which Duber scooped up in his helmet. At the next break fish was frying for a select group in company headquarters. Deer were also Duber's prey but the most dangerous because they were in the inventory of vigilant British game wardens. By Sink's orders, Lieutenant Colonel Wolverton was obliged to fine each man in his battalion a pound sterling for every deer that fell to Blue bullets. However, before their collective punishment could be imposed, milord's game warden had to produce evidence that his game was not just missing but had been shot.

What Duber did best was make things disappear. He could skin a stag, gut and bury it almost before the carcass cooled. Venison made great sandwiches to supplement K rations, appreciated by Captain Shettle and once even served to Wolverton, who was pleased enough to not ask about its origins. So, when approached with the question of brandy, Joe harkened to Duber, almost twice his age and respected additionally for having survived Currahee training that had washed out a third of Third Battalion's youthful candidates at Toccoa. His proposal was enticing:

"Listen up, Beyrle. So what if you don't drink much? You get two bottles for trading. Napoleon's brandy—I'm not shitting you—worth hundreds of dollars per bottle. *Hundreds,* Joe, more than two months' jump pay—and all you have to do is stand guard while I requisition it." This, said Duber, was a guarantee, not a gamble.

Shorty, the professional gambler, presently a stockade inmate somewhere in Britain, had convinced Joe to bet on himself, thereby adding the personal factor to an equation of chance, and always review the odds before a gamble. So before participating in the brandy requisition Joe asked Duber to describe the plan. He readily did, a reassurance but with a rebuke—he was doing Joe a favor by bringing him in, a favor for his contribution to pirate fishing.

Duber explained that for generations the earls of So-and-So had owned the estate on which men of I Company were now billeted. The manor house contained a wine cellar where famous liquors had aged for at least a century. When British authorities required the present earl to accommodate Americans, he had prudently removed his most valuable possessions, such as the brandy.

Upon evacuating, the earl had dismissed most of his staff. They were heavyhearted, having to find odd jobs around Ramsbury or being vacuumed up by conscription. Duber had met the out-of-work wine keeper at a pub, bought him some bitter, and learned of his unhappiness. A carton of Lucky Strikes was enough for him to divulge the location of milord's brandy trove—buried under hay in one of the manor barns. With that information, Duber said, the heist would be "easy as spitting."

Persuaded, Joe stood watch at twilight as a jeep coasted down to the barn. Four men piled out. Their silhouettes scampered between barn and jeep, careful to suppress clinking of bottles. Three men packed hay to cushion the glass, then climbed aboard to surround and protect the load. Duber quietly started the jeep and rolled away at a walking speed.

There was no immediate outcry. The earl, now living outside Wiltshire County, raised it at a high echelon, several removes from the concern of Wolverton, who had implemented two unwritten rules: (1) do your major drinking on pass to larger towns like Swindon; and (2) while in Ramsbury behave as if at home—that is, with your parents watching.

Wiltshiremen appreciated Wolverton's policy, and there was never much trouble, though there wasn't much to eat or drink either because both food and alcohol were far more tightly rationed than in the States. Petrol was even more precious, so that horse carts far outnumbered cars on lanes, called roads, which were designed for scenery rather than speed. Though GIs chuckled, locals thought it not funny at all for British officers in uniform and businessmen in suits to decorously ride bicycles.

GIs were not the only strangers in town. Three years earlier, ruthless bombing of English cities had forced evacuation of tens of thousands of the aged and underaged. Over a hundred were quartered in Ramsbury, along with young women placed by the Ministry of Labour to do farmwork, previously the occupation of Wiltshiremen now overseas. Additionally there were uniformed women doing administrative jobs for the Auxiliary Territorial Service, a factotum wartime agency. They came from every class and social background, less welcomed by the natives than were the Americans, whose presence had resulted in a famous British saying about their GI tenants that they were "overpaid, oversexed, and over here." To which there was a less well known American retort: "You're underpaid, undersexed, and under Eisenhower."

What cultural friction the Blues experienced was more within the U.S. Army. Though large-scale maneuvers took them farther and for longer periods away from Wiltshire County, they had made necessary adjustments with their hosts, which were not disrupted before regrettable incidents occurred when the 28th Infantry Division of the Pennsylvania National Guard moved in near Ramsbury. Their scarlet shoulder patch—to become known as "the bucket of blood" after horrific combat—was the icon of Pennsylvania, a keystone, so Duber labeled them Keystone Kops. They probably would have been tolerated had they not hustled girls whom Blues considered proprietary. Competition immediately flourished, and the legs turned out to be as clever as they were presumptuous.

While Third Battalion was participating in an invasion rehearsal, measles broke out among the female population of Wiltshire County. British authorities requested assistance from nearby 28th Division medics, who obliged and, with all professional gravity, concluded that because most local lasses had had contact with Blues, it would be prudent for a quarantine to be imposed between the two. Wolverton was in the field, so the medical recommendation went up to Sink, who, in probably his most unpopular command decision, acquiesced to a thirty-day quarantine.

This struck Jack Bray hard. He took his pleasure quietly, assuredly. There was a Swindon girl with the same tastes, and they had melded with none of the abruptness of a wartime romance. Now she was off-limits! He was quarantined! Something had to be done, and it was for Joe and Orv to help him do it, as Keystones were reveling in pubs once the preserve of Currahees, buying drinks for Blue girls. Only two factors worked in favor of the paratroopers: for the legs, new acquaintances had not yet taken firm hold, and the 28th Division also had a full schedule of training and maneuvers. If certain pubs could be denied to them, the thirty-day quarantine would expire before the fairest of Wiltshire were won over by Pennsylvanian treachery.

Joe and Orv consulted Duber, who, though he had a wife in the States, was courting a lady of Swindon and was said to be engaged to her. As in his fishing technique, Duber believed in demolition solutions. The quarantine called for smoke grenades. Designed to guide resupply parachute drops and air strikes, they produced voluminous smoke in a variety of colors. The Keystone color was red, but Duber felt green would be better—the signal to go (and don't come back). He directed that Orv, Jack, and Joe hit three pubs simultaneously. They knew the proprietors and felt bad about anonymous bombing, but when Keystones piled out of every door and window, that was compensation. The girls, now changing hands again, were initially angry, suspecting Blues and no one else. But a short time healed. Bray's lover was the first to forgive and led a movement back to the paratroopers.

Joe had been a reluctant smoke grenadier, but to support his tripod of buddies he'd joined the fray. For a GI, Joe was more serious than most, while Jack was the leading fun lover. He had fun training, and fun afterward, and he thought even war would be fun. Joe hadn't had much fun in his life except with family and in athletics. Coming at fun from different directions drew them togther.

Orv fit somewhere in between. He'd had a serious girlfriend back home and wrote to her steadily, but she jilted him before the 101st went overseas. That was as serious a tragedy for Joe as when his sister had died of scarlet fever. He and Jack mourned with Orv, trying to direct him toward local girls but mostly watching him because they cringed to see him change very much, as vicariously they were much a part of him, sharers of experiences and what was to come. Joe, Jack, and Orv were a trinity, three in one and one in three. There were pairs like that and a few quartets—the largest such group a squad of twelve—with overlapping bonds of different strength and codependence.

The communication squad of company headquarters was where the three worked under Sergeant Todd, closely integrated with officers. Because of his build and stamina, Joe carried Captain Shettle's radio, a forty-pound SCR 300, plus a small walkie-talkie. Joe knew his job and liked it for keeping him Best Informed about I Company in the field. Being around headquarters also kept him current with the concerns of Wolverton, Sink, and even some of the commanding general, Maxwell Taylor. What concerned them all was lack of jump training. Scarce aviation fuel was the reason, and balloons became an expedient, "barrage" balloons levitating all over Great Britain to snarl German bombers.

It was widely though not officially recognized that Joe had done a lot more parachuting than most paratroopers. Back in Georgia he had jumped illicitly for others who were afraid that a bad landing would result in injury that could put them out of the Airborne, reducing them to legs. Such worriers paid Joe five bucks per proxy, a reward for what he would have done for free because he loved to jump. Impersonation at Fort Benning was easy because jumpers had only numbers on their helmets, not name tapes on their chests.

Joe made over a hundred dollars that way till his shambling gait became familiar to the parachute-school cadre (not part of the 506th). One day a cadre jump master consulted his manifest, stopped in front of Joe, and asked if he had a brother going through the school. Joe sounded off, Yes, Sergeant, he did, that his was an Airborne family. Good, said the jump master, knock out twenty-five push-ups for your brother and twenty-five more for yourself. This was a tip-off that Joe was under suspicion; it took Jack and Orv to convince him to give up proxy jumps, so as not to risk splitting the triune by way of either a broken leg or a court-martial.

Now, for approved jumping, he began to be split from his best buddies. Based on sub-rosa reputation, Joe was selected to experiment with new techniques of putting a paratrooper on the ground with more equipment within reach. The 101st's planners reasoned that if each jumper could drop something ahead of him, something tethered, his payload could be increased significantly. This load carrier became known as the leg bag. A yardlong sack of strong canvas, holding up to 125 pounds of gear, ammo, demolitions, anything, it was wrapped around the jumper's leg. After opening shock he was to pull a cotter pin, dropping the bag on a thirty-five-foot tether. Because it hit the ground before he did, the additional weight would not make his landing harder.

A valuable innovation, the leg bag, but one that Joe demonstrated was unworkable after many balloon jumps. The problem was the standard landing method, called the British tumble, which all paratroopers had been taught. With two years' head start on the U.S. Airborne, the British had favored a landing where the jumper tucked his knees, then rolled like a tire bouncing on the ground. Joe could do the tumble in his sleep and in any direction, but with a leg bag ahead, acting as an anchor on the ground, he couldn't tumble at all. Division observers watched him in jump after jump. Wherever he tried to tumble, his leg bag jerked him back. He arose slowly, feeling fortunate, like a test pilot who'd completed something as dangerous and problematic as it was necessary.

After a particularly violent land-tumble-jerk, an officer from division G-3 went over to Joe, helped him to his feet, and murmured instructions for the final balloon jump of the day.

"Beyrle, when your feet hit this time, just kind of collapse. Relax and crumple, don't tumble."

Joe did, landing as close as he could to his leg bag. They both stuck like darts on a board, the tether slack in between. Consequently the British tumble was discarded in the 101st, to be replaced by what became known as the PLF—parachute landing fall. Joe practiced it day after day till G-3 decided he was ready to demonstrate the PLF for the British, sort of a courtesy, saying thanks for pioneering in this field, but, respectfully, we are bent another way.

In a demonstration at an RAF airfield, Joe did PLFs forward, backward, and to both sides, with leg bags. He sensed a certain rubber-meets-the-road stardom and for his final jump showboated with a "standing landing," outlawed in the 101st but admired by the British. With the parachutes of the twenty-first century, a standing landing is easy, but in 1944 the jumper had to judge very accurately how fast the ground rose, chin on his risers, then release them at just the right moment so that his body weight bounced up exactly enough to counteract the rate of descent. It all happened in a moment when Joe landed on his feet with no more impact than stepping off a curb. The Brits loved it. Wolverton heard about it.

ON A MISTY MORNING in April 1944 Sergeant Kristie looked at him warily and muttered, "Get in that jeep, Beyrle. Report to Wolverton at regimental HQ." It was a long drive to Sink's headquarters, an ivy-walled manor house in Littlecote, giving Joe time to nervously speculate about the summons. Smoke grenades? No, Joe was never implicated. But the brandy? Civilians, acting like detectives, had been browsing around Ramsbury, and Duber was unusually silent. Joe's orders were to report to the CO himself, not to his first sergeant as an enlisted man normally would. He sensed this would be face-to-face, only his third time with Wolverton.

The first had been more than a year earlier in North Carolina, at a camp named for PFC John Mackall, the first U.S. paratrooper killed in combat, a member of the 82nd Airborne Division, already fighting in the Mediterranean theater. At Camp Mackall Wolverton had struggled with the perpetual problem of paratroopers: assembling after being scattered in a mass drop. Flares and smoke grenades were one way to guide them, but he needed something audible. Combining a classic instrument of war with the most advanced means of warfare, Wolverton came up with a way to sound the call. It was a bugler named Ross.

Joe knew him; all the Blues did because of the innumerable mornings Ross had woken them at reveille. He blew loud enough to be heard a half mile away. Wolverton's idea was for him to blow assembly (the traditional bugle call that draws racehorses to the starting line) after a battalion-size drop, then everyone would head for the sound, whether in daylight or darkness.

But Ross blew a lot better than he jumped. He had been tucked in Wolverton's stick with orders to follow the CO's canopy down to the ground, then start bugling. But he kept his eyes closed till his chute opened, then couldn't find Wolverton's among dozens in the sky, then got caught in a tree a quarter mile away, where he frantically started bugling—and as planned, everyone headed in his direction.

That was the opposite direction from where Wolverton had landed and the battalion was supposed to assemble. When Joe got there Wolverton was beside himself, but with few others, while a hundred Blues helped Ross out of his tree. When Sink heard how the experiment turned out he sent a memo down suggesting that Wolverton either learn to bugle himself or try a drum.

Joe's first occasion with Wolverton was at the end of Third Battalion's 142-mile forced march in December 1942. The Currahees were to move from Toccoa to Fort Benning, on the opposite side of Georgia. They had taken a train to Atlanta when news reports—all grim and disheartening in those days—carried a Japanese boast that their army had set a world record for endurance by marching 130 miles in eighty-five hours while whipping the British in Malaya. Those numbers rang Sink's chimes. He ordered Wolverton to break the record and made sure there was plenty of press coverage.

With full combat loads, including mortars and machine guns, the Blues indeed beat the Japs by several hours, Wolverton leading the whole way, at the end shod in only socks after swollen feet had herniated his boots. Only eleven of the seven hundred Blues who'd set off in the rain from Atlanta failed to complete the march. Blues knew Wolverton was proud of them but also that he was less talker than walker, a foil for Sink whose strong craggy face and Clark Gable mustache seemed designed by Hollywood for a "full bull" colonel's role.

Wolverton had given Joe a pat on the back for assisting Bray across the finish line, but this summons at Littlecote was unlikely to be a reminiscence. The CO was in the midst of training and planning for the invasion of Hitler's Europe. It was hard for Joe to imagine what possible interest Wolverton would have in him, a lowly tech-5, equivalent of a corporal. The only possibility was chilling: warm, ancient brandy.

Values clashed traumatically in Joe as he straightened his fatigues in the orderly room. He would not draw in anyone from I Company and was steeled to accept Wolverton's penalty for remaining silent. Unless it meant expulsion from the Airborne. Joe was inveterately stubborn but not sure if he could accept that ultimate punishment. It would be the excruciating test between pride and loyalty. He'd do anything to avoid it, call upon Wolverton's sense of soldierly honor as best he could and if he could find the words.

Like a criminal about to receive sentence, he knocked on the door, was admitted, and snapped his battalion commander an Airborne salute. Wolverton looked like a lumbar support when seated at his desk. He was short and, despite paratrooper fitness, appeared more fit for logistical staff than leading men into combat. He returned Joe's salute, gestured for him to sit down, then nodded to a civilian seated next to him. Joe suspected he was a local constable, but he spoke American English.

"I hear you're called Jumpin' Joe," he said as an icebreaker. "Why do you like to jump?"

"Fifty bucks, sir." That was the monthly premium for enlisted paratroopers.

"What else?"

That would take a long explanation, and Joe was never long on words. Neither was Wolverton, but he provided an answer. "There's nothing like the blast, is there, Beyrle? The opening shock, the coming down." He shoved Joe's brief military résumé over to the civilian for his next question.

"I see here you had a classified jump. What was that about?"

"Sir, I was in a squad-size drop into Panama to test the range of walkie-talkies in the jungle."

"Fun?"

"No, sir. The bugs ate us alive."

"Glad you're in the ETO instead of the Pacific?"

"Yes, sir."

"How many jumps have you had?"

The official number was right in Joe's file, so the question seemed to lead to his unauthorized proxy jumps. Joe did not try to dissemble. "About forty, sir. Maybe fifty, counting balloon drops." Among real paratroopers, the latter was considered sissy because there was no opening shock.

"Quite a few more than average," the civilian noted. Wolverton nodded. "Would you be interested in another one? Sort of like Panama."

"Yes, sir."

"You'd be going to where *brandy* comes from. You know where that is?"

"France, sir."

"That's right. And you'd be going solo. Think it over."

He didn't need to. "I volunteer, sir."

"Currahee," said Wolverton—high praise from him—"there's a jeep outside. It'll take you to division G-2." Joe rose to salute. "You know where I remember you from, Beyrle?"

"At the end of the march, sir?"

"No, after that, at Camp Mackall. "Assembly—*ta-ta-te-da*." Joe grinned. "Ever see Ross?"

"I think he's carrying a mortar in G Company, sir."

"I'll see you again, trooper. Don't worry about anything while you're gone."

That was reassuring. Whatever Wolverton said, he meant, and he never promised what he couldn't personally deliver. But how could he this time, Joe wondered as he began his second jeep ride of the day. His destination was division headquarters about fifty miles away at Greenham Common, near Newbury. There Joe saw more officers than the total number he'd seen so far in the army. At Greenham Common, captains were like privates, majors like sergeants, and lieutenant colonels like Wolverton scurried around like somewhat important clerks. Joe even got a glimpse of the division artillery commander, Brigadier General Anthony McAuliffe.

In the G-2 (intelligence) office no one knew why Joe had been sent for; eventually a major appeared to ask about his background, as if Joe were being considered for a security clearance. This was the pretense for a sizing-up, a checking-out for general steadiness. Joe had it; he spoke slowly while keeping eye contact. Now, what about his German name? How close were his ties to Germany? The question offended: both sides of his family were devoutly Catholic and American. There had been a Berlin, Michigan, but during World War I German-Americans, like the Beyrles and Schmidts, had changed the name to Marne.

Joe's interview was interrupted by a phone call, then quickly ended. A lieutenant from G-2 drove him back at top speed to Ramsbury, telling him to pick up just overnight stuff as if for a weekend pass. I Company was out in the field as usual, so Joe didn't have to do any explaining. At even higher speed, honking most of the way, the lieutenant drove him to the Hungerford railway station. The jeep sped off, then hit the brakes. The driver had forgotten to give something to Joe, something important. He went into reverse, tossed Joe a bag, and was gone. Inside were new coveralls, called a jumpsuit, dark but otherwise the same as paratrooper fatigues. Joe was elated to have them, as his fatigues were tattered from training.

In the stationmaster's office he saw three Americans in identical jumpsuits. They gestured and pointed him to the men's room to change. His new comrades weren't like any GIs he'd seen before—one spoke with a European accent—but on the train to Middle Wallop they brought him into their conversation, which he perceived to be that of college guys after mentioning his scholarship to Notre Dame. Like Joe, none of them had seen much of England except its woods and weeds, so they all felt like tourists for the first time. The towns en route were drab and beleaguered by war, but the Americans felt vital, confident that this war's course could be changed to their expectations. Among the passengers they seemed to be the only ones enjoying themselves as the musty coach rocked along.

It stunned Joe when the man with a foreign accent leaned over and whispered, "You from the 101st?"

"Can't tell ya."

"Hell, we saw the markings on your jeep."

"Where you from?"

There was no answer, but it was the fledgling OSS, predecessor of the CIA, as Joe would learn years later.

At the Middle Wallop station they were collected by an RAF airman, who drove them to his base. Joe wasn't sure, but it looked like the air-field where he had done his standing landing for the British. The four were received fraternally. "Ah, come in, lads," a lieutenant greeted, and led them to a secure map room. "I'll take Beyrle first. You other gentle-men can wait in the canteen." They departed. "Corporal Beyrle—am I pronouncing that right?" he began pleasantly. "I'm sure you've been a good American soldier. Now we'd like you to do some good work for the Allies. We have friends over in France. True friends. They perform indispensable tasks, especially in keeping us informed about what Jerry is up to. These courageous people are called the French Forces of the In-terior: FFI for short. Ever heard of them?"

Joe had not. Papers back home ran apocryphal stories of the brave French resistance but said nothing of how they were cagey polypolitical cobelligerents whose principal value to Eisenhower was real-time, on-the-ground intelligence about German forces—increasingly vital intelli-gence as time tolled down to invasion. In return for their services, the FFI wanted money as much as demolitions for sabotage. Money to bribe gendarmes, government clerks, truck drivers, and switchmen on the rail-roads—even money for select Germans whose loyalty to Hitler was tepid and who found the good life of occupying France a bit costly for their military pay.

That thoroughly interested Joe from his worm's-eye perspective of the war. Speaking to him was this Allied officer, explaining matters Joe imagined were known only to generals. As always there was nothing like being Best Informed.

"Yes," the lieutenant continued, "so we must deliver rather large quantities of money to the FFI. Gold, actually. That's what they prefer. How do you suppose we deliver it?"

"Parachute, sir?"

"Quite. Now we'd like for you to do that. Be a paymaster, as we call it. Give it a go?"

"Yes, sir."

"Fine fellow. Now, it's all very simple. And not much risk, I'd say. We've been doing it for years. Here's this bandolier." With both hands the lieutenant hefted it. "It contains rather much more than you and I together will likely make in our lifetimes. So please don't lose it, will you? Just strap it on, fly off, jump out, and become an honored guest of the hospitable French. *Voilà.*" Before continuing, he handed Joe a receipt for the bandolier, its contents, and a .45-caliber automatic with holster. "Now, we certainly expect those who greet you to be the Frenchmen intended. To verify that, your challenge is 'A breezy night'—in English of course. You don't speak French, do you? The appropriate answer will be 'Yes, let's go sailing.' "

"Sir, what if that's not the answer?"

"Well, if he answers in German, you might try bribing him with some of that gold!" The lieutenant managed to make Joe join him in a laugh, then started speaking quickly: "You have your dog tags, so you're entitled to prisoner-of-war status. This hasn't come up at all, Beyrle. Our chaps always come back complaining that they couldn't do any shopping. Beautiful tapestries where you're going." He tapped the map near Alençon, at the southern border of Normandy. "And don't worry about getting back. The FFI handles that admirably.

"Now, off to the canteen with you. Ask the next chap to come in, please."

THE FLIGHT BRIEFING was also genial, and the drop plan perfectly simple. If the pilot saw a certain pattern of lights below, the first jumper would go; if not, he stayed in the plane, which would fly on to the next jumper's site. This would be repeated three times before the plane dodged back to England, carrying any jumpers whose drop had been aborted.

Putting on the bandolier was enough to make Joe's knees bend. He was worth several hundred thousand dollars, a million today, and it felt like all pennies. If being rich weighed a man down this much, Joe didn't mind being poor. What he felt most was relief and excitement. The brandy guilt was behind him; instead he was still very much in the Currahees, indeed now representing them as a star parachutist. Sure there was danger, but danger was the elixir of youth.

An hour after moonset Joe and his perdu comrades climbed into a Lysander, a single-engine British airplane with its machine gun removed to accommodate three jumpers jammed together like a bobsled team.

Joe was the only one burdened by a bandolier, and though the plane had been stripped of any unnecessary weight it nevertheless seemed over-loaded while taking off.

The route was southwest across the mouth of the English Channel, which was surging with whitecaps. The Welsh pilot hummed as he dove and wove to avoid radar detection. The Luftwaffe had nearly aban-doned these skies, yet he zigged, zagged, and rose a few times but came right back down to wave-top altitude as if a Messerschmitt were pursu-ing him. He was good, better than the jumpers' stomachs. One man (Joe suspected he was hungover at takeoff) popped an airsickness pill and managed to slump into sleep.

For the other two, bladders filled distressingly during the two-hour flight. Only a pee tube, venting into the slipstream, had been provided for relief. In the cramped darkness the small hose was passed around. When it reached the man beside Joe, a kink had formed, causing his urine to backflush. The wet and stench added new discomfort to the longest of Joe's sixty flights, in the noisiest, most rattling airplane he'd ever flown in, and never had he waited so long before jumping.

Paddling his thighs in anticipation, he thought of people he wished could see him now. Not his parents—they'd worry too much—but the sisters and kids at Saint Joseph's, Jack and Orv back in Wiltshire (proba-bly out on a night exercise themselves), Wolverton, Sink . . . Currahees, Screaming Eagles . . . Gee, it occurred to Joe, he might be the first of them all to get into France. That would be hard not to tell Jack and Orv when he got back. And he would get back, of course. He was twenty, in-destructible, and besides, the RAF said this would be a piece of cake. He hoped not too easy. He remembered Hollywood movies where Nazi sen-tries were garroted in the dark. He'd learned how to do that at Toccoa, something daring, something dangerous, what being a man was all about at his age.

But first what must be done was what he did best—if this plane would ever stop weaving. At last it did and Joe grew tense, profession-ally tense. The pilot gestured for him to hook his static line onto a thick cable running across the top of the jumpers' compartment. They roused and patted him on the butt. Through the open hatch by his feet was France, under no moon, perfect for the pilot to see a lamp pattern below. Joe looked up at him for the jump signal. It was a downward-thrust index finger and the inaudible cry "Go!" A step through the hatch and Joe was blown into the dark. And into history as the first American paratrooper to descend on France—and high among the ones most welcomed by the French.

Joe yelled, "Currahee!" *Pop.* Opening shock wasn't bad, leaving him just bouncing a little in the night. The only sound was from the Lysander veering away. Jump altitude was a thousand feet. The drop-zone lamps, which he'd never seen, were already extinguished. All there was to steer toward was one of the pale patches on the ground. The darker stuff was trees. Joe tried to sense wind direction and slip against it, but there wasn't much wind, so he prepared for a neutral landing and just went limp. The best way to land on unfamiliar terrain was like a rag doll.

At the last moment Joe worried about injury, imagining himself spending the rest of the war hidden by the FFI while his broken leg mended.

The ground came up like an elevator. *Thud,* a heavy landing—all that gold—on a hard meadow with knee-deep grass. The canopy descended on him while Joe broke out of the parachute harness. He was down, safely down, the first step—the longest one—taken. The next was upon him as he unholstered his .45 because figures hurried across the meadow. Despite feeling foolish, he hollered, "A breezy night!"

A voice in Oxford English answered, "Yes, let's go sailing."

Someone gathered up his chute as Joe was silently led away through trees. Beyond the grove they arrived at a large hay shelter where kerosene lamps were lit, the same that had marked his drop zone. In the unsteady light Joe looked around at his reception committee. They were five men and a woman who, with her lover, was there to do a distracting scene if a German patrol happened by.

Naturally the French were glad to see him, especially his bandolier, which had been promised by the British but delayed. The FFI leader had lost three fingers to Rommel's panzers in 1940 but was still able to do a quick count of the gold. Satisfied, he pulled bottles of red wine out of the hay. Only he spoke English. Recognizing Joe's accent he was pleased to tell the others that their paymaster was an American, the first they'd ever met.

So too for Joe; except for the British, they were the first foreigners he'd ever met, and it occurred to him why he had been picked as a paymaster— to show the flag to the French resistance, let them know that America was in the war with them too. Representing America was headier than his second jelly jar of red wine, raised by his hosts in toast to Allied victory. Here he was, treated like a hero, and all he'd done was jump. It reminded him of his little speech last year at Saint Joseph's.

The FFI reassured him that now he was in their hands and they'd handle things from here; so feeling pretty safe and secure, Joe slept like any tired GI. The next morning (awaking in a bird-shooting blind) he began to reflect on how unexpectedly he had been brought into this war that meant everything to his families. All three of them: his parents, his army, and his nation. Clearly his army parents considered him expendable, a youthfully ignorant courier, chosen from on high by those who would trade his life for the likelihood of an important delivery. Yet no one had forced him. Far from it. Bring on more. Bring on more adventure because this sure beat humping the English countryside carrying a ton of radios.

Joe was now in the FFI network. Western cloak-and-dagger doctrine prescribes that an infiltrator-agent should stay in one location for minimum hazard of discovery. But the French constantly moved him, on roads, all back roads, in vehicles subject to search at German checkpoints. Frequent movement was a way the FFI distributed risk by requiring that a host harbor an agent only one night. The next morning he'd be gone and so too his host's exposure to the Gestapo.

That's the way it worked with Gallic guile. At daybreak Joe was alone and edgy till a retarded farmhand arrived in a one-horse cart, dressed him in peasant clothes, and handed him a brief note instructing him to also act mute and retarded. The farmhand then burned the note. He spoke no English, so the two sat silently for a clopping ride of several hours to a house far out in the countryside where the proprietress prepared a ravishing brunch of ham and eggs, croissants, café au lait, and red wine.

After a nap he was handed a one-sentence note and put on a horse, which carried him for hours on game trails to a small hunting lodge deep in a forest. The horse knew the way from repetition, a perfect agent for the FFI. If Joe were nabbed, he wouldn't know his destination and the horse wouldn't say. The note, nevertheless, said to shoot the horse if Germans were closing in. There was only a caretaker at the hunting lodge. With nothing to do, they listened to the BBC describe the Allies' slow advance on Rome. Joe helped him with the English and in return was taught a few French phrases that might come in handy if he met Germans.

The next morning Joe was transported somewhere else, the beginning of more moves than he can remember. Several times he was buried in hay with a clothespin on his nose to stifle sneezing. He still had his .45 but felt unready to use it; the foreign strangers who were his only protection were unarmed; it was their game Joe was playing, and they'd said nothing about shooting his way out of a tight spot. It seemed in some ways there was almost an arrangement being observed with the enemy, that the French and Germans were occupied in matters that didn't much involve each other. At one halt he heard German spoken. It startled him to hear his family language in such a different context. He could make out some bilingual banter, and that his cart driver didn't sound tense or the German soldier threatening.

It was difficult to keep track of time, but it was probably about a week till one night Joe's cart halted in the woods next to a long narrow field of mown hay. His escorts fanned out, apparently to secure the field, but it had so many dips and rolls that he didn't expect this to be the exfiltration site. However, after midnight, under a quarter moon, a dark Lysander glided in as if the hay field were Heathrow Airport. Joe guessed, correctly, that this was the paymster system: jump in new ones, then pick up returnees before flying back to England.

There were no ground lights, so the pilot had obviously landed here before. Out of the woods came a big wagon drawn by two horses. Off came the hay, revealing a huge vat, maybe a wine vat. Four Frenchmen took hoses from the pilot and began refueling the plane. No doubt some of Joe's gold had gone to buy gas on the black market. That made him uneasy about the quality of the gas. But if the pilot would fly with it, why worry?

He had expected to be snatched off the ground in seconds, but there were long minutes before the engine coughed and turned over, during which the pilot had an amiable chat with his fuelers and exchanged something for wine. He finally climbed into the cockpit, gave a V for Victory and thumbs-up. From the woods a Norman cheer erupted that made Joe jump as he crouched in the brush. But if this was the way the French did things, why worry?

They had gotten him this far. He hugged the men who'd delivered him, received kisses in return. A bottle of cognac was shoved into his hands, then he raced for the Lysander. From woods on the opposite side of the field another American, also with a bottle, sprinted for the plane.

The exfiltrators sipped cognac during the flight home, which was direct, as if the Lysander were just a lagging aircraft from one of the increasingly frequent bombing raids on northern France. Guardedly the Americans probed each other about their time with the FFI. The other man talked like a demolitions specialist, joking about how his leg bag had been so full of explosives that he felt like a parachute bomb. Though the cabin was dark, Joe noticed how the man, presumably from the OSS, kept glancing his way as if trying to place him, at least by his voice. But then clandestine protocol was respected, and for the last hour of the flight the topic was girls of the FFI. Was there a love scene set up at your DZ? Joe asked. Oh, yeah, his companion said, nodding. That's standard FFI procedure.

Like a homing pigeon, the Lysander landed at the same RAF base from which Joe had departed. He was immediately separated and debriefed by a British lieutenant, who concluded by sternly warning Joe not to indicate to anyone in any way where he had been or whom he had seen. This routine admonition affected Joe unusually, forcing him to reconsider himself no longer as Jumpin' Joe but as someone holding secrets that could change, even end other people's lives. This induced in him a subconscious defensiveness about the possibility that unknown enemies might try to search through his mind; it was an inchoate fear, different from that of impending combat for which months of intensive honing had prepared him.

IN THE FOLLOWING DAYS the whole paymaster experience, carrying with it his secret fear, became a dormant memory like last night's dream—a short, strobelike interlude between the hectic time before and after—so Joe found the debriefer's orders easy to follow. Gone was the urge to share his foreign adventure with Bray and Vanderpool; he would keep it to himself like some attraction for a girl he didn't want them to know about. Wistfully he looked back on France as an experiential vacation, a romantic getaway from hard-time soldiering.

Surely if another classified jump came up again, he'd volunteer with gusto. That seemed improbable, and after his solo Joe stepped back into a half-million-man chorus preparing for the premier performance of World War II.

CHAPTER THREE

ON BOTH SIDES OF THE WALL

Except for Jack and Orv, there was little curiosity about Joe's absence. It was nothing unusual for a radioman to be pulled out for days of specialized training, like how to guide fighter-bombers onto targets because the 101st would have little of its own artillery available when they first met the enemy. Such training would have been excuse enough for Joe, but division G-2 went further. Realizing that Joe's absence might be open-ended, they provided a cover story that Bill Beyrle, stationed with the air corps in Kent, had taken seriously ill, so Joe had been granted emergency leave to see his brother. Upon his return from France, Joe deflected questions by asking them.

"Yeah, Bill's okay now. What's been going on in I Company?"

From everyone the answer was exercises like tactical drills, maneuvers, and night movements after company-size jumps, followed by critiques, cleaning equipment, and preparation for the next drill, maneuver, et cetera, to the point where a graffito went up in Ramsbury latrines: "One more exercise and we'll be too tired to make it over the Wall!"

That's what all the Screaming Eagles' preparations were for—to vault what Hitler called the Atlantic Wall of Fortress Europe. No one expected an easy landing. Indeed, German radio made specific reference to the 101st, how a warm welcome awaited them if they survived parachuting into minefields, plus acres of sharpened stakes known as "Rommel's asparagus" to impale gliders. Never had an invasion been so taunted by those defending against it.

But the taunters had immense problems themselves, starting with where was Rommel to plant his asparagus and sow his mines? Between Spain and the tip of Denmark were sixteen hundred miles of potential invasion sites. To defend that span Rommel and his boss, Gerd von Rundstedt, had thirty-five divisions of widely varying strength. Rommel wanted them all, especially panzers, close to the coast, where they could go into action with much less interference from the Allied fighter-bombers that now ruled the sky.

Rommel knew the fighter-bombers could paralyze movement on the ground, for he had suffered their devastation in North Africa. Rundstedt had had no similar experience and wished to concentrate most panzers well back from the coast to counterattack when the invasion site was confirmed (a preliminary Allied feint was anticipated). Moreover, Hitler reserved unto himself the decision of where and when four of the ten panzer divisions in France would be committed. Consequently, German deployments on and behind the Atlantic Wall were a compromise between contrary defensive strategies.

Even if Rommel had commanded all thirty-five divisions, the Atlantic Wall, like the Great Wall of China, was too long to be impregnable for its entire length. Hitler, Rundstedt, and Rommel knew the Mongols were coming, but where? A wily deception plan, featuring a phantom army, commanded by Patton and apparently poised to strike across the Strait of Dover, kept the German high command befuddled.

Currahees were also guessing, but because of huge bets placed on where they would drop. Otherwise location didn't matter much. They were the Mongols, ready to breach the wall anywhere. All they had been told was that the 101st would go in ahead of amphibious forces and hold off counterattacks against the beachheads. Yeah, we can do that. Let's get on with it. What are we waiting for?

Of more immediate concern in I Company was repercussions from the brandy heist. During Joe's absence, the heat was on. An eminent earl had raised it to the point that General Taylor was obliged to admonish Sink to recover the brandy or hang the thieves. Briefly the 101st's intelligence resources turned from the Atlantic Wall to domestic sleuthing.

A noose tightened on Duber but, aware of Sink's fondness for fine spirits, he found a loophole by approaching a trustworthy officer with this proposition: if the heat was turned off, two cases of brandy would be found under the canvas of Sink's jeep trailer. Through intermediaries the deal was cut. Duber sensed that no enlisted man in I Company seemed to be in better favor with Wolverton than Beyrle, no one less likely to be punished if something went awry in transferring the brandy; furthermore, Beyrle would be the last man to squeal on his buddies if the deal turned out to be a trap.

But Joe, remembering his trepidation when summoned for his unexpected interview at Littlecote, was not an easy sell this time. If another paymaster opportunity came along, he was not about to jeopardize his favor with Wolverton. So Duber's offer of prime venison cutlets was declined (Joe had had better in France). Okay, what about four bottles of the brandy? No thanks, Sarge. Joe still had the two that had been his reward for standing guard during the heist. They might be worth hundreds of dollars—as Duber averred—but a price could not be established while no one dared put Napoleonic brandy on the market. When Sink gets his cut that's going to change, said Duber. Maybe, said Joe, and he took the offer back for consultation with Jack and Orv. They both advised him to pass. Duber had too many irons in too many fires, and it was always someone else who got burned.

So Joe declined again, but Duber took that as an objection, not final rejection. He claimed to be a trustee—at what level, no one knew—of the invasion-site gambling pool. For transferring the brandy, he would let Joe in on how the betting was going, very confidential, very valuable insider information. This appealed to Joe's bent to be Best Informed, and he proposed that if Duber put in five hundred of his own money—but as Joe's bet—then he would participate in the transfer.

This counteroffer revealed his Class Shark trait, but compared with Joe, Duber was a great white and glided to another inducement: he would give Joe a secret weapon—a crossbow—easily fitted into a leg bag. That was enticing. Already the Screaming Eagles were arming themselves for the invasion with personal weapons like shotguns, six-shooters, and German machine pistols.* Joe asked for time to think about the crossbow.

---

* In armies other than the Wehrmacht, a machine pistol was considered a carbine, in the shoulder-fired species of submachine guns, sten guns, and tommy guns. Hitler, as a corporal in World War I, had had bad experience with carbines, so when he

A significant part of the 101st's training in England had been devoted to operating French civilian vehicles and German weapons, even tanks. Paratroopers were expected to capture such munitions in the enemy rear, then use them till resupplies arrived amphibiously some thirty-six hours after jumping. Till then, the Screaming Eagles' logistics were in their leg bags and whatever they could seize ("liberate" was the term, as "requisition" was in England), most important, German weapons and ammo.

This expedient was debated at division headquarters. Do we really want our men firing German weapons in the dark? How will anyone know friend from foe? The problem was a factor in a command decision that in the dark no one should fire *at all* unless fired upon by an identifiable foe. The preeminent factor was to conceal planned drop locations. Widely dispersed beyond the DZs, hundreds of mechanical puppets were to be parachuted into Normandy. Hitting the ground, they set off loud bursts from firecrackers, hopefully drawing Germans into a wild-goose chase, while Screaming Eagles assembled and organized on relatively silent DZs.* So Sink's policy was to stay silent, stay concealed for as long as you can. Till situations sorted out in the morning, the approved weapon was your hand grenade.

Currahees were skeptical and felt unreasonably constrained if they had to wait hours before pulling a trigger. They had a particular fondness for the enemy's Schmeisser submachine gun; its rate of fire was so fast that it went *burrrrp* while a hundred rounds filled the air in a few seconds, hence the Americans called it the burp gun. A model of German engineering excellence, it was a Mercedes compared with crude Model T's like the Sten and the tommy gun. No one could wait to capture a burp gun. Somehow Duber already had one, dismantled and concealed in his footlocker. It could be Joe's for transferring the brandy, but again he passed.

---

became führer of the Third Reich, he banned them. That didn't at all alter the Wehrmacht's need for a rapid-fire assault weapon; technically theirs was a folding-stock carbine, but they were compelled to call it a machine pistol.

* The firecracker paratroopers and unintended dispersal of real ones thoroughly discombobulated German intelligence, which reported on the morning of June 6 that 94,000 Allied paratroopers had landed in Normandy the night before—more than seven times the actual number.

The "don't shoot unless fired upon" policy was not pronounced till the eve of D Night, but much earlier most Screaming Eagles comprehended the value of a well-aimed silent weapon, no matter what its rate of fire. Consensus had developed that initially they would be fighting singly and in the dark, when a firearm gave away its origin much more than by day when a thousand weapons were crossfiring. The troopers deduced their jump would be at night because the amphibious invasion would have to be at dawn so that legs like the Keystone Kops could locate their objectives.

So, while declining the burp gun, Joe remained curious about a crossbow. Did Duber have one? Yes. Did he know how to use it? Not yet, but he was practicing. Joe said let him know when a crossbow was as good as the silencer on his deerslayer.

Duber was persistent, but he was down to his last fillip. How was Joe dealing with censorship? Were the folks back home reading what he wanted to tell them? Were there some confidentialities he'd rather keep from Blue officers?

All mail—V-mail it was called, letters on special folios that could be photocopied for minimum bulk—was censored by officers whose unwanted duty was to expunge references to unit locations. A trooper's letter that mentioned pubs meant head scratching for his platoon leader because it was supposed to be a secret, despite the taunting of German radio, that his unit was even in Great Britain. Hundreds of V-mails like that kept censors reading late by lamplight, often with embarrassment. If the officers didn't know their men already, they surely learned more than they wanted to after reading love letters. When they sent men into combat, it affected them, sometimes acutely, knowing the names and feelings of loved ones they had never met but would never forget.

To have an officer figuratively reading over his shoulder was not disturbing for Joe, so Duber's last enticement of bypassing censorship fizzled. Unlike most of his buddies, Joe didn't have a girl waiting for him back home, so he never gave a censor cause to blush. Dating had been too expensive while the Beyrle family was down and almost out before the war. In England, camaraderie was stronger for him than companionship, though after his paymaster adventure there had been a lass named Greta of the Auxiliary Territorial Service who took a fancy to him. He never mentioned her in any letters to his parents. Joe only suggested that he was chased and no longer chaste.

Letters from home (also by V-mail) were not censored, and for Joe they were an increasingly remote connection with the past. Whatever was back there had already exerted its influence, a vital impulsion but expended, a booster rocket that had done its job. Now, to finish the job, whatever it entailed, was the be-all and end-all for Joe and those around him, no matter how much they joked or pretended otherwise.

The paymaster experience had sparked his sense of being special, as part of what mattered most. It had developed an expanded and novel perspective of the war, a vague but keen appreciation of components previously beyond his ken. Joe declined Duber's blandishments because he wanted to remain eligible for more uniqueness—someone else would have to carry out Sink's conditional return of the brandy.

Duber recruited Jack Bray, leaving Joe nonplussed. He had acquiesced to Jack and Orv in turning down anything Duber offered. Now here was Jack picking it up like a girl Joe was no longer interested in. Okay, buddy, what's going on? Well, Jack said, this was an investment. Four bottles, sure to appreciate, were worth the risk. Yeah, he had counseled Joe otherwise, but . . . hell, this is going to be fun! Joe, you got in on the fun (and the reward) when you stood guard for the heist. On a maneuver while Joe was away, Duber had poached game in Sherwood Forest, gotten caught, and told the sheriff of Nottingham that he was America's Robin Hood—and he got away with it. Duber was a proven winner. His plan for the brandy transfer was simple, the odds very good.

Then why, Joe demanded, didn't Duber transfer the stuff himself? Well, the heat was on; Duber was under suspicion and maybe under surveillance. You've been the risk taker, Jack said, referring to Joe's proxy jumps; now *we* want some fun-risk-reward. We joined the Airborne for that. And Duber is a sergeant. We do what he tells us in the field and will in war, so you can't separate that from off-duty.

Jack and Orv were basically mild young men, resembling each other in their countenance and slim physiques. Neither of them took to Airborne bravado. Each felt, as General Taylor was to say, that he didn't much like jumping out of airplanes but loved being around men who did. As only soldiers do, they loved Joe, he loved them, and they proved to be right when the transfer went down as smooth as the brandy—brandy with which Sink and his staff toasted the crumbling of the Atlantic Wall hours before they took off to vault it.

With the transfer accomplished and the heat off, the Blues' attention spun down to a shrinking vortex of concentration on what they were to do and how to do it. It didn't help when Captain Shettle moved up to be Wolverton's operations officer, replaced as CO of I Company by Captain McKnight, a taciturn, Lincolnesque man.

As McKnight's radio operator, Joe was his shadow in the field and had to understand his unrevealing personality, anticipate his orders, actions, and inactions. This resembled a new libidinous relationship: a complicated ebb and flow of affection, admiration, incomprehension, and fury. Nothing had gone outstandingly well under Shettle; there were no particular plaudits from Wolverton or Sink but no pratfalls either. McKnight was comfortable with that, satisfied with continuing Shettle's high standards and not pressing for major changes. As the man closest to McKnight's shoulder, it was for Joe to reassure his fellow enlisted men that though I Company was changing quarterbacks before the big game, it was still a winning team. The game plan was so immense and comprehensive, I Company's component so subordinate, that staying the course was tantamount to success.

McKnight's attitude was the prevalent one in I Company: let's just get to the kickoff fairly rested. Those above him, however, Wolverton and especially Sink, felt their team could not be overtrained—latrine graffiti notwithstanding. Lives lost from inadequate training would be the colonel's responsibility, as would the onus of writing letters to widows. Better to be safe than sorry, even if Blues felt overworked. Like Antaeus they were expected to regain strength as soon as their feet struck the earth.

During this exhausting run-up to a marathon, flashbacks came to Joe: how the FFI were over there, not that far away, waiting to detonate in the German rear somewhat as the 101st would, albeit the latter explosion would be infinitely stronger. He wished he could have told the FFI how strong. His mind encompassing both sides of the Atlantic Wall, Joe longed for the day that would link them. He felt it would be during the invasion.

Not quite.

———

NO CIVILIAN WAS PRESENT this time, and Wolverton had even less to say, yet when they saluted, something passed between them, an acknowledgment from the officer that the enlisted man had been there, done that—a tip of the hat. With nothing prefatory, Wolverton smiled and said that brother Bill had taken a turn for the worse. Did Joe wish to visit him again?

Yes, sir! A week of escape and evasion in France would be like rest and recuperation. Once again Joe was jeeped to the Hungerford train station and again joined there by two men. This time, to his surprise, they claimed to be Screaming Eagles. Their cover story was special training at Bournemouth Airport. Joe didn't tell them he'd been through this before, and it was their turn to be surprised when the three went out to a hangar and drew golden bandoliers.

More excited than apprehensive, the paymasters joshed with their pilot that they would skyjack the plane and spend the rest of the war in Swiss luxury. He was a Battle of Britain pilot whose wounds had disabled him from ever flying Spitfires again. Without irony he announced that these days the RAF never put enough fuel in paymaster planes to reach Switzerland.

The young Americans looked at one another, unsure if he was kidding. They had little comprehension of British weariness, how years of mortal struggle against Hitler's tyrannosaur had either killed, drained, or enervated the few to whom so much was owed by so many. In 1944, from sheer fatigue, Great Britain was not reluctant to hand off the heavy lifting to America, rightfully considered to be both the United States and Canada. Like a tag team the three nations were hellbent on taking down Hitler from the west, but with the freshest members wondering why their veteran partner seemed most patient for victory.

IN FLIGHT JOE'S PARTNERS nattered so much about going over the wall, going to France, that he worried whether they could stop talking about it when back with their units. We're going to be the first! they exulted. No, you're going to be the second and third, Joe reflected, wondering if there was something he should say about their upcoming FFI experience that would help them get through the adventure. He held his peace. Though his tips would be useful, what if either of these guys was captured?

Joe wouldn't be—he refused to believe he could be—but what about the others? If his description as a second-time paymaster circulated in German security channels, it might make it more difficult for the FFI to move him to exfiltration. That was his apprehension now, as fear of a broken leg and convalescing with the FFI had been on his first pay-master jump. This time he wanted in and out of France quickly, like a senior-class outing before high school graduation.

It was another two-hour night flight, bobbing and weaving. In the blacked-out cabin the jumpers were shadows swaying against one an-other. Being the veteran among them was a peculiar feeling for Joe. They asked him nothing, said nothing. It occurred to Joe that maybe they weren't Screaming Eagles at all. Maybe they all had clandestine covers like his. Maybe they were supposed to test Joe's ability to keep his mouth shut. Things didn't add up, but he felt higher-ups were doing cal-culations that would work. Wolverton backed what he was doing, and that was good enough for Joe.

The engine shook the fuselage, rattling the deck on which they sat with increasing pain. This time Joe was scheduled to jump last. At some signal Joe couldn't hear, the man nearest the cockpit pushed open the hatch. Joe slid closer for his second look at France. Currahee! Joe yelled to the first jumper; he received a nod in return, then the man was gone. Joe was more excited watching him than he had been when he first jumped a month before. He grew increasingly excited as his re-maining comrade crouched in the door and disappeared into the rushing night. They leaped out about ten minutes apart. No aborts. That was encouraging—the RAF-FFI system was working smoothly.

Then he was sitting alone as the slipstream screamed by that black hatch that seemed to suck at him like a whirlpool. It was the alone-ness that troubled him. Yes, there were allies down there, but he wouldn't know any of them from before. Almost sentimentally Joe wished to be back with Jack and Orv as he fidgeted, waiting for the command to go.

The pilot was an RAF sergeant with a regimental mustache curling at the ends. He flicked his hand up, and Joe wasn't sure if that meant to hook on to the anchor line. The pilot nodded but was more concerned with finding the pattern of lamps a thousand feet below. Quickly he reached back and gave Joe a rap on the shoulder.

"Currahee!" he yelled into the wind that in seconds was hurling him a hundred miles per hour horizontally.

The shout spit out any misgivings. Life at twenty could be no better than this. No matter that the night was even blacker than the first, without any horizon between an earth and sky that were equally dark. His chute blasted open for that moment of suspended animation when he was neither falling nor parachuting. It should take about three minutes to descend. Joe lost count on the way down, too eager to pick up a light source somewhere.

There were a few, scattered and distant, probably isolated farmhouses. Normandy wasn't completely blacked out despite the German curfew. In England even little lights like those would have brought the police in minutes.

Some murky colors emerged below him, the kind a scuba diver sees when approaching the bottom of an opaque sea. Joe steered for the palest patch within a spiky collage.

At the last second he prepared for a tree landing by crossing his legs. Joe's children are glad he did. His feet crashed through twigs; the trunk swayed as he knocked off branches and hit it bruisingly hard. With all of that tree holding him back, touching the ground was soft. His jumpsuit was ripped, as was his skin beneath it.

In a spider's web of parachute cords, branches, and twigs, Joe noisily freed himself as leaves floated down like a light snow. He scrambled away more afraid than ever in his life. Another ten yards of slip would have missed the clutching tree and set him on a meadow. Silently, from the perimeter of the meadow, a dozen figures stepped out in silhouette like the chorus in an opera.

"I'm off to see the wizard!" Joe yelled. The answer should have been, "The wonderful wizard of Oz." But there was a quizzical silence.

The British briefer had advised, "Now, dear fellow, if they're Germans, it will sound like 'vonderful vizard.' You should then take appropriate action."

"Yes, sir," Joe had replied. "What would that be?"

Some of the silhouettes appeared to be in uniform, and all prickled with weapons. Appropriate action for the moment was not to go for his holster. A figure stepped forward, a woman, to say, "Do you have something for me?"

That was good enough for Joe. He unsaddled the bandolier and gave it to her like the offering at mass. With that, as suddenly as they had appeared, ten Frenchmen disappeared into the woods, leaving him with two English-speaking guides. No wine this time. Grimly Joe was offered a burp gun, as if the three might soon be in action.

A burp gun was better than wine, and he longed to take the weapon but couldn't figure out how he could explain his possession of it to Jack and Orv, and especially to Duber. So Joe declined the gun, indicating that his hosts' valor was all the protection he needed. Such sangfroid ingratiated him with the FFI. Once more he was taken to safe houses, fed, and bedded. He ate very well and slept very soundly.

One morning from the foot of his bed he was awakened by a dog barking, one who didn't like strangers and hadn't been briefed that Joe was an ally. Bijou was the dog's name, like Joe a fugitive because she had bitten a German of the SS who had intruded on her mistress. Consequently Bijou had been marked for execution. She was hostile to Joe because of his black jumpsuit, a uniform the same color as that worn by the SS. For reasons he never asked, during this sojourn with the FFI Joe was never disguised as a peasant.

One morning he woke to a serene view of rolling farmlands with squares of tidy trees. It was hard to comprehend that there was a world war going on, that he was behind German lines, especially when he was served breakfast in bed as if he were lord of the manor. If this was war, Joe wanted more of it. But he noticed something different in the eyes and attitude of the FFI. They were noticeably tense, more impatient. They had expected the liberating invasion by now. From large-scale maneuvers in England, Joe had sensed the Anglo-Americans were headed toward the Atlantic Wall like a locomotive; but to the French who had waited four years it was different, the occupation apparently a permanent humiliation, and they let him know.

"We are called the resistance," one of them said, "but our countrymen's resistance is weakening. There has been too much time for them to adjust to life under the Germans. Too many of us are adjusting to it. When are you coming?"

"Wish I knew."

Between sleeping and eating there was a languid time for such talk in safe houses. When a guide's English was good he'd draw Joe out about Franco-American relations. Joe knew only about Lafayette and the First World War. The FFI tried to indoctrinate him, and he didn't mind at all even though European politics were way beyond his pay grade.

But when the invasion? The recurring question was put subtly, put bluntly, put in every way. Joe wasn't about to tell them his guess, which was that they could expect to see him again in the next month or two; but he did divulge the latrine graffiti that said much more training would exhaust the Americans to the point where the Atlantic Wall would be too high. This went over well with the FFI, most of whom had been soldiers in the French army when it was blitzed in 1940. Okay, they liked to say, the invasion must be coming. Joe's question to them was where.

Just prior to exfiltration, the local leader, Camille, made a pitch to him: Joe could play a much more important role in the war if he stayed in France rather than returning to England and the fate of infantrymen, most of whom, said Camille assuredly, would be killed during the invasion. It would be like attacking the German trench lines in World War I, when Camille's father and all his uncles were mulched by machine guns.

No, it would be *German* infantry slaughtered this time, Joe corrected him. Camille toasted to that but went on; French and Americans were the most freedom-loving people in the world and should be the closest allies, work hand in glove, forget the British. Joe liked to blow up things, didn't he? During his stay in safe houses he had provided the FFI some valuable instructions on how to mold charges (delivered by the OSS) for maximum damage with minimum explosives. He'd shown them that by packing a little nitro starch on the outside of a railroad track the blast effect would also clear the opposite track like a bulldozer blade.

Camille rubbed his hands. There was a railroad junction about twenty-five miles away that Joe should see and advise on how best to destroy it.* Stay with us a while longer, dear ally. You will never forget our hospitality, nor the hostesses of Argentan.

Argentan? Joe perked up. Camille seemed to know some practical information. Might it include the location of the invasion? His answer came with a sigh as if it embarrassed him how ignorant Joe was of grand strategy. "But of course, my friend, the landings will come between the Seine and the Somme. Why else did the Canadians rehearse at Dieppe?" Then Camille commented on how Churchill sacrificed the French-speaking Canadians in a cold-blooded experiment.[†] So the location of the upcoming invasion could not be more obvious: "*Normandie, n'est-ce pas?*" So apparent that Joe should support it from behind German lines.

So it would be Normandy; he had it straight from the horse's mouth. Joe was wondering how to change his bet from Picardy and double it without arousing the curiosity of Duber, when someone interrupted Camille, causing him to bilingually curse.

Word was that a German patrol had come across Joe's drop site and noticed the tree he'd torn up when landing. It had torn him up too, leaving multicolored bruises. The Germans had also discovered scraps of his jumpsuit, deducing that there had been an aerial infiltration. Joe was impressed by their sleuthing while Camille railed against the crew who were supposed to sanitize the site. They had reached it too late the morning after Joe's jump.

The heat was on, in a way as it had been in Ramsbury, Joe thought

---

* Most important transportation targets, like this railroad junction outside Argentan, were "dual-targeted" by the Allied high command—that is, assigned to the FFI as sabotage missions but also struck by bombers. This redundancy policy exasperated the FFI, who would risk lives, and often lose them, hitting a target that subsequently was obliterated by heavy American or British bombers. Because the FFI received missions through well-established British channels, of which the paymaster system was a part, guerrillas like Camille blamed the British.

† Dieppe (August 1942) was a raid in force, meaning a short heavy strike with a scheduled withdrawal rather than the objective of holding ground permanently. As such, Dieppe was the largest raid in history and probably the least successful, though British commandos and American Rangers significantly contributed. The Canadians sent 5,000 of their best men across the Channel to Dieppe and returned with but 2,200. The raid was an experiment to test the prevailing Allied thesis that a sizable port must be seized by direct assault immediately, as had been accomplished in North Africa. The well-learned lesson of Dieppe was that, in the face of Rommel's defenses, the way to success was to first seize beaches before attacking ports. That was done to perfection in Normandy; the port seized was Cherbourg.

at first. Things get screwed up and involved, but the Dubers of the world (Camille, evidently, was one of them) dodge or deflect bullets, and things turn out right. But now Joe heard a different chord being struck. Camille reported random arrests and interrogations, safe-house keepers declining his requests. French eyes and attitude now expressed hatred of the occupiers, whereas previously there had been nonchalant distaste. Before, the FFI had referred contemptuously to the Germans by their World War I sobriquet, *boche,* which Joe took as the GI equivalent of "clerks and jerks"—drones of the occupation administration.

The Gestapo were appallingly different, their very name uttered quickly and quietly. Joe asked more about them, as he felt responsible for their present focus. He learned they were despisedly professional as well as sinister, most of them police officers before the war, now with five years of international experience. In Normandy the Gestapo studied the flow of money and transients in the province. Their principal means were records of the French police and cooptation. For that reason the FFI dealt with local gendarmes only through intermediaries. In Camille's plans, all gendarmes were considered Gestapo auxiliaries: bribe them if possible; kill them if necessary.

The Gestapo's duties in France were far more immense than their manpower. Rounding up Jews and other "vermin" was the task for which they evinced the most enthusiasm, but the Gestapo (an acronym for Secret State Police, an arm of the SS) was also responsible for Rommel's rear-area security and counterespionage, normally military functions.

Corpulent Hermann Göring was godfather of the Gestapo, whose original success was to ferret out Communists in Germany. Moving up as Hitler's deputy in 1934, Göring turned over the Gestapo to its wartime chief, thirty-five-year-old Heinrich Himmler, a prim, pedantic headmaster and professor of agriculture. At all concentration camps—the Gestapo ran them—Himmler directed that there be an herb garden. His eleven-year reign of terror, carried out by twenty thousand secret policemen, would cover Europe to the Volga. His was the key instrument of Nazi power, the knife at the throat of every German, the scourge of conquered peoples, the flywheel that kept Hitler's war machine functioning to the end.

The Gestapo's charter in France was Himmler's 1941 decree, titled

Nacht und Nebel ("Night and Fog"), which stated, "Measures [to date] taken against those guilty of offenses against the occupation forces are insufficient, and even penal servitude or hard labor sentences for life are regarded as signs of weakness. An effective and lasting deterrent can be achieved only by the death penalty or by actions which leave the family and population uncertain as to the fate of the offender."

Himmler's frustration, expressed in *Nacht und Nebel,* was because hostage taking had not worked well in occupied France. Indeed, in Camille's opinion, it had helped FFI recruitment. If a Norman feared a midnight knock on the door, Camille could rusticate him as proprietor of a country safe house like those that had harbored Joe; thus a fugitive and a potential hostage found shelter together. What infuriated Camille now was that Himmler's intimidation might be succeeding through the heat applied after discovery of Joe's drop site.

The Gestapo's unblinking eyes scanned the entire Atlantic coast, too wide a panorama for constantly detailed surveillance, so it took an incident, some evidence of underground resistance, before they focused on a locale. The evidence of Joe's jump near Alençon was such a precipitator. Though sanitizing the drop site was not his responsibility, he faulted himself for not avoiding the trees, thus bringing *Nacht und Nebel* upon his hosts. He needed no instruction that Nazis were as bad as anyone in the world, but up till then they'd been simply the enemy, rather than perpetrators of terror and torture. Now Joe heard Camille's reports on the Gestapo, and his offer of a "kill pill" for the possibility of capture. Joe asked instead for the burp gun he had previously declined.

With the heat on, movement to exfiltration was slower, the stops longer. In transporting Joe, the FFI took any encounter with Germans as a failure of their intelligence sources, their strongest and utterly vital asset. Someone had not posted himself as a lookout on schedule, or had left her watch early. Or the bought corporal at the Germans' motor pool had not, as promised, reported the departure of several vehicles, his quid pro quo for a gold coin. Camille had led the corporal to believe that his bribe was from black marketeers wishing to move contraband on the roads.* If his officer discovered that treachery, he would be demoted and

---

* The FFI were major players in the black market, though of course they never identified themselves as members of the resistance when they approached Germans with bribes. However, a nonperformance, like that of the motor-pool corporal, re-

packed off to the Eastern Front; however, if he had knowingly been an accomplice for the FFI, his penalty would be execution, either by interrogative torture or firing squad, with his company formed up to witness.

When they torture their own, Camille had informed Joe, the Gestapo use whips and cords. For French victims, they start with things that burn the skin. They have written instructions for what to use on different people. Obviously it's different for males and females, he noted, downing another jelly jar, and who do you think holds out longer? Not us but the women, once they get through the initial humiliations. What do you think, Joe—is it because nature endows them for the agonies of childbirth?

"I've tried very hard to obtain the torture instructions," Camille said, "but we haven't yet been able to bribe a Gestapo."

"Why do you want their manual?"

"It helps to know what they'll do to you. You're better prepared to hold out as long as possible. We pledge ourselves to four hours. Could you do that, Joe?"

"Hell no. My body'll look like a Swiss cheese before they get it."

JOE WAS THINKING THAT way when his cart made an unexpected halt. Stuffed under hay with his clothespin and burp gun, he heard imperious German commands. That was unnerving for him, but the French had always demonstrated an effective sense for what worked. Laugh it up, play the drunk or the flirt as necessary. Other times be very correct and respectful—that always meant a German officer was present at the checkpoint. No bilingual joking by his driver this time, only short, polite answers. And a long, quiet pause.

Joe listened for one word, *Merde!*, the emergency signal to burst from the hay firing his burp gun. Waiting for the probe of a pitchfork, he strained to hear what the driver would say now. What he heard was a German curse, a resounding slap, the horse neighing from pain and surprise as the cart jerked forward. The driver said something servile, clucked, then the cart creaked and slowly moved on.

---

sulted in effective blackmail when the FFI informed him of the true source of his bribe.

At the next safe barn, Joe came out sneezing. His driver apologized as if Joe were a mistreated dignitary and congratulated him in a way he couldn't understand till shown two small gold coins. Joe had brought them from England, and another of his coins had just bribed his way through the unexpected roadblock.

That outcome was rewarding, but being behind enemy lines had definitely lost its appeal. The powerlessness, more than the danger, grated on Joe. It was hard to be clandestine cargo when he was a soldier longing to do what training had taught. On his last day he was moved nearly thirty miles. Itching from hay, this time Joe was glad to exfiltrate. Darkness came very late, with the Lysander right behind it; he was the only agent to be recovered. The FFI departure committee was grim and their kisses hasty. No cognac this time, no one to talk with in flight. As he snuggled behind the cockpit, Joe wondered about the two jumpers who had accompanied him outbound. They'd probably exfiltrated earlier while Joe was delayed by the Gestapo dragnet. Or had they been caught in it? How could he find out? Reluctantly he realized that he probably never would.

The RAF debriefing was brief—obviously much more was now in the wind than single parachutists supporting the FFI. Joe was sent off with thanks but no transportation and had to hitchhike to the railway station. That didn't bother him; he had a greater gratitude, for it was certain that his next jump into France would be with six thousand Screaming Eagles.

He'd missed the 101st's final dress rehearsal, called Exercise Eagle. Vanderpool said he was one lucky guy: five hundred troopers couldn't jump because their planes didn't even find the DZs at night. There were also four hundred jump casualties: broken bones, sprains, and cuts from farmers' barbed wire. And that wasn't even under fire.

"We'd better go soon, Joe," Orv said, "or there won't be many of us left."

CHAPTER FOUR

D NIGHT EVE

THIS TIME DUBER WAS MORE PROBING. "BEYRLE, HOW THE HELL did you get two leaves when nobody else gets any? You're a sergeant, and the colonel can't even take one."

It was gratifying to see Duber suspicious that someone might be in on a deal that didn't involve him. His curiosity peaked when Joe casually changed his invasion bet from Picardy to Normandy. Could he have penetrated the ultimate secret? Secrets abounded, real secrets and not-so-secret secrets. Though Duber was now secretly married to a local woman, he also had hustled Greta, the ATS girl. He lost out to equally interested Currahee officers with whom she appeared at Red Cross/USO dances. On the arm of two majors, she turned up at a big party in Newbury where Yehudi Menuhin played "Turkey in the Straw" as an encore. Despite these attentions, Greta seemed to have time for Joe, a high sign he deflected because there was something about her that said stay away. The paymaster debriefings had emphasized not getting too close to any civilians, and grimly illustrated posters admonished, A SLIP OF THE LIP MIGHT SINK A SHIP. Standard warnings like that were ignored like familiar furniture.

Imminent combat absorbed attention so extensively that even officers became lax about counterespionage until they were "bigoted." A bigot was the code name for anyone who knew the location of invasion landings or objectives. Of course Eisenhower was the first bigot; after him those shiveringly important secrets sifted down in tight, controlled steps through the highest ranks, not to reach the lowest till they prepared to board ships, planes, or gliders for the great crossing to France.

When that would be, not even bigots knew. It all depended on a weather window. Ike himself could not predict exactly when the invasion would go through. Movement of millibars over Greenland was as important as the movement of panzer divisions in France.* Thus Allied plans, extremely detailed, did not include the vital date on which they were to be carried out, instead designating it as "D," from which the term "D Day" became immortal.

About two weeks after Joe's second paymaster jump, Third Battalion moved out to a marshaling area near Exeter to be locked up with no outside contact, there to be briefed on the purpose of Exercise Eagle, about which Orv had reported so bleakly.

"Remember what you did, what you were to accomplish," Wolverton announced solemnly. "That's what we'll do in France. The operation is called Overlord. Our part in it is called Neptune because we'll be protecting the amphibious forces."

Two days later, under even tighter security, the Currahee enlisted men were bigoted, then confined like prisoners. It seemed that if all the MPs guarding them would ship out for France, Ike might have an extra division to hit the beaches on D Day.

Screaming Eagles were to jump into action hours before the landings; D Night it was called unofficially, and D Night objectives came as a surprise to many. Most bets had been on an invasion east of Normandy, but thanks to Camille's tip, Joe had a winning wager because Normandy is such a big province. Duber approached him as soon as I Company was bigoted.

"Good guess, Joe, but sorry, you can't collect right away. This whole Overlord-Neptune thing could be to fool Rommel. Bets will be paid off if we actually jump on Normandy." Joe began to exhibit his Most Obvious Temper. "Not my policy, trooper," Duber said. "It's the guys run-

---

* One of the smallest and most obscure—but far from the least important—battles in the ETO was for weather stations in Greenland, a Danish territory that fell to the Germans when they overran Denmark in 1940. For the purpose of reporting storms to their U-boats, two German radio teams set up clandestine transmitters on the frozen coast. By intercepting their signals, the British located those stations, then liquidated and replaced them with their own. Consequently, by 1944 the Allied high command had better foresight of impending weather than did Rundstedt and Rommel, who had to rely on irregular reports from U-boats.

ning the casino." He held up his hand. "I know you're pissed, but I'll make you a side bet, double or nothing. I think Normandy is just a feint." Duber threw out his left, quickly pulled it back. "To see what Rommel does. We're going in somewhere else, pal."

The Class Shark took him up: a thousand dollars if they indeed jumped into Normandy. Collection shouldn't be hard because Joe and Duber were assigned to the same D Night stick. Macabre joking like that became common between creditors and debtors, how the former if necessary would heroically save the lives of the latter in combat.

At Exeter there was but one more rehearsal, a full-dress battalion tactical jump that didn't go much better than Exercise Eagle. The 101st didn't participate in the worst rehearsal snafu, a practice amphibious landing at Slapton Sands. Reconnoitering German torpedo boats slipped in and sank several ships with great loss of life. There was no official word about Slapton Sands; Screaming Eagles learned about it through the grapevine. What it told them was that Rommel knew the invasion was coming but not when or exactly where.

The grapevine constantly carried negative information, so officers were constantly admonished to ignore it. Naturally Currahees didn't, but when rumors circulated about how final rehearsals for Operation Overlord had been botched, the negativity was shrugged off. In bull sessions they reasoned that their job was doable—not that they understood everything, but they knew enough so that if they landed anywhere near their objectives, those objectives would be seized. Yes they would, no matter how many Germans stood in the way.

At the same time, what the Currahees would do, they realized, was but a small patch in the stupendous parquetry Eisenhower had put together. That was Ike's ultimate talent, demonstrated from 1943 to 1945, for which the world owes him ultimate homage. Neither Joe nor his buddies knew anything about Ike except that he had come up from the Mediterranean Theater and had a German name. That seemed ironic, and they wondered if it did to the Germans too.

Ike was a principal archangel, God being Roosevelt. As remote as he was, Eisenhower came down to the 101st several times, including a last visit as they loaded up on D Night. His British air adviser had told him that 80 percent of them were being sent to certain death. Paratroopers are picture takers. From D Night the most famous of their photos was of Ike speaking with vehemence to a Screaming Eagle lieutenant as black-face troopers listen with intent seriousness but scant worry. Depicted is the paradox of the Allied supreme commander, visiting to encourage his men and instead finding encouragement himself.*

The other big-name generals were better known to Screaming Eagles than Eisenhower. Omar Bradley had commanded the 82nd before it split into the 101st, so Bradley was okay even if he was a straight leg. He'd lived up to his nickname, "the GI's general," and they were glad he had overall command of the American half of the invasion. He'd know what the Airborne could do and the kind of support they'd need to do it. Joe had heard of "Blood and Guts" Patton but in a negative way because Ike had relieved him for slapping a GI in Sicily.

The other celebrity general was Field Marshal Bernard Mont-gomery, the overall Overlord ground commander. The British put titles before a man's name, like Sir or Earl or Duke, but also after his name if he had won some famous victory. For that reason Monty—a nickname as well known as Ike—signed himself "Montgomery of Alamein." In Ramsbury Third Battalion had been shown a British-produced docu-mentary war movie, *Desert Victory,* about how Montgomery finally routed Rommel in the desert at El Alamein. Jack liked the film so much he asked Joe and Orv to see it again with him. This was after the second paymaster jump, and Joe declined because he was separating war movies from war experience in his mind. Clips of German POWs, hands on head, jarred with his memory of German voices snarling behind guns. To capture those guns and the men who held them, he had come to realize, was not going to be the romantic adventure that Jack looked forward to. There was no one to dissuade him, for there were no combat veterans among the Currahees.

At Exeter came the last sign that combat was nigh—the issue of live ammunition. In exercises, maneuvers, and rehearsals there usually

---

* When Ike showed up on D Night he nervously took very hot coffee from a Red Cross worker. She noticed his hand trembling so much that he was in danger of scalding himself, so she withdrew the cup till it cooled. "As the 101st took off," she recalled, "tears rolled down his face and he didn't even accept a handkerchief. Ike just kept waving till the last C-47 disappeared into the night."

weren't even blanks because it was feared that if civilians heard what sounded like torrents of gunfire, they'd think the Germans were invading England. So if a trooper carried a rifle, he went, *"Bang-bang."* If he was a machine gunner, he went, *"Duh-duh-duh-duh."*

Now dumped in Joe's platoon bay were clips, bandoliers, and belts of sharp-pointed, hard-metal bullets. Troopers dipped into them and looked at one another. What weighed on their minds was the weight of the ammo. They'd have to saddle it on like burros, jump with it like anchors, pick it up and carry it till they could unload on the Wehrmacht. Nevertheless they liked the heavy lethality of what was called their "basic load." The *bang-bang, duh-duh* of "voice fire" had made the most serious rehearsals a little childish.

Now they were no longer boys doing a man's job, they were unquestionably the men. Yet they rubbed their peach fuzz when orders for D Night came down: don't shoot until fired upon. Throw grenades instead to keep the DZs secret. Bullshit, Duber snorted; six thousand parachutes would give that away like a circus coming to town.

In addition to his basic load, each paratrooper was to carry ammo he'd never personally use, like a howitzer round in his leg bag. He would carry it to someplace near the DZ assembly area and leave it for artillerymen who would arrive later. Joe's nonpersonal munitions included an antitank mine and belts of machine-gun ammo he was to drop off by a certain barn after finding Captain McKnight and moving out with him to I Company's objective.

Yes, real objectives were at last revealed. Finally, at the eleventh hour, the troopers were shown exactly what they were to do in the vertical invasion. Maps and aerial photos were unsealed, sand boxes with models unveiled, and everything put on display for excruciatingly serious study. *Memorize, memorize* was the watchword and requirement for repeated quizzes. Study that barn from every angle, Beyrle. Imagine how it's going to look at night. What color is it? It appeared tan from the photo of a prewar tourist. Brochures from travel agencies were also helpful for appreciating the landforms, agriculture, and foliage. Details—for example, the cows around Drop Zone D were predominantly white— were provided by the most titanic intelligence effort in the history of warfare.

What to do if, despite intimate knowledge of the barn, Joe never found it? That was up to him. There were dozens of such dumps planned on the expectation that many would never be established. Not everything had to work for success, just enough things that exploited possibilities till they became probabilities. Combining good odds, the planners reasoned, put the overall odds in the 101st's favor. That too was the way Joe's young mind was thinking as, around midnight, he saddled on a herculean load for his third jump into Normandy. H Hour of D Night was scheduled for 1:40 in the morning, double daylight saving time, so in that part of the world midnight in midsummer is not very dark, especially with a moon.

For Screaming Eagles, D Night Eve produced tension like a turn-buckle, not so much seen as felt: a trooper scribbling a last letter, another sharpening his knife even though it was already so thin it seemed nearly transparent, someone else practicing pigtail splices on commo wire. And briefings, briefings, briefings. If the vertical invasion failed, no one could be blamed for not repeating enough the plans of what had to be done and how to do it, even if little went according to plan.

Plans focused on objectives, soon firmly planted in everyone's mind. The 101st's initial objective was to seize and hold the exits from Utah Beach where the 4th Infantry Division would be coming ashore. Protected by the 101st, the 4th would swing north to capture the vital port of Cherbourg. That was the overall plan, and every trooper knew how his DZ was located to support it. If you land somewhere else, join up with whoever is there and help them take their objective. At some point the generals would sort things out. This was inculcated by briefing after briefing.

Briefings and brief-backs definitely kept the troopers occupied, but what to do with the extra time after a twenty-four-hour weather delay was announced? Officers feared a nervous idleness—it could lead to greater fear. The chain of command felt their men should concentrate on what was coming up but at the same time not think about it too much, a most difficult balance to strike.

Troopers took it upon themselves to show what they were thinking and how to deal with it. A buddy of Joe's from Michigan, George Koski-maki, kept a diary of what was going on: crap games clustered everywhere, other little groups who tested their memory by sketching the

Norman road net without looking at a map. Each man had been issued a silk map in three pieces. When the pieces were joined it was about a yard square and showed the whole Cotentin Peninsula, the portion of Normandy to be invaded. Most troopers wore the map as a scarf.

They were told the challenge and password for the first twenty-four hours of the vertical invasion. It was reckoned that the Germans couldn't pronounce the word *thunder* the way Americans did. They'd say *donder*, so for D Night the challenge in the 101st was "flash" and the password was "thunder"—pronounced like an American.

But the 101st obtained a better identifier than that. Cautioned by his staff about the hazard of friendly fire when Screaming Eagles used enemy weapons, and from experience with the 82nd's jump in Sicily, General Taylor was vehement about the need for an audible and unmistakable recognition signal for paratroopers milling around in the dark among Germans. He asked an old friend on Eisenhower's staff to come up with a solution. It was both lightweight and lighthearted, the simplest of toys, not much bigger than the trinket that amused children when they emptied a Cracker Jack box. Taylor's toy made the sound of a cricket; research by an army entomologist confirmed that there was a similar species native to Normandy. The FFI was requested to send some over. The insects were auditioned and the mechanical cricket tuned so it could be distinguished from a real one.

Not long before D Night, the Overlord pipeline spewed out enough mechanical crickets for the 101st, the only division to use them. The source was P. H. Harris & Co., a British toy manufacturer who must have been mystified when the Allied high command, at the crucial point of the war, ordered rush production of frivolous baubles—seven thousand of them.

The cricket went *click-clack*. That sound asked "Who's there?" Two *click-clacks* (no more or less) was the answer: "a friend."

From his French experience Joe didn't have to be told that the cricket could mean life or death. Duber kept saying that on D Night there would be more to fear from Screaming Eagles than from Germans. So the cricket couldn't be buried in some pocket, taking seconds to retrieve. Each trooper punched out a hole allowing it to be laced onto a cord around the neck; then all he had to do was reach for his throat and make the cricket chirp.

AT EXETER EVERY MAN checked over a personal arsenal in light of his D Night tasks. Viewed officially, Joe's task as a radioman called for him to be armed with a folding-stock carbine—regarded as not much more than a peashooter—so he had added a pistol and Thompson submachine gun, both firing .45-caliber slugs. In the 101st that wasn't considered heavily armed at all. Unauthorized weapons proliferated because officers were taking along plenty of extra firepower themselves. Sink's was said to be a sawed-off shotgun.

Besides two half-pound blocks of nitro starch, Joe stuffed grenades in his cargo pockets and taped blasting caps to his ankles and helmet. Bray looked at him skeptically: "Joe, if a bullet hits your pot, don't worry about a headache; you won't have a head."

More important than his head was Joe's back, to transport the most vital radio, an SCR 300, the principal way for McKnight and Wolverton to communicate. All told, Joe's load, no heavier than most, was hundreds of pounds, so it took two men to raise him up the ladder into his C-47.

Instead of a million-dollar bandolier he'd been given ten dollars' worth of crisp new French money just minted in Washington. Little brass compasses and big English life vests were issued. Troopers were encouraged to shave their heads because it might be a long time till the next haircut. Many did to look more warlike. In the marshaling area everyone was engrossed with skin and helmet camouflage.

Before loading out from Exeter they cased their weapons, some in leg bags; they checked ammo for dents that could cause misfires, broke down K rations, and lined up kit bags containing their chutes. Then it was waiting time—waiting, the synonym for worry—waiting for something, whenever it came. In the next hour, line up chutes and leg bags, then form up by sticks. In the next minutes, assemble at your plane. In the next seconds, gather your thoughts. Waiting time divided quite like the jump commands they knew as well as their names: Stand up. Hook up. Stand in the door.

Something was stronger than even tension as the clock ticked down on D Night. Currahees felt beyond ready to do what training had exhaustively prepared them for. For eight months they'd been at it in England, a year before that in the States. They had reached the peak, with no further to go before falling on the Wehrmacht, the most feared and infamous force in the world. The whole world would be watching.

The 101st had no combat experience, but that didn't preclude a cocky attitude. They'd be rushing in, but that didn't make them fools. Youth and testosterone were big parts of it, but the biggest part of all was the unwavering will to fight to the death for your buddy, the death of either or both of you because you knew he felt the same way. That feeling was the strongest, but unspoken.

The overarching motivation was that Overlord must not fail. If it did, everything had to start over, with thousands fewer buddies. The Wehrmacht too had its ultimate motivation—that if they couldn't repel the invasion, they didn't have a chance of stopping the Red Army that had pulsed out from Stalingrad like schools of piranha attacking a bleeding crocodile. If the Russians weren't stopped, that meant the end of Germany's version of civilization. That was evident enough even at Joe's level, though in one briefing he learned that some of the static troops the Blues might fight were Russians who had thrown in with the Germans.

D NIGHT COUNTDOWN RESUMED fretfully after Channel storms caused the false start. Like a temporary reprieve before execution, the weather delay deflated much of the bravado and some of the emotional high. Eisenhower's army had hurried up only to start waiting again. The face painting, the Mohawk haircuts, the whole metaphor of war dance subsided for its inability to sustain energy.

Two Screaming Eagles, David Webster of the 506th and Tom Buff of division headquarters, noted the waning hours contrastingly. Webster mulled how the June sun didn't go down until 9:00 P.M., how he could sit watching the soft hills of England darken and wonder about the time of day in the States. Gripped by solitude, he gazed south down a valley winding to the sea. That's where the Germans were, over the southern horizon. What are they thinking? he mused. Of their own homes, their chances of ever returning to them?

"When will it get dark?" Webster wrote. "What chance does a paratrooper have then? Stay light, stay on forever—and we'll never have to go to Normandy."

Buff noted an entirely different attitude among his buddies who would *not* be jumping into Normandy:

> Every one of our friends whom Fate had placed in the rear echelon [to cross by sea] was there to tell us goodbye. Just before we got into our trucks they took photos of us with rolls and rolls of film. How those guys wanted to go! Even though I had a compass, Bill Urquia of our Aerial Photo Team gave me his, saying: "Tom, this is a lucky compass. It's been through North Africa, Sicily and Italy. Take it to France for me. Dammit, I'm not going . . ."
>
> Everyone shook hands, then we drove off for the airfield. We later learned that those fellows just roamed around, killing time until far into the night so they could count our planes as we flew over, wave to the sky and pray Godspeed.

President Roosevelt was also composing a prayer, his for a radio message to America on D Day: "Almighty God—Our sons, pride of our nation, this day have set upon a mighty endeavor."

After those words resounded, the nation came to a halt. The stock exchange, courtrooms, school classes, professional baseball games, traffic in every city and activity elsewhere froze to mark the moment as America collectively prayed as never before—nor since, till September 2001. Church bells began to toll, perhaps in contemplation of the many American lives that had already ended in Normandy before Roosevelt announced the invasion's site.

As it so rarely has in all of history, on D Day oratory matched the occasion. To his corps and division commanders of three nationalities, Montgomery had restated the mighty endeavor with verse from the marquis of Montrose:

HE EITHER FEARS HIS FATE TOO MUCH,
ELSE HIS DESERTS ARE SMALL,
THAT DARES NOT PUT IT TO THE TOUCH,
TO GAIN OR LOSE IT ALL.

Colonel Sink's message to the 506th was read inside C-47s:

Tonight is the night of nights.

Tomorrow, throughout the whole of our homeland and the Allied world, bells will ring out the tidings that you have arrived, that the invasion for liberation has begun. . . .

The confidence of your high commanders goes with you. Fears of the Germans are about to become a reality. . . . Imbued with faith in the rightness of our cause and the power of our might, let us annihilate the enemy wherever found.

May God be with each of you fine soldiers. By your actions let us justify His faith in us.

With such words in their ears, Currahees were pawing to "put it to the touch." The feeling was that their chutes couldn't get to the ground fast enough so they could start working over the Wehrmacht. That feeling intensified as Joe watched the first wave of transports slowly climb into an aerial armada.

Here was the big roll of the main game, even though it had been Japan that had shoved the United States into World War II. Joe could see that priority right in front of him, behind and all around. He saw I Company on the tip of an immeasurable, irresistible spear. It was hurled from the heart and arsenal of democracy—Rosie the riveter, war bond drives, around-the-clock shifts throughout Michigan—the whole wholehearted American effort at its zenith, circling to poise over the dark and choppy English Channel. Minutes before him, thousands like Joe were already flying off to their rendezvous with destiny. *Rendezvous with Destiny* became the name of the 101st's march and the title of its book recording the Screaming Eagles' wartime history. The rendezvous began with troopers strapped onto bucket seats in a surreal state of mind where more was to be won than could be lost with their lives.*

---

* Major General William C. Lee was named the 101st's commander when it was activated in August 1942. He may have recalled "rendezvous with destiny" as the phrase applied to the United States in a speech by President Franklin Roosevelt some years earlier. In any case Lee first addressed his fledgling Screaming Eagles this way: "The 101st has no history but a rendezvous with destiny. . . . We shall be called upon to carry out operations of far-reaching military importance, and shall habitually go into action when the need is immediate and extreme."

That was how Joe, Jack, and Orv felt, representing the bachelors. Family men had more on the line. Their bedrock sentiments were expressed, if at all, during some earlier time of contemplation, like those of Phil Wallace, Joe's buddy in a sister regiment:

SUNDAY, MARCH 19TH, 1944, NEW YORK CITY

My Dearest Jo,

You are now reading my last letter from NYC. All letters after this will be censored, so—if there is anything to be said I must say it now.

You already know that my heart and thoughts remain with you there in New England. No matter what happens to me overseas, believe that your Phil has given all because of deep love for his wife and baby. To die for you both would be an honor, far surpassing the Jap's honor to die for his emperor.

But to live would be an even greater achievement—and to this end I shall strive. Jo, you never need fear for my safety for it is far better to believe that God takes care of these things. What happens will happen, beyond our understanding. That's the way it goes and will.

If it is written in the Book of Fate that I shall return to you then we will forget our worries, our sorrows, our heartaches, and forever enjoy that God-given day when your Phil comes home to spend the rest of our lives in happiness. This war will make me appreciate that so much.

So your husband must leave you and Baby Sue for now. He has a job to do, a job that is not to his liking but he must do it to the best of his ability. You will see him again, even if not in this life. No power can keep us apart.

I am not alone in my travels. Millions of American soldiers are crossing the waters this spring. May most of us return, God willing.

CHAPTER FIVE

HIDE-AND-SEEK

AT THE DEPARTURE AIRFIELD A RADIO WAS PLAYING THE *Moonlight* Sonata. Oh, brother, Duber muttered, is that telling 'em we're coming by moonlight? There had been other music, live music by bands playing favorite marches, as Third Battalion assembled. This seemed a breach of security, a tip-off that something special was in the air or soon would be, but instead it reinforced Duber's hunch that such obvious activity must be to provoke German reactions for study. So he began taking bets that this run-up would be another dry run rather than the end of a weather delay as had been announced (the rain hadn't been too bad around Exeter where they'd marshaled).

Wagers like that revealed some amazing sangfroid among the paratroopers. Even when they blackened their faces with charcoal some did Al Jolson imitations. Banter between sticks continued up to the C-47s' ladders. English villagers had also been deceived into nonchalance. They'd just waved and given thumbs-up to each truck convoy as they had during the many, so many rehearsals.

Consequently a good number of Blues were feeling déjà vu when they reached the airfield but had second thoughts when they saw all the VIPs there. That's when Joe became convinced this was it; others were still smokin' and jokin', which seemed to cheer up the VIPs but also puzzle them. Don't these troopers know what they're going into? Didn't we make the training serious enough? The Currahees took their cue from Sink, who didn't seem at all worried.

Before wrestling into his chute Joe ran over to the next ship for an encouraging handshake with Bray and Vanderpool. However, they had already loaded, so he just waved at portholes, hoping they'd see him. Their jump master, Lieutenant Johnston, was the last to climb aboard. "Good luck, sir!" Joe yelled. Johnston nodded and confidently returned his salute.

Like all the others, Captain McKnight's stick was so heavily loaded that they had to be boosted up one by one into the narrow fuselage. Now even jokers were quiet. Several men popped airsickness pills as soon as the propellers turned over, were snoring by the time they reached altitude, and remembered nothing of the ninety-minute flight to their rendezvous with destiny.* Every trooper was in some degree of sleep deprivation because of the twenty-four-hour weather delay. They jumped at around 1:00 A.M. on June 6 but, except for catnaps, hadn't slept since the night of the fourth.

The moon was a fluorescent lamp, illuminating a sky jammed with planes, many of them pulling gliders. Joe had seen pictures from the Pacific war showing ships spread from horizon to horizon. The heavens over the Channel were filled the same way but in three dimensions and more tightly. *Awesome* didn't nearly describe it, even though Joe's porthole was no more than a peephole. Inside, the only light was from pulsing cigarettes. Joe's mind was in four places—the past, present, future, and a little of the beyond. He tried to take the best from them all.

Not much from the present; that was all watching and waiting as the armada turned south. The past was about his parents and people who he wished could be watching him now. The future was not far away, a product of his training that required a leg-locked exit, tight body position, and counting to four. If the main chute didn't open then, pull the rip cord of the reserve. It wasn't much to remember but it was everything that mattered during those first four seconds, then would come a bent-leg landing, sorting his gear, finding McKnight, and moving out to the company objective.

With everything at stake, such unique concentration was unforced but set off a riptide of thoughts in all directions. More than anything

---

* The pills were so strong that a medical investigation revealed some troopers were half asleep when shot by the Germans.

else, the mind, even the most highly disciplined mind, needed distraction from an overload of concentration. As chewing gum for their thoughts, men hummed or silently whistled vacuous tunes of the times like "I Want a Zoot Suit with a Drape Shape."

Joe indulged in such mind occupation but kept his thoughts close to what he knew he could do, not what luck could do to him; at the same time he realized that the future was no promise, only potential to continue. The priorities of the immediate future had to be taken in sequence, or the sequence would end.

Beyond was what would happen if the sequence did end. How he'd be killed didn't matter much. He imagined two doors. If he couldn't get through either one, it didn't seem he would suffer—he would instead be whisked away to a new reality.

CROUCHED AT THE HEAD of the stick was McKnight, the jump master, who checked off landmarks and bellowed them back so that if the plane got hit, his stick would know where they'd be bailing out.

"The English coast's behind us, men . . . here come the Channel Islands . . . whoops, they're shooting at us."

There was a German division stationed on Guernsey and Jersey. The aerial armada skirted them with enough distance so that antiaircraft guns were ineffectual, though it seemed sure that their fire would alert batteries on the Norman coast. That didn't happen—there was only a dribble of tracers from Cotentin—perhaps because the coastal batteries were fooled into thinking that the initial wave of the armada was just another of the big bombing raids that had become so common they flew over unopposed.

Duber cursed that he'd lost his bet—they hadn't come this far to turn around and go back. Joe knew he'd won the larger wager because that sure as hell was Normandy coming up. At one thousand feet it looked as dark and still as it had for his paymaster jumps. Once again he would arrive in France a rich young man.

So as not to pass above Allied navies (nervous naval antiaircraft gunners had riddled the 82nd's jump into Sicily), the aerial armada approached the coast from the west, the opposite side of the peninsula from Utah and Omaha Beaches. Upon landfall the pilots started a gradual descent to the planned jump altitude of seven hundred feet. Joe's stick sensed they were lower, much lower, around four hundred feet. The ever-calculating Duber did some calculations. He determined that at that height a reserve chute would be useless. McKnight agreed, so one by one his stick chucked the reserve packs to the back of the plane.* Same thing with gas masks and life vests. The troopers were over land now, and poison gas was at the bottom of their fear list.

"Get ready!" McKnight shouted, a standard prejump command, quite unnecessary except for a few troopers coming out of a sleeping-pill stupor. Joe's thoughts flashed for a moment to the FFI. Here we come, Camille—you won't be disappointed! God had been away from Europe for five years, replaced by the Gestapo. Now He was back. Yet the Germans prayed to Him with a motto embossed on their belt buckles: GOTT MIT UNS. God is with us. It seemed impossible for God to receive so many short messages, from both sides, as D Night unfurled.

"Check your equipment" was McKnight's next command.

Even while descending to four hundred feet the C-47s applied full power, though they were supposed to throttle back to the maximum safe jump speed of 120 miles per hour. Evidently many pilots found that was too slow for safety as each wave of transports felt more shocks from guns below. The German "88" artillery piece was originally designed for antiaircraft use and against the vertical invasion did much damage. Moreover, the armada was flying in formation. To slow down to one hundred miles per hour was to risk being rammed from behind. Thus the waves reached drop points at the speed of the fastest rather than the slowest planes among them.

Concussions from 88s multiplied, bouncing C-47s around like speedboats in a typhoon, as eight hundred of them—wingtips scant yards apart—struggled to hold formation and continue inland. Hunched on metal benches, troopers lurched against one another, helmets striking the fuselage as it whipsawed from explosions that flashed and thundered like a lightning storm, first remote, then rolling by, then rumbling else-

---

* Without a reserve parachute there was life or death in a hundred feet of altitude. Some sticks didn't have enough. They went out without enough altitude for even the main chutes to open, and troopers who had already landed heard a sound like pumpkins smashing on the ground.

where, then returning as antiaircraft batteries ahead searched for new targets. Between thunderclaps a face would appear momentarily in the flare of a cigarette lighter. Otherwise the fuselage was a dark cave of prayerful impatience united in a single plea—Let us out!

But first the Germans broke in. Joe heard a scud of shrapnel pepper the left wing. Suddenly a long stitch of heavy-caliber machine-gun fire shrieked up through the belly of his plane, punching jagged mouths across the deck. As one, the stick shouted and pulled up their feet. Spent slugs rolled around on the pitching deck. A trooper bent over and picked one up, perhaps the first war souvenir on the Western Front. No one seemed to have been hit. A good omen, and a taunt from the Germans that had to be answered because several men exclaimed that their precious jump boots had been gouged. No one's going to get away with that! Let's jump!

Ground fire and concussions abated when the armada, its formations broken beyond reassembly, entered a belt of fog. Germans could shoot only at sound, which five hundred feet overhead was like elevated trains. In the fog McKnight and the pilot saw no landmarks, relying entirely on a luminous compass, a wristwatch, and dead reckoning. The fog opened. Once again tracers reached up. Most missed, some hit, one with a huge flash and jolting explosion dead ahead. Lieutenant Johnston's ship—Jack, Orv—all aboard were consumed in a falling flame.

TWENTY FAMILIES LOST their men in a moment. It would be days before Joe knew, weeks for them. The fireball superheated a fury to get at the antiaircraft gunners. Till then jaws were locked, but someone yelled at the pilot, "Lemme at 'em!" But it was not quite yet time.

Emerging from the fog bank the armada was scattered, storm-tossed, its pilots confounded and confused at every altitude. Red lights went on, the alert to watch for green. McKnight yelled the long-awaited commands:

"Stand up!" Troopers struggled to rise amid flashes in darkness.

"Hook up!" Attach to the anchor line.

It was hardly an anchor, rolling, slanting down as if the plane had crested the ultimate dip of a roller coaster, the pilot as eager to disgorge the jumpers as they were to escape.

A trooper blurted that his boot was full of blood. The crew chief pulled him from the stick where he slumped against the pile of reserve chutes, fumbling for his first-aid pack. He'd been hit by the earlier stitch of machine-gun fire but didn't notice the wound till he tried to stand. No one said anything when he apologized for not going with them. His was just an early rendezvous, they'd think later, but not be able to remember his name.

Tracers streaked outside while in the black tube of the cabin Joe's stick swayed, groping for balance, every man bent by his load, which seemed welded to the deck. As the C-47 fishtailed, its crew chief man-handled cargo bundles to the door. Out they went.

"Shuffle to the door!" was McKnight's last command. Belly to butt, the stick jammed up behind him moments before a green light suddenly glowed in the fuselage: the signal to *go* from their pilot, from Wolverton, Sink and Taylor, Bradley and Ike. From America, to go do what had to be done.

Joe's stick was hell-bent to set a new record for sixteen men evacu-ating a C-47. They probably did so in under ten seconds. Photos were to show that many Screaming Eagles flung themselves out "ass over ap-petite," as if they'd never received jump training. McKnight led, fol-lowed by Duber, then Joe, who took a firm grip on the door and exited professionally like a Toccoa trooper. He yelled, "Currahee Three!," un-heard by anyone else as the prop blast ripped his words away.

"Hup thousand, two thousand." The overstressed harness wrenched his shoulders up to ear level, the opening shock estimated after analysis as the equivalent of several tons. Though Joe's didn't, leg bags burst like fountains of confetti because most planes were going so much faster than jump speed.

The correct and inculcated body position was to be tense above the waist, chin down on the reserve chute. By choice Joe had no reserve, but in other sticks jumpers were knocked unconscious when metal rip-cord handles hit chins with unprecedented force. These jumpers did not re-vive, if at all, till they crumpled in trees or on fields. It was as if astro-nauts, seconds after pulling incomparable Gs, had to strip off their space suits and immediately fight with ferocious aliens. All this happened for D Night paratroopers within less than a minute between exit in the sky and combat on the ground.

The uproar of war was all around, yet the night was cool and clear, the air rising from farmland fragrant of long grasses that descending jumpers were surprised they could smell. There were muzzle flashes but no Germans to be seen below, the only movement from disturbed shadows of horses and cows. With neurons still vibrating from the ultimate opening shock, Joe gaped and gawked from sensory contrasts. The night glowed as if God had lit the lamps of heaven to watch.

Thus commenced by far the largest and most sudden scattering of a major force in military history. Twenty thousand (counting British paratroopers) rendezvous with destiny began with a green light. For some men the rendezvous would end before they reached the ground, for many as soon as they did. The rest would start savage battles to control the ground, and remember that nothing was nearly the same thereafter. Not for them, not for the Germans, not for the world.

THERE WERE ONLY SECONDS for Joe to realize that he was drifting toward a steeple coruscating with rifle flashes. From briefings he felt pretty sure it was the steeple of the church, the only church, in St. Côme-du-Mont—unless his C-47 had been way off course, and conscientious McKnight never indicated that it was. If Joe was right, he was also lucky because the village of St. Côme-du-Mont was only about a half mile from Third Battalion's drop zone and less than three miles from their objective, two wooden bridges across the smallish Douve River. Seizing the bridges and defending them would foil a German drive against Utah Beach. The intense briefings, the pictures and sand tables, had embedded that big picture in his mind.

Tracers perforated his canopy, leaving circular glows in the silk. Joe climbed the risers to side slip, at the same time releasing his tethered leg bag. In free fall it hit the church roof like a wrecking ball. Two seconds later so did Joe, with a force that buckled his knees. The roof sloped sharply. He tumbled and slid down it till boot soles and fingernails stopped him spread-eagled at the eaves.

For his second jump of the night, Joe rolled off the roof, grabbed the eaves to slow his fall, and dropped about fifteen feet to the ground, landing on his side and carbine. Even with the wind knocked out of him, earth never felt so good. The shadow of the church provided some con-

cealment as he unharnessed, retrieved his leg bag, and for a few moments took stock. All the while tracers crisscrossed in the night, with no
counterfire from the hundreds of Blues who must already be on the
ground. That amazed and perplexed him. Here at last, after the desperate flight to reach them, were Germans as targets, the enemy to kill. Why
aren't we doing it?!

The Germans had torched a house nearby. It was burning like a bon-
fire at a football rally. Snipers in the steeple were using the illumination
to shoot at planes and jumpers. Joe, as the Most Obvious Temper in his
class, began planning how to climb up to the belfry and tommy-gun
those snipers. It was an infuriating and nearly irresistible impulse; then
it dawned on him why Blues had not attacked the church and snuffed its
antiaircraft fire. Where were they? Well, they must have already set off
for the objective—the Douve bridges—and the objective came first, as
had been repeated in every briefing. It was for him to join them, all the
more important because he was carrying I Company's most vital radio.

Where were they, his single-minded buddies? Another briefing point
came to him. Wolverton had said over and over, "Remember, men, our
objectives are *east* of the DZ. That's the direction the C-47s will all be
flying. If you get disoriented, just look up and follow the planes." They
were still roaring overhead, still fired upon from the steeple. Grinding
his teeth, Joe concluded that eliminating that fire must be left to others.
But he'd leave something for them. Gathering up his gear, Joe be-
queathed the heaviest stuff like the land mine and machine-gun belt.
When troopers from later sticks attacked the church, probably soon,
they could use it.

Unburdened, he took off in a crawl through the cemetery, dragging
the radio. It reminded him of Toccoa times when Currahees had to belly-
crawl a quarter mile in under ten minutes. The tombstones were good
protection, but when Joe reached the wall it had to be vaulted.

With a heave and walrus jump he did it. No fire was directed at him
from the steeple, for the Germans were focused on planes and jumpers,
exchanging yells when they scored a hit. That was more than Joe could
bear. From a ditch he let loose tommy-gun bursts at the steeple some fifty
yards away. Divots of plaster spouted where the few bullets hit, very satisfying for Joe, though the snipers paused just momentarily. Firing on the

enemy was a rite of passage, whetting an edge to see them fall next time. That could wait till he had some Blues beside him.

His stick had dropped a half mile west of almost all the others in Third Battalion. Though he didn't know it while slinking toward the Douve bridges, Joe was bringing up the rear. He'd seen aerial photos of the hedgerows for which Normandy is famous. Now he was encountering them in the dark. Thick mats of vegetation, they rose from solid earthen berms, marking off and walling in rectangular fields for crops or cattle. Hedgerows could not be crawled through or climbed over; neither could they be skirted except on cart lanes. Through hedgerows there were no more than two openings between fields, usually at a corner. At these corners were most of the clashes on D Night. Joe could see muzzle flashes flickering behind distant hedgerow shadows, hear burp guns versus tommy guns like dogs fighting.

Until he joined a pack, Joe could only come up to a hedgerow and listen for anything on the other side. Once or twice there seemed to be some kind of scuffling sound and he'd cricket, but never got a response. He was tempted to toss a grenade over but incapable of handling what might come back at him. Probably most of what he heard was cows.

So if the sound went one way, Joe went the other. Even with a compass, this back-and-forth disoriented him. He was playing a version of hide-and-seek that little resembled his childhood game. Am I the only guy by myself? Where's the rest of the company? he kept wondering. It seemed they had vanished, transplanted to another battlefield.

"Stand alone" was the Currahee motto, but to survive in the vast grid of hedgerows required at least two men, one listening for what might be in the next field and the other to watch his back because some Germans could be coming into their field from the other corner. A squad leader lucky enough to assemble his men could move right along like a king in checkers. Enter a square, and if unoccupied, it was his. If not, he had men to seize the corners, then, holding a hedgerow square, his squad could repel almost anything. The same was true for German squads, fewer in number but more intact because they had not been dispersed like the paratroopers. In general, on D Night, the Germans knew where they were but not what was happening, whereas the Allied paratroopers were positive about what was happening but uncertain where they were.

Like a demolition derby, firefights for squares progressed east. Following them, Joe came upon bodies, German and American. The first sight of dead men did not much affect him because his mind was filled with determination not to join them. More than anything else he wanted to find some living buddies.

More hedgerows thwarted, kept turning him back. Now heavier-caliber fire was moving farther east and he was farther behind. He turned on the SCR 300. If Third Battalion was in hot action, he'd surely hear about it. But there was only static on the company frequencies, and he had memorized them all. He tuned all through the band every half hour for a couple of hours.

By then the hedgerows had curved him around, back toward St. Côme-du-Mont. In the distance he could see flames still leaping from the house that was the Germans' torch. Antiaircraft fire had ceased because the aerial armada was gone. For the last time Joe turned on the radio. Hearing nothing, he switched the frequency, smashed the set, and buried it in the corner of a hedgerow.

That represented failure, the first of any significance since Joe had joined the army nearly two years before. How significant he didn't know, but he felt that was the right thing to do. Despite all his efforts, he was alone, quite killable, his radio a prize for the Germans to take from his body. That's how Joe was coming to view himself, somewhat as he had as living cargo with the FFI: a potential find for the enemy who outgunned him. He also reasoned that there were plenty of other radios in I Company—if I Company still existed. What if every one of its C-47s, except Joe's, had been fireballs? There was little reason to feel otherwise, at that age, at that time, at that place in the darkness of D Night.

Joe's primary job was radioman; his secondary, demolitions. The blocks of nitro starch were for blowing the Douve bridges in case of German counterattack. It didn't look like he'd get to those bridges soon, not the way D Night was going for him. He needed a change of luck and, crouching in the corner of a hedgerow, decided to make it happen.

St. Côme-du-Mont, now a lurking silhouette in front of him, was just a minor village, but according to briefings, the Germans had installed a small power-relay station there. Joe crawled up to the outskirts and cased the village. The relay station, he remembered, was a fenced enclosure between buildings on Highway 13. Joe crawled closer. Sure enough, there was a square of high fence. It had a gate and something that looked like a small bunker inside with cables and wires running out.

The briefers' description of the relay station was exactly right, information that must have come from the FFI. Joe's memories are like glimpses of a mountain range through turbulent clouds. What he remembers about the relay station was, "I'd paid the FFI, and now they were paying me back."

While Joe watched, he listened to a lull. As if in some spectral intermezzo, smoke from the burning house drifted toward him over the roofs of St. Côme-du-Mont. The moon had set; the village was nearly silent, seeming abandoned, as if the war had departed. The French were hunkered in root cellars, keeping their heads down till one side or the other exerted firm control. What control Joe could detect was German.

For what seemed an hour he staked out the relay station. Not a light, no movement around it, though out on the edge of his vision he detected a soldier or two moving between cottages. He was determined to get ahead of them before they reached the objective he had set for himself.

But Joe became distracted. Studying silhouettes, he could see some Wehrmacht vehicles parked helter-skelter as if they had been abandoned in a snowstorm. They were unguarded. Whether or not there were Germans inside that relay station, he wasn't sure, but he was the Class Shark, an opportunist who saw an opportunity, with no sergeant or officer there to gainsay him. With the knife he'd used to extricate himself from his harness, Joe crawled around slashing tires with glee and a rationale: "General Taylor said that our hell-raising was his biggest problem in England. Just before we took off for Normandy he told us, 'Okay, *now* go out and raise all the hell you can!' "

So Joe just followed orders, slashing and crawling while there was still enough darkness to shadow him. If this was combat, he thought as he heard tires deflate, the more the merrier. Then there was no more rubber to slash. It was time to face up to the relay station he had avoided, indeed past time to just move out, be a Currahee, straight to the gate.

As Joe came closer he could see that the gate was open about an inch. "Okay," he said to himself, "you *can* do it, now do it." The last twenty yards remain engraved in his memory. He wanted to kick open the gate and throw in the nitro starch like grenades. He'd already fused the blocks and primed the caps. Then he lectured himself as if Sergeant Lincewitz, his demo instructor at Fort Benning, were lecturing him: go up and open the gate, soldier. If no one's home, *place* the nitro on the target. Throwing close is only good for hand grenades and horseshoes.

Okay, Lincewitz, he thought. Approaching closer, Joe could see a generator or dynamo larger than an office desk. Whatever it was, it was silent, apparently not operating. Too bad, but he put one nitro starch block on each side of what looked like the most important machinery, then popped the fuses and walked away (Lincewitz had said a good demo man *never* runs).

The fuses were set for forty-five seconds. Joe was looking for cover when they went off together, a muffled explosion that puffed some white smoke from the bunker; but much to his disappointment, nothing changed in the darkly silent village. He broke into a run, rationalizing that even if lights didn't go out—there weren't any on before—some German radios went off the air.

THE WEHRMACHT HIGH COMMAND was slow to size up the scale and objectives of the vertical invasion, how it was designed to seal off Utah Beach, where seaborne forces started to come ashore with the dawn of D Day. In a disorganized night fight, with communications often cut, Rommel's forces were largely immobilized, hard-pressed to defend where they stood while awaiting orders for the next day. It was this quiescence Joe had noticed, but hiding by a brush fence he sensed that his opportunity to raise hell was ebbing with the night.

Toward the relay station Germans began moving around. Had they really heard Joe's charge go off there, or was it another random explosion in the night? He heard them coming down Highway 13 as if there were no danger. He was one happy hell-raiser when a group of them stopped twenty yards away and started talking. He could have sprayed them with his tommy gun but adhered to his D Night orders not to shoot unless fired upon, which made sense in his situation.

Joe carefully pulled the pins from two grenades, one to roll down the road, the other to lob over the group for an airburst.

Like parachutes, grenades are timed for four seconds. For the air burst Joe released the handle (muffling its *ping*), counted "Hup thousand, two. . . ," and threw a grenade high. In the next second he bowled the other grenade down the road; he heard it bounce before his air grenade went off, followed by the second small boom.

He expected to hear screaming and yelling, but there was hardly any. Shit! This war wasn't like any war movie he'd seen. Knocking out a power station didn't bother the Germans, now he'd peppered them with grenade fragments and they'd hardly reacted. He'd have to get another shot at them, if only to reestablish his self-respect. There seemed to be plenty of opportunities ahead. Joe took off in a crouching run, putting hedgerows between himself and the road. Hide-and-seek had been no fun, but this was almost like playing kick-the-can on a summer evening in Muskegon.

The Douve bridges were east, but hedgerows deflected Joe south, while overhead the main lift of gliders arrived at dawn. He could see them angling down, often under fire. Many were to land or crash nearby but always inaccessibly behind hedgerows. Thousands of Screaming Eagles were all around him, but still Joe could not link up with any. Better to wait for the glider men chancing upon him rather than search for them. That's what he decided, his cricket in hand.

Before the jump Joe had been a one man arsenal. Now, with his land mine, machine-gun ammo, nitro starch, and grenades all gone, he felt lightly armed with only a carbine, tommy gun, and pistol—maybe enough for self-defense but no more. Joe was less frightened by his predicament than frustrated at not doing everything possible for his buddies. Unified with them but in a way AWOL, he felt he had contributed little. While he was within earshot, so much was being done by others.

He hid out on D Day, the day Rommel called the longest. It was long for Joe but also the shortest in his memory because it contained no events, no change in his predicament. He'd move a little this way, that way, look at the compass a lot, more a fugitive than a soldier while historic fighting raged within a few miles' radius. On D Day he was just one tiny eye watching inside a hurricane, hearing more than seeing it.

Fatigue was taking over. All of Colonel Sink's training had been about functioning while more tired than ever before. That made Currahees "body-conscious" decades before the rest of the country. Joe began to look at himself as if he were his own doctor, an ability he would cultivate.

He'd notice himself staring at a barn a hundred yards away but unable to put it in perspective. A place to hide? A good machine-gun nest for the Germans? He was a decisive youngster, in tactical drills quick to see what was key terrain. Now he was failing, and it enraged him. Everything seemed to be in slow motion; he felt his judgment was poor. That's what alerted him. "Hey, Joe, what's going on?" he asked himself. The answer was exhaustion after being awake for dozens of hours, most of them in an adrenaline rush. Adrenaline is a supercharger for emergencies, it allows you to floorboard the gas pedal to avoid a crash but empties the gas tank very fast. As the driver of his body, he was nearly out of control.

INCREASINGLY INTENSE COMBAT focused on St. Côme-du-Mont, now behind him, and he heard the heavier calibers, mortars, and howitzers joining the battle. To the village was where Rommel, at the end of D Day, moved the first of his reserves, the 6th Parachute Regiment, to throw back what he was now convinced was the main invasion. Hitler, however, still vacillated.

Once more darkness set in. Joe took off his helmet so that it wouldn't affect the magnetism of his compass, but then he couldn't find the helmet. His nose was the last of senses to lose keenness, for he noticed his caustic miasma as he slumped on the ground for longer and longer periods.

The freight-train rumble of glider-towing C-47s had ended, replaced by a stupendous naval bombardment of the beachheads. In that direction Joe persevered—east—a solitary soldier, scared by exhaustion but still daring. He kept putting it to the touch, through another hedgerow maze, instinct his only guide. He poked his head into a field, sniffed around, felt he was still alone.

Crawling along the hedgerow he heard a rustle. Joe cricketed. There was a shout, *Hände hoch!* before many hands grabbed him as if he were a girl.

CHAPTER SIX

IN THE ORCHARD

Wᴴᴬᵀ JOE HAD STUMBLED INTO WAS A PERFECTLY CAMOU-
flaged machine-gun nest of nine German paratroopers—*Fallschirmjägers*.
Evidently he wasn't their first capture; they went through his equipment
and uniform like experienced garage-sale shoppers. The jump jacket and
cricket were prizes, while the folding-stock carbine and .45 made Joe's
captors think that he was an officer, granting him a bit of respect as they
throttled him.* It was a paralyzing, out-of-body feeling to watch himself
being frisked.

Captures, recaptures, cross-captures, and uncaptures were occurring
all over the Cotentin Peninsula, the thumb of Normandy that was invaded.
War stories would emerge from the Airborne, typically of a trooper getting the drop on a German, taking him prisoner, only in the next minutes
to be ambushed by the German's comrades, who reversed the roles but
were subsequently captured themselves by a larger group of Americans.†

From such stories emerged a grim variation of the Golden Rule.‡

---

* The 101st's planners, assuming there would be some early captures by the Germans, intended the cricket for use only in the darkness of D Night. Troopers were
told of this reservation, but with no implication that after D Night their cricket
might, as happened to Joe, be an identifier for the enemy. Everything considered,
the cricket most likely saved many more lives than it cost in prisoners.

† Screaming Eagles had been taught *Hände hoch!* to demand surrender. This must be
considered a humane measure, allowing that German soldiers would hardly have
been instructed to learn the equivalent English command—hands up!—when all
their training had been to fight to the death.

‡ Many enlisted men in the 101st swear that in D Night briefings they were told, literally, to take no prisoners. Obviously this was not official division policy but

Such was the chaos because, even after the advent of helicopters, never have major forces mixed so suddenly and violently as when three Allied Airborne divisions landed in the dark upon the Wehrmacht. General Marshall would withdraw his faith in division-size night jumps, and none was ever again attempted by any army. Third Battalion's chain of command was riddled because of errant drops, losing almost all the senior officers.

Benumbed, Joe didn't realize at first that for the third time he was headed toward St. Côme-du-Mont. Two *Fallschirmjägers* took him there, an encouraging thought: if the Germans could afford a double guard, they must not have many prisoners. For Joe this was a stimulus for stubbornness: he would be a model of noncooperation for his captors. Yet to show them he was a hard-core soldier he followed their orders strictly, keeping his hands folded behind his head, saying nothing, and staring straight ahead.

The three paratroopers heard, somewhere in twilight, the *chunk* of a small-caliber mortar. *Vorsicht!* a guard whispered, and simultaneously they went to ground. It was an American 60-millimeter, its rounds landing elsewhere. The three rose, and for the first time the guards addressed Joe in German. He shook his head. As they wended toward St. Côme-du-Mont, Joe realized that he shouldn't have reacted to *Vorsicht* (heads up), a word not in international parlance like *Achtung* (attention).

Off and on, his guards probed further as the grim march continued along lanes between hedgerows, many with gaps blasted out of the foliage where he could see crashed gliders and wrecked jeeps. His captors didn't gloat. They were Hitler's Airborne, accustomed to victory starting in Crete. Joe heard that word as he listened with a new ear, his ear for German. But it was difficult to conceal it. *Wie heist du?* (What's your name?) a guard asked casually. It took a suspicious moment for Joe to nonreact.

---

rather that of some officers who realistically foresaw the circumstances under which Germans would be captured in the crucial early hours. There would be no place to send them, no secure rear area for POWs to be collected and effectively guarded. This was a dilemma peculiar to the Airborne; infantry divisions establishing beachheads at Utah and Omaha could send POWs back for pickup by vessels returning to England.

HE WAS DELIVERED TO an apple orchard of some twenty trees. Beside it was a small stone farmhouse with a chicken coop and pigsty enclosed in a crude courtyard. With permission from the sergeant in charge, Joe's two guards took a bottle of calvados from the wine cellar. Apparently that was their reward for each prisoner brought in, and they departed with a swagger and a promise that they'd be back with more.

"Ja, hoffentlich." Yeah, I hope so, the sergeant replied, but with little conviction. It was late evening yet still semilight. Background war noise flooded and ebbed with little indication of which way the tide was running; consequently the sergeant and his comrades were antsy.

The orchard was their POW-collection point, while the farmhouse served as a medical-aid station for a dozen American and German casualties, wounded or otherwise disabled. Most of the Americans had suffered bad jump injuries. What Joe immediately noticed was that the POWs were guarded closely, the casualties much less so, so the Class Shark convincingly faked a fractured back.

Sometime during that surreal night, Major Kent, the 506th regimental surgeon, was brought in to examine the most serious cases. Joe was glad for the wounded but also worried because if Kent had been captured, that meant the whole vertical invasion had not gone well. Joe could only get in a few words with Kent, who said he'd allowed himself to be captured with the American wounded in his care. The Geneva Conventions required that in those circumstances he be given unique status, a doctor for both sides. The Germans very much respected Kent in this capacity, addressed him as *Herr Major Doktor,* and deferred to his every medical judgment.

From his paymaster jumps Joe knew a little more about the Geneva Conventions than other men of his rank.* In all the Currahees' preparation and planning for the vertical invasion, the only order was that if captured they were to give the enemy no more than name, rank, and

---

* Germany signed the Geneva Conventions before the Nazis came to power. The Soviet Union never signed. If the Soviets weren't bound, the Nazis weren't either. This was an excuse for reciprocal atrocities on the Eastern Front, in contrast to the relative chivalry observed by Germans on the Western Front.

serial number—not a word about how difficult that might be. Maybe no one knew because in Europe few Americans had been captured since the First World War, when prisoners were routinely treated well.

Determined not to be a prisoner much longer, Joe took a place in the farmhouse with the real wounded and wondered what to do. To lie there among them was a trauma of tense guilt. They were in extreme pain, not faking it. For lacerating wounds there was only a sprinkle of sulfa powder and maybe a self-applied pressure pad to slow the bleeding. No painkillers, though every trooper had jumped with a morphine surette in his first-aid pack. That was the first thing Germans took away to use themselves.

In the farmhouse, Jack Harrison from Third Battalion was the worst off. He'd been gut shot by a burp gun. Joe could feel, because he heard, every outcry as Harrison struggled with his agony. That got on the Germans' nerves too. Joe understood that they were debating whether Harrison should be delivered from his misery. The guards were for it and put the question to their chain of command.

The answer never came—too minor for consideration while the war hung in balance. The battle din grew louder. From one hour to the next, the Germans didn't know if they might be overrun by paratroopers, maybe by Harrison's battalion. So the guards punted to Major Kent. Exhausted from lifesaving emergencies outside the orchard, he nevertheless came around whenever possible. Kent, of course, was not advised by the Germans that Harrison had been nominated for execution but told them that his life was savable.

Late that night or very early the next morning, Harrison's travail became too much for Joe. The hour fit his plan: when the guards were sleepiest, he'd fake the need to flex his back and hobble over to the stairs. If no one stopped him, he'd go up to the loft.

No guard was present when he rose achingly to his feet. The wounded were moaning, some calling for their mothers. Joe had to get away from that. Their crying was undoing his training. It was too much to be around them any longer.

The stairs were like a steep ladder. At the top was a farmer's attic, just junk piled up, but in the dark Joe saw a sliver of faint light. He tiptoed to it, but the attic floor creaked a lot, and the window tapered into just a slot, not big enough to get through. This wasn't going to be his chance, so he backed away. The floor creaked again. Then he heard the stride of jackboots.

The German at the foot of the ladder seemed drunk, enraged, and desperate. He pointed a machine pistol. If he'd stitched Joe, it would have been just another unrecorded incident during the fury of the invasion. Like the opening shock of his cherry jump, Joe for the first time felt a man's lethal hatred, saw it in a tightening trigger finger and spittle on the guard's lips. The Germans had something of his, even more than freedom, that would be awfully hard to get back. He'd need every bit of himself to recover it.

He raised his arms fast, felt like a kid caught stealing hubcaps, while the guard ranted and cursed. Most of his steam seemed about Joe's bogus injury, but he was also called a gangster fighting for Jews while Germany held off the Bolsheviks. Joe meekly came down the ladder to be knocked against a wall. The guard shouted to others, identifying Joe as an uninjured actor who needed watching. He was shoved into a corner to squat with hands behind head.

Joe's Currahee training had developed strong squatting muscles, but in an hour they began to give out as his morale also slipped. Though he'd destroyed the company radio for a respectable purpose, that thoughtless escape attempt had no merit but audacity. Even if he'd made it through the window, he'd still have been in the courtyard with no idea how to get out. What he'd done, Joe berated himself, was not brave but brainless. When a guard came over and gave him a random kick in the kidneys he only grunted as if receiving fair punishment.

He could hear what was going on behind him. Harrison was gagging as if his throat were being slit slowly. Joe exuded sweat, thinking that no matter what pain was his it didn't compare with what he heard from Harrison. He also listened for sounds from the guards. It seemed the one who'd caught him didn't want to be around for Harrison's final agonies and went off-duty. That's when Joe decided to slip down on his butt, hoping the new guard wouldn't notice.

He didn't, and soon Joe was pushed across a dirt lane to the orchard where about twenty unwounded POWs were seated in rows on the ground. The sergeant in charge denounced Joe to them: only a malingerer; no real soldier pretends to be wounded. A rabbit punch sent Joe sprawling. His fellow POWs were silent. He took a place among them. In the next hour he strongly needed to piss and raised his hand for permission. The answer was in German: piss where you are. It was important to pretend not to understand, so he kept his hand up and finally heard an impatient "*Ja,* okay."

As he got up a burst of machine-pistol fire made him jump, but all the other POWs stayed slumped on the ground as if this were nothing unusual. There was another burst, this one closer. Daylight had returned. He looked over into the orchard to where the fire was directed. Hanging from a tree, about ten feet off the ground, was a body so swollen in a parachute harness that it bulged as if to explode. German reinforcements marching by were using it for a little target practice.

The body was Robert Wolverton's, pitted, caked with blood like hardened lava. With each burst Wolverton vibrated and twisted, his head tilted much farther back than it could bend naturally because his throat had been cut almost in two.

Squads continued to swing down the lane, some whistling a jaunty marching song that goes, "When we march through the German gate, you, Madeleine, come out to watch . . ."

As a German-American Joe had never used the word *krauts* before, but now in his mind that's what the Germans became—for lack of a more despicable term—overriding a respect he had grudgingly developed for the *Fallschirmjägers* who captured him. Considerable soldiers they, from what he knew of their record and had seen himself. Now the entire Wehrmacht were hardly soldiers at all by any definition he'd learned with the Currahees.

Joe began to cry like the wounded he had tried to escape. Blues believed in their commander as much, sometimes more, than they believed in themselves. In the army he was their foster father. Before D Night Wolverton had gathered his battalion together to announce plans for the first postwar reunion, whenever that would be, but it surely would be because "we're going to win this war. We have to. All of us, no matter what happens to any of us."

Wolverton announced that the reunion would be be at the Muehlbach Hotel in Kansas City, Missouri. He'd buy the steaks—cheers—but couldn't afford the drinks—boos—then he asked them all to kneel and pray, pray as they were dressed and primed for kill-or-be-killed battle.*

He asked God to notice that their heads were bowed, not downcast for themselves, but so they could then look up and see Him better.

That's the way Blues remember Bob Wolverton: humble, not a rah-rah leader but one of the battalion, the one who led.[†]

Joe seethed with a virulence that had to be converted into some directed action, as when boiling water becomes usable steam. He collected himself enough to ask a guard for permission to take Wolverton down and bury him. Joe did this by gesturing. The guard looked like he understood and agreed but shrugged—it wasn't his decision, and he wasn't about to bother an officer to ask.

Almost like the answer of God, a huge projectile ripped overhead. Everyone ducked, the guards first. The POWs glanced at one another. That message was from a cruiser in the invasion fleet, firing a huge warhead with very high velocity and flat trajectory so that if it was off-target, the shell kept going for miles.

The navy spoke again with the sound like a ripping newspaper, followed by another. The cruiser seemed to be ranging in on the steeple of St. Côme-du-Mont, the same target Joe had peppered on D Night. It was now shot ragged, just a quarter mile from the orchard. The Germans were probably still using the steeple for observation, so the 101st wanted it leveled.

His mind filled with jagging emotions, Joe didn't know what he wanted. Like all POWs in the combat zone he longed for the Germans to be plastered by shells and bombs but not to suffer casualties themselves, something like watching a tornado head toward them while grappling

---

* Wolverton's instructions were carried out in 1947 at the Muehlbach Hotel, where Blues assembled for a reunion with the theme "J-57." Three years of research had revealed that his stick had jumped fifty-seven minutes after midnight.

† In the 101st, casualties among high-ranking officers became so heavy that General Taylor had to publish a stern advisory—to wit, that leading a charge in battle was the job of lieutenants and captains, not majors and colonels. His admonition was ineffective. Of the four infantry regimental commanders on D Day, only Sink stood unscathed at the end of the war. The Screaming Eagles lost a brigadier general, two colonels, and ten lieutenant colonels killed in combat. Twice that number, between the ranks of major and major general (including Taylor), were wounded.

with a deadly enemy. Around St. Côme-du-Mont they were prepared to take their chances because a full-fledged attack by the 101st might free them.

Their captors were thinking along those same lines. Late in the morning a tired squad came with bayonets to herd the POWs through woods and across fields. Joe tried to get a sense of direction and whispered about it. The consensus seemed to be that they were being moved a few miles southwest of St. Côme-du-Mont.

But the seriously wounded were left behind. Some of the Americans had objected, a brave thing to do. The wounded were out of the war anyway, so for the Germans it made sense to leave them where they would be an American burden. Relying on Western humanity, they often left their own seriously wounded on the Western Front. What enraged Joe's group—and they said so loudly—was abandoning Harrison in his death throes with no medical help at all.

This unexpected protest had caused a delay. Before the POWs were marched off, a German lieutenant came over and told them that Harrison was too far gone; to give him anything would be a waste of medical supplies, better used for casualties (German and American) with better chances. Harrison heard that and began wailing. His countrymen started to yell, though a few kicks and bayonet prods shut them up. The lieutenant was genuinely surprised by the outcry. He'd explained his logic and couldn't understand why it wasn't accepted. In the orchard, in the eye of a hurricane, he'd shouted, "Who do Americans think they are?"

TO THE VINDICATION of the lieutenant, Harrison died where he was left. When Screaming Eagles recovered Wolverton's body it was so mutilated he could only be identified by his dog tag, which had slipped down the trachea.

CHAPTER SEVEN

HIGHWAY 13

Joe's NEW POW COMPOUND WAS AN APPLE ORCHARD ENCLOSED by both a fence and a hedgerow. This told him that the farther back the prisoners were moved, the tighter would be their security. His group from St. Côme-du-Mont was joined by about twenty more. They arrived bedraggled, hands on head, eyes on ground, as if shame were the worst of their predicament. Joe looked for a familiar face, saw none, and felt that he too would not want to be recognized among the losers, those who a few days before were as potent and powerful as the *Fallschirm-jägers* now guarding them.

For a while the prisoners could mingle and talk, learning what misfortune had brought the others here. It was consoling for Joe that most had been captured as he had, alone.* Some had been dropped twenty miles from their intended drop zone. They'd fought till their ammo ran out, and all appeared benumbed like survivors from a train wreck. This initiation to captivity was unlike anything they'd ever experienced in the hardest training, nothing in the past they could relate to, contradicting what had been vital in their lives, which was to take prisoners, not become one. Addled by lack of sleep, Joe's thoughts drifted a lot, but he found some vitality in reconnecting with his countrymen. The previous days had been an evil epiphany for which he needed some sort of

---

* Like the American Airborne, the German *Fallschirmjägers* were not above braggadocio. After the war, 6th Regiment veterans convinced British author Robert Kershaw that twenty men of their bicycle company had in one swoop captured a complete American battalion of thirteen officers and six hundred GIs.

sounding board. The incoherent, the babblers he shunned as he had the wounded in the farmhouse, but huddling with grim POWs encouraged him, and vice versa. He kept hearing that what happened was a crap game. Snake eyes had come up, but they still had the dice to roll again. Joe saw God as his croupier, taking chips when he lost but also pushing enough across the table for another bet.

However, there was also Third Battalion's collective gamble, which meant infinitely more, and Joe knew nothing of how it had turned out. It seemed that the Blues had dropped off the map and out of the war. Now, Joe wondered fitfully, was he their only POW, maybe the only survivor?

Down narrow lanes like those on which the FFI's horse had carried him, he was marched with the others southwest. Guards and prisoners froze when P-47s, General Bradley's ground-support fighter-bombers, called Thunderbolts, thundered overhead. The march resumed, despite interruptions by P-47s, till in a copse the POWs were halted and seated in a circle, facing inward with one German rifleman behind them. If there was a signal, Joe pondered, they could all rise at once and overpower him. But what then? They were farther from American forces than ever before.

One by one the prisoners were pulled to their feet and led away, never to return. Joe knew his turn was coming. He was taken into some heavy woods and nudged to stop; he looked around, got another nudge, then noticed a hole with a dark stepped passage into the ground. Guards ordered him to descend. Belowground was a huge bunker expertly excavated, perfectly camouflaged from someone walking by, even less detectable from the air. Entirely subterranean, it accommodated the headquarters of a battalion of the 6th Parachute Regiment.

Joe was faced against the bunker's earthen wall. Suddenly his knees buckled and chunks of wall calved off from an explosion above, the largest and most shaking he ever heard. It was probably one of the naval projectiles hitting a huge German ammo dump miles away. It took a moment for him to understand that this was friendly fire. It took longer for the Germans to start talking again, their voices lower than before.

That was a morale lift for Joe. He was their prisoner, but the krauts were the ones in trouble, an impression they strove to change right away.

As soon as the earth quieted Joe was shoved into a small room and stood at attention in front of a seated lieutenant who spoke with an Oxford accent.

"Name, rank, and serial number," he commanded.

"Tech-4 Joseph R. Beyrle, 16 085 985."

"Unit." Joe stood silent. "Beyrle, I can *see* the escutcheon" (what was that? Joe wondered) "on your sleeve. We are required to confirm that you are a member of the 101st Airborne Division, which so obviously has had no combat experience."

Joe flushed from the insult. "Sir, I am required to tell you only what I've told you."

"How do you expect to receive Red Cross parcels if we cannot identify you?" Joe had no idea what Red Cross parcels were and, having said what he was going to say, said nothing. "Near here we have Red Cross rations designated for confirmed prisoners of war. I request confirmation of unit so that you may be fed. Nothing more." He looked for reaction from Joe, but there was none because he was suddenly overcome by exhaustion. His eyes drooped, bringing a smile from the lieutenant. "The International Red Cross is, of course, a humane organization trusted by both sides. Would you like to meet their representative?"

Joe may have nodded, for the guard pushed him into a second room as the lieutenant looked at the top file on a thick pile of papers, then called for the next POW. In those moments Joe came wide awake as he realized that the Red Cross representative must be a fake. After closing the door of the second room, another lieutenant seated himself behind a field desk. Greta was sitting on it with her legs crossed like Marlene Dietrich.

"Hello, Joe. I've been waiting for you," she said with convincing sincerity but belied by the lieutenant's grin. "How 'bout a dance? Remember those times in Ramsbury? Newbury? I always wondered why you wouldn't dance. Well, there's time now. Nobody to cut in, and we've got music." She gestured to a gramophone on another desk, but Joe shook his head. So Greta tacked. "No, I don't feel like dancing either." Her handkerchief stifled a sniffle. "Lost too many friends the last few days."

Joe indeed believed she had. Wolverton was very social. Greta mentioned him first. "I can't get over what happened to Bob. Harwick was luckier. McKnight too. But the Blues were pretty much wiped out, Joe. There are not many of them left. This is a horrible, horrible war. Let's get on the same side. Please?"

Joe wouldn't reply, so the lieutenant started off on how we of the West were really together against the "Bolshi." Joe felt like puking. The Russians hadn't cut Wolverton's throat and used his body for target practice. Greta chimed in with names of more Blue casualties, starting with officers. Joe shrank from her when she began to get very friendly.

"I understand, trooper." She sighed. "I just want to show you that there can be love in all the hate of this war. I know what you love— you're Jumpin' Joe. You love it. Lieutenant, Corporal Beyrle was the 101st's most accomplished parachutist." The *Fallschirmjäger* officer nodded respectfully. "Joe, this is an Airborne outfit you're with now," Greta continued. "It was those lousy static troops who killed Bob. They're going to be punished by the 6th Regiment. I know them—they're jumpers like the 506th Regiment, Joe. You're among brothers here."

"Did you have a hard landing in Normandy?" the lieutenant asked in a brotherly way.

Greta winked at him. "Which one?" she asked, then exchanged some quick words in German with the lieutenant, who looked at Joe appraisingly and jotted in his file. With a flick of the hand he beckoned for the next prisoner to be summoned. Joe emerged from the bunker into daylight, then was stood in a line parallel to one entering for interrogation. He recognized the face of a Screaming Eagle, Fred Berke.

"Watch out for Greta," Joe muttered before he was pushed along, his head shaken as after the opening shock of D Night. She seemed to know everything. Probably, Joe suspected, what Greta wanted from him was the frequency of I Company's radio, but it was her wink and rhetorical question that unnerved him. Whatever she was after, he had deflected in the only way he could, by a soldier's silence. Joe felt he had passed a minimal test after his failures so far.

CARENTAN WAS THE 101ST'S final objective, and the Screaming Eagles were closing in. Under savage attack, the *Fallschirmjägers* moved their POWs south at twilight, scores of them, a long column with just a platoon of guards trudging down Highway 13. Some miles to the east, combat sputtered and roared like an untuned carburetor, over a constant background of two-sided sniper fire.

The road sloped down imperceptibly toward Carentan. Faking a bad leg, Joe dropped back through the shadowy column, muttering, "Sink Blue." He was answered by Captain Harwick from H Company and PFC Tucker of I Company. The guards were nervously alert but widely spaced, so the three Blues were able to talk unheard. They guessed the krauts wouldn't move this column many miles because with deepening darkness it would be relatively easy for someone to slip away. That was the premise of Harwick's plan—that this was the time, in front of them the place, to put it to the touch and make a break. In England he had memorized the Norman terrain so well that he knew the roadside for the next half mile was flat with few bushes or trees.

The roadside was now unnaturally marshy after Rommel had flooded the lowland to slow down the invasion. Harwick scooped up a chunk of broken asphalt, as did Tucker and Joe, to be flung far out into the marsh for a splashing distraction when they darted in the other direction. The signal to do so would be Harwick's throw. He studied the terrain ahead while Joe and Tucker trudged along whispering as they watched his arm.

"Who do you know about?" Joe asked.

This was hard for Tucker to tell him. "Lieutenant Johnston's ship . . . they got it . . . all of 'em."

"Jack Bray? Orv?"

"Yeah," he murmured. "They're gone, Joe."

THAT KIND OF DISMAL information was going up and down the column—who'd been killed and how, who'd made it out with wounds, who'd been captured. Everything later was words, words, words—in telegrams, on citations, in tributes, on tombstones. Everyone who'd put on a parachute or strapped into a glider had anted up. For the first time Joe learned who had lost their bets.

The image of Jack and Orv consumed by a fireball was a blow to Joe's stomach, not his head. They'd never reached the ground. Joe had.

That was something more he owed them. They'd been incinerated, mangled in jagged metal, maybe charred pulp in some of the smoldering wreckage Joe had passed on D Night. The impact on him was not immediate, rather a feeling that those killed were not dead, only gone—like jumpers ahead of him snatched by the prop blast, standing one moment, invisible the next, a flashing pair of dice in the great crap game. Irretrievably, numbers came up, winning or losing, ever-changing yet constant, to appear in every combination of life, death, and in between. Jack and Orv seemed out there waiting for Joe on a drop zone toward which he was descending.

Tucker whispered more, glad to change the subject to other results. Currahees smoked the krauts at exits from Utah Beach (the 4th Infantry Division consequently came ashore largely unopposed). Blues seized and held the two Douve bridges, under command of Captain Shettle, the highest-ranking officer left in Third Battalion.

That's what Jack and Orv had set out to do. It had been done, and that seemed like a temporary memorial to them.* Now the impact of their deaths came over Joe like the onset of flu. It drained his heart to think about the trio's last pass together in the States: the visit to Forty-second and Broadway, their glitzy introduction to a world-famous place, to be part of it for some hours, the experience and youthful accomplishment. Joe moved away from Tucker, who understood why.

There was slight time to grieve before the night was ripped by a huge missile. In the same seconds it was heard, the naval shell erupted in the middle of Joe's column. The 101st had probably slipped an artillery observer up to watch the Carentan road. In the gloaming and at a distance he saw a column of troops, not knowing they were prisoners. On his command a cruiser in the English Channel delivered sudden devastation on friend and foe.

The earth jerked sideways. Joe felt a sting burn in the butt, smelled the scorched rent in his pants, with dreamlike detachment saw how the fringe of wool still smoldered. He'd been blown into a ditch and penetrated by

---

* Postwar, it was for the next of kin to decide where their dead would be interred. Many, including General Patton, were buried near where they'd fought, in awe-inspiring cemeteries like those in Normandy and Maastricht. Most American families, however, wanted their children home: Jack Bray to Louisiana, Orv Vanderpool to California.

a shell fragment at sonic speed, but that didn't register at first because all along the dusky road hands clawed the air as bilingual screams merged like their blood. Two guards closest to him looked like shark food, not quite digested, not quite quiet.

Despite the carnage, somehow Tucker found Joe, pressed a hand-kerchief to the wound, and led him off to Harwick, who, not aware that Joe had been hit, appeared pleased. He whispered that sooner or later they'd have to move east of Highway 13, so better do it now in the confusion—odds in the crap game had changed in their favor, and they had the dice.

They stumbled over two mangled bodies in marsh water. Tucker looked them over and recognized one was a Currahee named Richie Johns. Most of one leg had been blown away. He was so covered with blood they assumed him dead. Then he groaned. So did the other man. Harwick took off his belt and twisted it into a tourniquet. The other "body" had lost both legs. Belt tourniquets were tried for him too but could not stop spurts from femoral arteries.

With a faint hope that the Germans would sweep up survivors, the amputees were pulled onto the cratered road. That's what Harwick told them, though they were too much in shock to understand.*

In hiding, Joe watched the remaining guards reassemble prisoners and continue toward Carentan leaving blood trails on the road. Tucker tapped him, asked if he could follow; if so, it was time to go. Into the marsh and deeper darkness Joe limped behind Harwick, the trio's guide, east toward sporadic flashing of naval gunfire. They paused at a stream close to Highway 13 and drank noisily. A German patrol squirted automatic fire in their direction. Harwick and Tucker dodged one way; Joe heaved himself in the other.†

---

* A German patrol did come by and found Johns, the only one alive. Twenty-seven years later, at the dedication of the 101st Memorial at Arlington Cemetery, Joe and Johns stared at each other's name tags. Johns had lost a leg, but eventually the Wehrmacht turned him over to the Red Cross in Switzerland, where he was exchanged for a German prisoner with an identical amputation.

† He learned what happened to them when Tucker showed up on "Starvation Hill" near St.-Lô. Sometime in the early morning of their getaway, Tucker and Harwick were taken under fire, split, and couldn't get back together, just as had happened with Joe. German outposts were radiating from Carentan; one of them recaptured Tucker. Harwick made it back to American lines, was later promoted to major, and became a battalion executive officer in the 506th.

He listened for their splashing but heard none and made no sound himself. On elbows he pulled along like a turtle with a bad rear leg. In the excitement of escape he'd ignored his butt wound, but now it throbbed with a piercing ache. He felt very much alone again. The second time was like the first, but he resolved to do better from his experience. From what could be seen at dawn the Germans were thick east of Highway 13, so he pulled back to the west side where there was a little more conceal-ment. With Carentan as their final objective, a lot of Screaming Eagles must be headed that way. Joe decided to lie low and let their attack sweep him up.

But German skirmishers were deploying to meet and feel out the weight of the attack. Joe could see *Fallschirmjägers* in camouflage smocks darting north—riflemen, machine-gun crews—all hardened troops, fin-gers on triggers. Even at a distance they scared Joe out of hiding like a flushed quail; he could stay beyond their range only by heading north, back toward St. Côme-du-Mont. From what he could hear, it sounded like the Germans were in trouble there, even that the village might al-ready be in American hands.

P-47s regularly machine-gunned Highway 13, preventing any move-ment of vehicles, but when not being strafed German troops dodged forward from ditches. They were gaining on Joe, yet he felt almost privi-leged to watch what was coming up, a helluva clash when German para-troopers ran into American. West of Highway 13 was a solitary hill that despite its middling size dominated the flatlands and the impending bat-tle. Joe knew it would be a strong German position that he'd have to avoid like a dinghy rowing away from an iceberg. But constantly he was funneled toward the hill by American artillery and strafing; yet if he stayed put, the krauts he'd watch deploy would be upon him, seeking the same concealment from the air that he was seeking from them.

That dilemma, whether to move or not, ended the thrill of regained freedom, leaving Joe with a hangover of hunger and weakness. He wouldn't admit what was wrong with him, rationalizing that it was from loss of blood. He couldn't see his butt wound, but it felt swollen to the size of a grapefruit, and how it throbbed. What could not be rationalized was that someone would find him, friend or foe, and he didn't have much control over who it would be. Joe felt like a slow-moving rat in a maze, going in one futile direction followed by another, stopping only to wheeze. He began to notice a buzzing in his ears.

Bleary thoughts resolved into a dubious decision: he had to get around that hill, no matter what his chances. Midmorning offered some hope when a new sound growled from the battlefields, far off to the east but unmistakably headed his way. A tank sounds like a Greyhound bus going through its gears. What he heard meant that the seaborne forces were ashore and the 101st would be supported by tanks—just the encouragement Joe needed. He left his hideout, a spray of reeds, and sneaked along parallel to the road toward the sound of distant approaching armor.

Starting up once more, Joe collapsed from lack of energy. Instead of watching for Germans he kept looking for apple trees. All the fruit had been blown down by concussions, and what lay on the ground was putrid. He devoured what he could find, cores and all. Several times during the day Joe fell asleep wherever he happened to be lying. That may have helped him. There were bodies strewn across the countryside, so he looked like many others, one with blood caked on his butt.

Highway 13 became an iron curtain: he couldn't get across or around it, and that was his situation for the next eighteen hours or so. Finally, when dusk settled in again, chances looked the best since he'd separated from Harwick and Tucker. German positions could be identified when they fired at fighter-bombers, which kept strafing all through the night. Apparently the Germans had lost St. Côme-du-Mont. If he could reach the oncoming Screaming Eagles, he'd have some very timely information for their attack on Carentan.

Be cunning in doing the Lord's work, a nun at his high school had once told him. He felt now that cunning, more than courage, was what would get him through. From the Germans' antiaircraft fire Joe had a mental picture of their strongest positions. There was a stretch of Highway 13 that looked blank, the gap covered, it seemed, by interlocking fire from two small elevations about a half mile apart. When there was complete darkness Joe limped for the middle of that gap, where a low hedge had been mulched by strafing and artillery.

Joe's try-or-die lunge for friendly lines was like his D Night jump. He thought about parents, country, Saint Joseph's, buddies living and dead, how they were all behind him in spirit and prayer. But it also occurred to him that many men like him had probably died in that state of mind.

There was the cricketing sort of silence when he crawled up to Highway 13, now more narrow than its two lanes after P-47s had furrowed it like a farm field. This was the place to do it, put it to the touch. As fast as he could hobble, Joe crossed the road and crawled into reeds and water. His face was down and wet when he heard, *"Hände hoch!"*

JOE'S SECOND CAPTURE was like his first, except for his captors. Instead of helmets they wore forage caps, the mark of static troops.* They pinned him down in the mud. With neither a weapon nor a helmet, Joe was evidently an escapee, which angered them to sadism. Pungent with the smell of sweaty wool and leather, they tried to pull off his jump boots but received a suicidal snarl: "You'll have to kill me first!"

So they started to. One of them found his butt wound and began jabbing it with his bayonet. Joe fought with unimaginable strength and fury, got in some hard blows but received overwhelmingly more. He was about to lose both boots and life, but there was a shout—*"Sei ruhig!"* ("Be quiet!")—with some German curses Joe hadn't yet learned.

The Germans beating him froze like statues. A silhouette appeared, two others beside it. There were some quiet commands, the forage caps stepped aside, and a panzer grenadier sergeant wrenched Joe to his feet. The other two looked him over, patted him down, and with a nod from the sergeant he was hauled away.

The following day a fellow POW confirmed that Joe was once again near St. Côme-du-Mont. The name caused him more pain than his festering wound, heightened a sense of failure—he had not worked hard enough or well enough to make good an escape. He was shattered,

---

* Static troops, as the Allies called them—the Wehrmacht's term was fortress troops—had not initially been stationed on Highway 13 but rather in bunkers to defend the beaches, such as they did at Pointe-du-Hoc, where Rangers scaled the cliffs to eradicate them as depicted in the movie *Saving Private Ryan*. The static troops Joe encountered had probably left their bunkers, against Hitler's orders to fight to the death, then been rounded up by Rommel's reinforcements and used wherever needed.

stunned: to be captured was a challenge; to be recaptured was a compounded defeat he could not comprehend. Joe had been a star athlete in high school, Third Battalion's premier jumper, but now, in the ultimate contest, he was a two-time loser. This was no longer a crap game if he couldn't make a single point. Shorty had a technique; Joe didn't, couldn't follow one.

Glum in a self-critical haze, Joe was with thirty new POWs. Confession seemed good for the soul, so he felt impelled to tell them that this was his second time through the wringer. No one cared. Their only concern was what would happen next.

The Germans were less organized, more flustered during this go-around. They seemed ready to retreat, so Joe's second interrogation (in a barn) was shorter than the first. The interrogator had a note telling him that Joe was an escapee but seemed otherwise uninterested in him. Except that he confiscated Joe's dog tags—strictly prohibited by the Geneva Conventions—and Joe's alone.

Dog tags didn't concern Joe while rain started coming down hard sometime during his second capture. There was no shelter; the prisoners were shivering, coughing, and falling sick. They were finally loaded onto trucks with POW lettered on the top to protect against strafing. Of course the Germans moved their own troops and heavy equipment in the same convoy, thereby presenting Allied fighter-bomber pilots with a wrenching dilemma.

Joe felt doomed as he remembered what strafing had done to Highway 13, the blasted road on which he was now headed south in a slow, exposed truck. Then, like the sound of hope, pelting rain turned up in volume to hailstorm intensity. It swept the convoy with a sopping chill, but the clouds kept P-47s away. The Germans weren't taking any chances, though. The convoy wended south like a cautious inchworm, so that the fifteen miles to St.-Lô took over twelve hours to traverse.

At one of many stops Joe's truck holed up in a farmyard with one exhausted guard. It was an opportune setting for escape, but still numbed by his failures and depressed by his luck, Joe just crawled into some wet straw and tried to sleep. He must have groaned because an American medic came over, examined his wound, and asked the guard for sulfa powder, a request that almost got the medic a bayonet in the stomach. He told Joe to watch out for infection, but otherwise the wound wasn't too serious, though the fragment was still in there. Yeah, until removed it would be painful, but pain was a good thing, a warning but also a sign that the senses were still functioning. If they stopped, he said, Joe was a medical crisis.

Before they got back on the truck, a German officer in a rain poncho came by and asked which prisoner was Beyrle. Joe was identified and stood up for inspection. The officer looked him over, noticed his butt wound, but didn't say anything and moved on. Shaking in fear that he'd get a special interrogation, Joe was very relieved when the guard told him to get in the truck.

CHAPTER EIGHT

GOOD COPS, BAD COPS

As HIS TRUCK, PACKED TWO DEEP WITH POWS, CONVOYED SOUTH, Joe had little idea if the semidarkness was twilight or dawn. Far-off U.S. artillery howled out projectiles from three sides like wolves converging on St.-Lô. Everyone could hear that the biggest inland battle so far was under way. The POWs prayed for their buddies' victory but prayed harder not to be caught where Americans would be killed by Americans. Indeed, just outside St.-Lô the guards yelled, *"Jabo!"* their word for fighter-bomber. They had well learned Allied strafing procedure: first the flight makes a pass to judge the target, then it either turns off or starts a hot run. This flight of three P-47s returned.

To hear their first burst was almost too late. Moments before, guards and the guarded dove for cover as *Jabos* rolled back to strafe from the other direction. Joe scrambled out, but there was no one to help the immovable wounded. Fifty-calibers blasted away canvas, hugely gouging truck beds and the stretcher cases on them. Joe trembled and crossed himself as a jaw, shin, ribs, and guts fountained onto the road. To see dead men had been melancholy, but to watch them killed like that was another shock like his chute opening on D Night. He tried to collect himself, tried to imagine that each soul was now with God, so it didn't matter what was left of his body.

The Germans were also hyperventilating. They collected themselves by ordering POWs to pile up remains in a ditch for the French to view. The convoy was now smoking and disabled. Ambulatory prisoners were marched through St.-Lô toward a town called Tessy-sur-Vire. Joe noticed the sign. North in the combat zone the Wehrmacht had removed all road signs. Seeing one alerted him that he was farther back in the German rear and closer to the FFI. He began thinking about escape again when his group was quartered in a stable with just a couple of tired guards.

But that night he doubted there would be a next morning. The whole town of St.-Lô surged with explosions. Under pass after pass of medium bombers, buildings fell as in movies of an earthquake. Rolled by each temblor, and showered with falling plaster, even exhausted POWs couldn't sleep, so Joe watched the guards. One was a teenager, scared to death and just as pale, perhaps not even German because he kept doing laps on a rosary, which Joe had never seen Germans do before nor would again. Both sides used "walking wounded" as temporary guards. The other wore a *Fallschirmjäger* helmet, and there was blood on his camouflage smock. He looked prematurely old, maybe twenty-five: months, perhaps years, of combat had accelerated his age.

Joe was semicomatose; his eyes kept closing as he watched this guard. Their glances crossed when a string of bombs rocked the stable. They could each be the last person the other saw before being killed, but that did not bond them. Fighting for one's country was understandable, respectable—but for the Nazis? Though his guard was a fellow paratrooper, if they both died that night, Joe was sure they would go in different directions. He said that with his eyes, and the German seemed to feel similarly toward him.

At dawn Joe saw few structures standing except his stable and a church across the street. The POWs were marched through the burning rubble and ruin of St.-Lô. When they passed dazed Frenchmen the guards pointed and said how this was all the Americans' fault. It took about seven hours—they frequently pulled off the road to avoid strafing—to reach their destination, a walled monastery named La Madeleine, previously a sanctuary for the blind. It was set atop a promontory. The monks had been run out of a three-story stone building strewn with books in braille. It was now the principal compound for American prisoners in Normandy—thousands of them—and they called it Starvation Hill.

When there was any food at all, it was a kettle of swill POWs called "whisper soup." Tom Gintjee, a man of wry humor, wrote in his memoir of captivity that when he first tasted it he had no idea that water could be diluted. With only two small bowls per day, prisoners weren't just weak, they were collapsing. Joe spent most of his time in a stuporous sprawl, and blacked out if he had to rise quickly for the air-raid siren.

Fortunately it sounded only false alarms. The monastery had been identified by the Germans with a huge POW lettered on the roof, saving it from the pelt of bombs nearby. Indeed, when P-47s finished their passes some would pull off and waggle wings as POWs waved feebly, a charged space between men in the air and those on the ground, expressing some kind of common will.

At all other times the slowly milling prisoners were as heartsick as they were hungry. Evidently Rommel had the invasion bottled up. The Germans, now that their panzers had joined the battle, seemed to have stopped the British at Caen and were holding around St.-Lô. French farmers confirmed this as each day more POWs of every kind trekked into the compound, Airborne and Rangers, infantrymen from the beaches, and a few British. Ironically, though salutes from fighter-bombers had caused weeping, a pilot was shoved through the gate, bringing tears of laughter.

Under his flight suit he wore a Class A uniform—"pinks and greens"—complete with ribbons and necktie. The famished, filthy GIs gawked at him. This lieutenant had a very sad story. Last night he was going to propose to his English girlfriend in London at a supper club where reservations had to be made a month in advance. His strafing mission was at six, his reservation for seven, not enough time to change uniform after landing. What made matters worse was that he knew of fellow pilots who coveted his fiancée-to-be. This he related to the POWs, whose reaction was such that the lieutenant was grateful to be taken away to a Luftwaffe camp before the Americans on Starvation Hill tossed him into the swill kettle, necktie and all.

Eventually a few cows were led into the compound and milked, providing a half cup per prisoner every third day. To Joe it tasted like the richest cream, even after being cut with an equal quantity of water. But the protein of meat was what was needed most. To get it, the milk had to be sacrificed, a decision made by the senior POW (a lieutenant

colonel) and approved by the Germans; so for a few days the whisper
soup had a taste of cowhide and contained tiny slivers of beef. Then two
old horses, wounded in action, were brought in and slaughtered. No one
had ever eaten horse meat before, but at the time it tasted like T-bone
steak. Cuts from the butt were called "sirgroin."

With Joe on Starvation Hill was Jack Brown from I Company. Like
Private Ryan of movie fame, Jack and his twin brother were "sole surviving sons." They hailed from Alaska. Wolverton had given them a couple of extra days' leave after Toccoa so they could get home and back. In
the D Night marshaling area he summoned the Browns because a new
War Department directive had come out prohibiting one or the other of
them from going into combat. The brothers looked at each other and
told him that if they both didn't go, neither would. What could Wolverton do—court-martial one of them for refusing an order? But which
one? He took it upon himself to disobey the War Department and let
them both jump on D Night. Jim Brown made it through Normandy and
the Netherlands but was killed near Bastogne.

On Starvation Hill Jack Brown plotted escape with another trooper
as Joe listened. The plan was to go over the wall. That didn't make sense
to Joe, who was too addled to understand, but he stood watch for the attempt, much as he had for the brandy heist. Brown got up on the wall
during a guard shift and lay there for hours in the ivy. At dark someone
threw a sheet rope up to him so he could go down the other side.

Currahee! Jack got away.

Joe thought about that a lot, wondered if he was losing it: the daring and determination, even the physical ability, to escape—the will and
guile to gauge the odds, then put it to the touch. This became a persistent uneasiness for him, like the compulsion of a race driver to take the
wheel again after a near-fatal crash. He tried to collect some sheets to
make a rope, but they were scarce and valued on Starvation Hill as bandages for the wounded. He was told no, but the asking helped him psychologically.

Anyway, whatever ambition Joe had to follow Jack Brown over the
wall was short-circuited a few days later when he was pulled out, with a
score of other troopers and glider men, to be packed onto another
convoy. From time and direction he figured their arrival was around

Alençon and mentioned it to the guards, but they said nothing and seemed to know no more about locations than the Americans did. Joe was developing an appreciation of the strata within the Wehrmacht—whom to fear, whom to test, who could be ignored. Watch, wait, pray, learn: these became articles of practice that induced patience. Patience did not come naturally to the Most Obvious Temper of his class; he would still seethe with anger, but indulging it was now a deprived luxury.

He was delivered to another stable, a small one, three POWs in each stall. Food was a little better than on Starvation Hill: cabbage in the whisper soup, a crust of black bread, sometimes something from a K ration. Whatever there was the POWs divided equally. Sharing hardship that way thwarted German policy to split solidarity among the prisoners by presenting food so that they had to divide it up themselves. With less resolute POWs the strong would take advantage of the weak, and that pointed out potential collaborators for the Germans. In Joe's stall, equal division was guaranteed because the man who did the dividing got last choice of the thirds.

The stable (probably about halfway between St.-Lô and Alençon) was a temporary respite from the war now evident only in the sky. A German medic pulled the shell fragment out of Joe's butt and patched him up pretty well, though recuperation weakened him. The relatively decent handling meant his group of POWs had been selected and collected by a high echelon of the Wehrmacht. Joe's comrades in the stable had reason, and some extra calories, to feel lucky, but his nervousness grew about the improved treatment; he dreaded Greta walking in and saying, "Joe, are you ready to dance?"

But she was not to be the celebrity.

The staff began looking their prisoners over, standing them up, sitting them down, moving them around like there was to be a big inspection. There was. At dawn they fell out into the courtyard while the guards kept talking about *Feldmarschall* while polishing boots and hand-pressing high-collar uniforms. The prisoners assembled as if it were their first day in the army. A parade-perfect *Oberleutnant* addressed them quickly, announcing that a preeminent visitor was about to arrive, that talking was strictly forbidden unless he asked a question. Now stand at attention to await the next order. The Americans ignored him, slouching till a Wehrmacht sergeant with a burp gun bellowed to march into the courtyard and form three ranks, *schnell*!

Minutes later they heard trucks. A flak (antiaircraft) wagon rolled in, its four-barrel machine gun trained on the POWs. Then a couple of Mercedes limos followed by another flak wagon. Generals and high-ranking staff piled out of the cars. The senior colonel adjusted his uniform and opened the back door. A small, very Prussian-looking officer stepped out and glanced at his watch. He wore a visored cap and carried a baton. Joe watched from the corner of his eye, and it was the baton that identified this impressive inspector. "Rommel," he whispered, and spontaneously the prisoners beside him came to attention. For Joe it was a strange feeling, showing respect for a great commander, at the same time showing him that here were soldiers for him to respect.

Starting in North Africa, *Feldmarschall* Erwin Rommel had obtained a feeling for the enemy by sizing up their prisoners. Joe squared his shoulders and popped his chest as if Colonel Sink were trooping the line. With head up he almost missed seeing Rommel, who was short like Montgomery (whose height had prevented Joe from seeing him when he went by during a regimental review in England).

Rommel trooped the POW platoon rapidly. Reading from a roster, his aide-de-camp mentioned each man's name going by. "Beyrle" drew a twitch of a smile but not a glance from the field marshal, who was said to ignore tall people unless he was far enough from them to neutralize their height. His momentary smile at Joe's name may have been from the thought that Rommel's family was living in Bayern; in fact he had been visiting them on D Night.

Rommel didn't say anything till he went around to the rank behind Joe where a trooper was barely able to stand because of a head wound. From what Joe could hear, Rommel asked the man if he was receiving medical treatment. Joe couldn't understand the answer.

The field marshal's visit lasted less than ten minutes. His motorcade roared away, and the prisoners were shoved back into their stalls. In a few days they were taken back to Tessy. Not long after Rommel's inspection he was out of the war himself, strafed and wounded. Not long after that he committed suicide rather than face trial for participating in the July plot to assassinate Hitler.

In the weeks without a calendar, Rommel's wounding (July 17, 1944) became a time marker for Joe's future experience and those of fellow "prisoners of the second front," as Germans called POWs from Normandy. The second and universally remembered milestone was the carpet bombing just west of St.-Lô (July 24–25), the decisive factor in enabling Patton's breakout into open terrain.

At Tessy, what Joe saw of the carpet bombing was the sky full of B-17s after they'd dropped their bombs in such tight clusters that craters overlapped. The bombers came on in waves, double the number in the D Night armada, using Tessy as their landmark to turn north back to England. For hours the ground shuddered and the air rumbled, as dust and smoke rose like a pall over some gigantic forest fire, the crematorium for thousands of German soldiers whose destruction opened a five-mile rent in the front lines. Joe's stable was solid stone, but he felt it would tip over. The POWs began to talk escape: if they could just get out and hide, Patton would overrun Tessy in a few days. In fact the general arrived the next week, but by then Joe was gone.

FOR THE FIRST TIME he was blindfolded, put in a truck with ten others, and driven east to a château estate (probably around Falaise) housing a high-level interrogation center. Again prisoners were stabled; this time each was put in a separate stall and told not to talk. Naturally they whispered at night or when vehicles went by, but for the most part there was only the quiet of the countryside, the war far away.

From the number of guards and staff, there must have been a hundred priority prisoners on this estate. All day long Joe could see them being led off to the château. It was several days before it was his turn. He knew it was coming when men in the first five stalls were taken away individually, an hour or so in between. Their stalls remained empty, and Joe's was the sixth.

Before the morning bread and water, a guard opened Joe's gate. Like a judge pronouncing sentence, he called out, "Beyrle." Handcuffing him, he asked with a laugh, *"Bist du aus Bayern?"* (Are you from Bavaria?) Joe was led to the basement of the château, into the servants' kitchen. It was about twenty feet square, and all the cookery had been removed. It

surprised him that the kitchen, appearing tidy, smelled like a public uri-
nal. He was turned over to two guards, who gestured for him to sit on a
stool high enough so that his feet dangled. They leaned their rifles in a
corner and conversed while waiting for the interrogators, two lieutenants who came in and took comfortable seats behind an ornate desk
(furniture no doubt from upstairs) facing Joe in the weak light of a dangling lightbulb.

The first lieutenant asked for name, rank, serial number, then continued with questions to which he already knew the answers, like "Where
were you captured?" and progressing subtly to answers he in all proba-
bility knew, like "When did your division arrive in England?" Joe's
steady reply was, "Sir, I'm required to tell you only my name, rank, and
serial number."

This went on for an hour, then another. The lieutenant was not at all
discouraged, his questions more probing (for example, "Where were
you trained?"), as if Joe had answered earlier ones. As he grew more
weary Joe began to wonder if he had. He lost much sense of the time but
tried to keep track of how often the door opened and closed behind him
when the guards went to chow or to take a piss. The first lieutenant
slowly grew annoyed. Joe could feel a guard close behind, ready for the
order to strike. It never came, and the first lieutenant got up, as if insulted by Joe's stupidity, and left in disgust.

The second lieutenant, the good cop, took over. His questions were
to put Joe at ease. Nothing military, but rather "Where's your hometown?" "What did you do before the war?" As bored as he was tired,
Joe was tempted to get into a casual conversation like that but decided
against it. He had to convince them they were wasting their time with
him. To the second lieutenant he either said nothing or repeated name,
rank, and serial number.

Then sometime during the hours Joe said something else (he can't remember what) because the good cop started in with a new approach,
how he was a Bavarian like Joe and couldn't understand why he would
fight his own people.

His own people! Fury rose in Joe's gorge as he thought of Wolverton's
throat cut almost in two. Good cop homed in on the new reaction but
followed up all wrong by asking how Joe could have been "traduced"—

Joe savors the word because he didn't know what it meant then—traduced by Roosevelt, Morgenthau, and all the other Jews who ran America. The lieutenant had a well-rehearsed pitch about the worldwide Jewish conspiracy. Listening to it gave Joe time to settle himself and go back to silence. Finally good cop tossed out a few common German phrases to note whether Joe showed some understanding, but he appeared as dumb as the FFI's horse.

At last the first interrogation shift went off-duty, turning Joe over to two other lieutenants. They took up the theme of how we westerners were killing one another while the mutual enemy was Russia. What do you know about communism? We will tell you. Marx was a renegade German, not a patriot for his country like us—like me and you, Beyrle. You're a patriot too, just a misguided one. We understand how you feel about America. We understand how democracy could appeal to you, but that's because there's no hostile nation next door, one that takes everything you have and calls it property of the people.

Hours and hours of instruction like that, hours with a question now and then to which Joe said nothing or recited name, rank, and serial number. His butt wound was agonizing, but he wouldn't let them see him squirm. It was early morning when he'd gone onto the high chair, nearly morning when they took him back to his stall.

He'd been without food or water for more than twelve hours, and lay in the straw in a stupor till he was hauled back to the château. The next session, he guesses, lasted about eight hours. Joe was hit a few times but only when he passed out and fell off the high chair. During the first session he'd always kept eye contact with the interrogator. The second and third sessions he couldn't keep his eyes open.

Randomly, like flashes back to consciousness, he heard, "What is your name, rank, and serial number?" determining if Joe understood where he was, what was transpiring. His rote reply reestablished a rough equipoise between him and the lieutenants. To all other questions he'd shake his head, so crumplingly tired and weak that the threat of beating didn't matter, but he was not beaten.* If there was any strength in him,

---

* The Gestapo's extensive experience with torture as a means of extracting worthwhile information had proven that insufferable pain was most often counter-

it was to not say anything or these professionals could lead him to the paymaster jumps. What had happened to him after D Night would be of no value to them. I Company's radio frequencies must have long since been changed. So it was the paymaster jumps that were his inner-sanctum secrets. There were times in those sessions when Joe imagined that they were learning about the FFI by monitoring his thoughts. The interrogators' alien voices were in his mind, the only thing in his mind, so it seemed they knew everything in there.

Most of his misery was an aching haze, but some moments were vivid. Once or twice the lieutenant would rise, push his face closer to say something very slowly. That jolted Joe awake. He'd stare and wonder if he'd babbled something. There was a gush of fear and bile whenever an interrogator's breath was close enough to smell. Joe's high chair was slippery with urine, one of the reasons he kept sliding off. What Joe had going for him was the way he stunk—even Germans couldn't stay close to him for long. He wore the same begrimed clothing of his capture last month; the closest he'd come to having a bath had been sitting in the rain in what he was now wearing, in a small room incomparably foul where prisoners equally filthy had been interrogated around the clock.

"Does your girlfriend write to you?" "How long do you think she will be faithful?" "Are you the only soldier in your family?" "Who will take care of your parents now?"

On and on like that. It is the singular talent of professional interrogators to come up with so many questions to fill so many hours. Joe's had been trained on British POWs and didn't know much about Americans. Late in the sessions Joe would come semiawake and notice silent stares, as if the lieutenants were examining a new, perplexing species.

Everything in Joe was stiffly hurt. It didn't help to pass out; right afterward the pain was worse. When he fell off the stool, guards were

---

productive; that is, that the victim would say anything for relief, whether truth or lies, and the two were nearly impossible to distinguish even by subsequent interrogation. Consequently, a combination of relentless physical and psychological pressure was demonstrably more effective than thumb hanging when information from the victim was the aim—a valuable tip the Gestapo passed on to the Wehrmacht as a professional courtesy. That didn't apply when a confession was the aim, and any combination of medieval and modern methods was recommended to obtain it.

allowed to administer kidney punches, something they enjoyed, if only to break the tedious routine. As hours crept on, the interrogators had to keep deciding whether he was conscious enough to understand questions. If not, there was no point in continuing and it was off to the stall. What the lieutenants wanted of Joe was that he be very weak and agonized but still conscious: a fine line, a close modulation in which their professional pride was expressed in enough stamina to surpass Joe's.

All Joe prayed for was that it would stop. Half his consciousness was in confrontation, the other in episodic prayer. He'd gone down the "no response" path because any other way meant the pounding questions would continue without end. They would anyway, but he was locked into a position beyond empathy, an unrecoverably altered state of mind.

THAT'S THE WAY the hunt went for a period of days. They'd revive Joe to a point where he understood questions. Then bad cop would mock him: "What harm is there telling us where your ancestors came from?" "We know you don't have any secrets, a mere technician like you. The guards here have more rank."

Then good cop: "I can't stand to see you suffer so much! I taught humanities at Heidelberg. You must be a conscript. Aren't you? I was too. You've been wounded, you've been captured—"

"Twice!" bad cop interrupts. "He's a bungling fool."

"He's right, Joseph. You have been foolish about your situation. If I were captured, I'd tell the Americans anything I've asked you. It's true. My army permits that. They'd want the Americans to understand me, just as I want to understand you. Germany has been at war a long time. We know what's important, what's not. Do you know what's most important? Surviving the war. No matter how it ends, we must survive so that the world can be better afterward. I want you to survive. We've been together a long time now. There's something about you. . . . I want you to survive!"

Bad cop rose in a rage. He started arguing with good cop, at first in English, about how Joe should be tied up and thrown into the pigsty. Good cop kept looking at Joe with sad eyes while he held up his hand. He seemed to outrank bad cop. That made bad cop even more angry, and he shouted to the guard, "What would you do?" They stepped forward so Joe could see them give the thumbs-down.

He became convinced that good cop was his only protector. In a cursing argument bad cop was sent away, then good cop turned to say, "I can't do this any longer. I'm going to get you some food and drink." He gave that order to a guard. German soldiers don't give their officers any back talk at all, but this one recoiled and muttered something before he left.

Good cop got Joe off the chair, steered him around the desk to where bad cop had sat. Grumbling, the guard came in with a plate on a tray. He tossed down a knife and fork while Joe stared at steaming heaps of chicken dumplings, baby potatoes, and red cabbage.

"You need to drink first," said good cop, setting down a tall cold glass of apple juice.

Joe feared it was spiked with truth serum but gulped it down. He wanted to drop his face into the food and suck it up, but good cop reluctantly slid the tray to the other side of the desk. He kept his hand on it, as if eager to slide it right back to Joe.

"I'm taking a great risk to feed you, Joseph. The other lieutenant is going to report this to my superior. I must prove to him that I've acted correctly. Just tell me anything you want: your hometown, your public school, your salary—anything at all."

"My name is Joseph Robert—"

"A little more, please. You see, if I can show my superior that humane treatment works . . . You're the first prisoner I've acted this way to! That's *my* meal in front of you. Think of the other prisoners. If my superior sees that there is just a little cooperation from you, he will permit me to feed the others. Joseph," he said softly, "do it for them."

Joe could not help crying. As he rubbed his eyes he realized he must have cried before, but he couldn't remember when. Good cop gripped his shoulder consolingly. He drew the tray over so Joe could smell the rising aroma. Something made him look up at the two guards. They were watching like chemists waiting for titration. That's what made him push the tray away.*

_____

* Joe still wonders if he should have eaten the food—in return for making up something like the name of his high school was Princeton—talking his way through a

Good cop's reaction was immediate. Joe was thrown into the pigsty as bad cop had recommended. When he was hauled out for the next session Joe knew there would be a climax because he was in some kind of fever, drained of everything except a wild faith, not a strong faith at all but one combining what he believed about God, his family, his country, his Currahees.

And he says today, "Some people call that corny. Isn't corny something that's so true no one thinks about it anymore? You do when you're falling over the edge."

Joe can't say that he had faith in his faith. Any minute he could have cracked and spilled his guts—that's admitted. What faith did was mute the little voice telling him to compromise: it's not that important; the most important thing is to survive (good cop is right); no one will blame you, no one outside this kitchen need ever know.

The next session Joe knew he couldn't withstand such temptation again. Caked with pig filth, he faced a new team of interrogators with handkerchiefs around their noses. Early on he fell off the chair and kicked at the guards who put him back. He spit at the good cop, refused to hear any siren song. Bad cop was very much into his role. Joe snarled at him, not giving even name, rank, or serial number. A power emerged in him, a strength like that of a drowning man just before he goes under for the third time.

The sisters at Saint Joseph's were very strict if he ever used profanity. Joe didn't much, not even in the army. But during that last session he yelled at the interrogators that they were sons of bitches. The next thing he remembered was about a week later.

---

meal, rationalizing that the food would have made him stronger, better able to resist. Over the years Joe has thought through that scenario. It might have meant a temporary reprieve, but then the Germans would have put him in a different category and the questioning would have gone on forever, and psychologically he would have been weaker. He faults no other POW who went another route, but for himself he had the great dread that any other way would have led to the paymaster jumps and vitiated all his previous resistance. The bedrock of his mind was an understanding that there is no return to virginity.

CHAPTER NINE

MUSKEGON

THE WAR HAD ALREADY BEEN A FEARFUL ORDEAL FOR JOE'S PAR-
ents, William and Elizabeth. Son John was wounded on New Guinea,
eventually to receive a medical discharge. Bill, in the air corps but on
the ground in England, had unknowingly been Joe's cover for the paymaster jumps. The youngest boys, Robert and Richard, lived at home
waiting to be caught up in the draft, which lowered the bottom of
the age barrel to seventeen as four theaters of war—northern Europe,
the Mediterranean, China-Burma-India, and the Pacific—demanded an
ever-expanding pipeline to replace tens of thousands of Johns and Joes.

General Marshall made it his practice to submit regularly to President Roosevelt the number of Americans KIA in the previous twenty-
four hours. One day that list included Marshall's stepson, killed in Italy.
Before V-J Day fifteen million youths would find themselves in uniform;
three hundred thousand would appear on Marshall's lists.

Celia, the remaining Beyrle daughter, married and had two children
before Joe went off to war. Besides her, both his grandmothers were in
Muskegon to help tend the home fires, where Dad was even more the
central family figure. On the living room wall he displayed a world map
pinioned with national flags to show fluctuations of the war. From newspapers and radio he became the authority and interpreter of all that happened overseas. As such he was also a buffer between alarming news and
the women's worries.

Despite censorship and because of brother Bill, the family knew Joe
was with the 101st and were sure he had taken part in the "mighty en-

deavor" of Overlord. Like everyone else, they had heard Roosevelt's D Day invocation with that phrase and like all of America had stood silent as bells tolled from every church. The Beyrles hurried to Saint Joseph's to offer prayers. It was so crowded they had to stand.

THEN BEGAN THE LONG wait of dread. Pre–D Day V-mail had been held up in case the invasion was significantly delayed, but in mid-June letters began trickling back to the States. In Muskegon, a town then of some thirty thousand, the arrival of V-mail was widely and quickly known. There was none from Joe.

The first communication about him was official, a telegram dated July 7, fully a month after D Day, from the War Department (today the Department of Defense). Mrs. Beyrle couldn't open it; she had to ask Richard.

"Joe's a prisoner of war, Mom."

She sat down with a shudder, read the telegram several times herself before calling her husband at work. The parents reminded each other that they should be thankful and bless God. Then Mom made fitful calls to find out how food could be sent to Joe, whom she remembered as ever hungry. There was a War Department phone number for such requests, but of course they were futile. Only letters could be sent to Joe; and besides, in his case no POW address had yet been provided by the International Red Cross (IRC). That would come, she was assured, once Joe was delivered to a permanent prison camp, what the Germans called a stalag.

In September, by telegram, came a crushing correction: Tech-4 Joseph Robert Beyrle, Serial Number 16 085 985, previously reported captured on 10 June 1944, had instead on that date been killed in action. Mrs. Beyrle, whose health had weakened since Pearl Harbor, was bedridden for several days.

The reason for the contradictory official reports was that Joe's identity had been stolen by the Germans.

Thanks to Captain Harwick's escape from the marshes, word reached the 101st of Joe's first capture. Paperwork on the status of casualties was not sorted out till the division returned to England in July, at which time Joe was reported captured on 10 June and his family so informed. Their telegram from the War Department included the caveat that his POW status had not yet been confirmed by the IRC, that is, that the preoccupied Germans hadn't completed their paperwork either.

It remains unexplained why the 101st considered Joe to be a POW when he was last seen, by Harwick, loose in the marshes. The appropriate status in those circumstances would seem to be "missing in action" (MIA). Probably someone like Jack Brown, after he escaped from Starvation Hill, later confirmed that Joe was again a POW.

Months passed, the summer months of 1944 when Patton won his fame racing across France. In September, with the Western Front approaching Germany's frontier, the battlefields of Normandy were being cleared of their dead, interred in temporary cemeteries. One such body, shattered by heavy-caliber fire, wore an American uniform and Joe's dog tags. The 101st was about to jump into the Netherlands. In Normandy there was no one from the 506th to confirm or refute that the mangled corpse was Joe's.

In Muskegon three pennants, each with a blue star, hung proudly in the living room window for view from the street, designating how many Beyrle boys were in uniform. Their father was supervising twelve-hour shifts, seven days a week, at Continental Motors. On his way to work he went down to the draft board that had produced the pennants. He brought a blue-star pennant with him. Very quietly he asked to exchange it for one with a gold star. The draft board workers, all local people, surrounded him in the love of tears. That's how death notices circulated in Muskegon, how "Gold Star Mother" became part of America's World War II lexicon.

Nothing needed to be said, for the pennant said it all. The war effort was consumingly intense but paused with each appearance of a gold star. A priest was at the Beyrles' door before the tragic symbol had hung for an hour. Every one of the sisters who had taught Joe came around to speak about him. The Muskegon Catholic community was ethnically divided, each with its own parish and school: Irish, Italian, French, and German, the last being the smallest. They united to console the family. The Beyrles spoke at length with clerics they had never met, but it was the teaching sisters who said the most and what was most remembered.

Neighbors offered words too, and merchants Joe had worked for briefly, nearly unknown by the family. They gave near-eulogies but were frank, as if by describing Joe in living terms they were keeping him alive. He could have been a B or even an A student but didn't apply himself so long as he could get by with C's. Yes, the parents nodded, that was their son. Though he had been voted Most Obvious Temper, he was well behaved in school, Sister Angelique, the mother superior, assured them—Joe took out his temper in athletics. Please tell me more, Mom asked each sister, until memories were exhausted like those of a long-ago movie. To continue talking about Joe kept him here, where he'd started, where he had rooted, where he would return at war's end, under America's flag.

The parents could delay but not prevent his inevitable slipping away, but not before Muskegon paid its tribute in an expression of unity and finality. The *Chronicle* requested a picture for the obituary. His parents could not bring themselves to reopen Joe's bedroom, the door to his truncated past. Robert and Richard were sent in instead to retrieve Joe's high school diploma for the funeral mass and the best picture of him they could find. It was Joe in army khakis and tie, featured in a double obituary next to Muskegon Marine Sergeant Emery Reagan, Jr., twenty-four years old, killed on one of the Mariana Islands. Reagan was survived by a son he had never seen. Both his and Joe's pictures were called Hollywood handsome.

Joe's funeral mass was on September 17, 1944, exactly one year after he'd arrived in England. Saint Joseph's Church overflowed. In the homily the priest spoke of how there are words like *orphan* and *widow* for the bereaved, but no name for the parent who has lost a child. It wasn't meant for children to die first, but in war they do, and that must be accepted. Each note of "Taps" seemed a tug to let go, acknowledge he was gone, but Mrs. Beyrle clung to Sister Angelique's scriptural reading at the mass: ". . . though he were dead, yet shall he live."

THE PRAYERS HAD BEEN for the repose of Joe's soul. That was premature, as if a reproach from God that the faithful were praying too small. On October 23 Mr. Beyrle was called to the phone at work. He could hardly hear over the roar of his assembly line. A Major Reidy identified himself; he was in some personnel office at the War Department. In bureaucratic language but with a tremor in his voice, Reidy advised that a message had been received from the International Red Cross that Joseph Robert Beyrle, Serial Number 16 085 985, was a prisoner of war held by the Germans.

Dad had to sit down, as much from anger as shock. No, he replied, that message had been sent before. The War Department had corrected it. Joe had been killed in the cause of the liberating invasion. The secretary of war and General Marshall had so written.

This was a further correction, Major Reidy assured him, because this latest message was from the IRC, who never confirmed anything unless it came from the captor's government.

The switchboard operator at Continental noticed that Mr. Beyrle was shaking when he put down the phone. He told her why. A replacement supervisor was pulled off the line. Word traveled fast along it. Those who couldn't pat his back pumped their fists and turned renewed to tasks. No, Continental's vice president ordered, don't call home, Bill, *go* home. Mrs. Beyrle's reaction can only be imagined because no one else was there when he opened the front door at such an unexpected hour.

Celia recalled how men did not express emotion as openly then as they do now, so Dad must have hidden his tears as he delivered the miraculous news. Mom would never say what she was thinking during that period of terrible confusion from September through November 1944. What she did every day was pray that Joe would survive, or not suffer before he died. It seemed those kinds of prayers shortened her life, as if fulfilling a covenant that if God sent Joe back alive, He could have her at any time.

No one in the family remembered eating anything for the next twelve hours. When Joe had been reported KIA, friends and neighbors delivered meals to the door for days. Now, during a miracle, no one knew what to do. Nor was there an army protocol for miracles, for on November 16 the Beyrles received a letter from Henry Stimson, secretary of war, that Joe posthumously had been awarded the Purple Heart medal:

We profoundly appreciate the greatness of your loss, for in a very real sense the loss suffered by any of us in this battle for our country is a loss shared by us all. When the medal, which you will receive shortly, reaches you, I want you to know that it goes with my sincerest sympathy and the hope that time and victory of our cause will finally lighten the burden of your grief.

A card from General Marshall added, "Your son fought valiantly in a supreme hour of his country's need."

On November 28 a brigadier general sent Mr. Beyrle the ultimate good-news/bad-news advisory. Joe's Purple Heart had been awarded

> . . . based on a report of death submitted from the theater of operations and, at that time, believed to be correct. In view of more recent reports showing that your son is a prisoner of war, I am happy to advise that award of the Purple Heart is erroneous.
>
> I would appreciate your returning the decoration and certificate to this office for cancellation. Inclosed are government franks for your use in mailing them postage-free.

Shortly there was more, this time from the army's Office of Special Settlement Accounts, which for reasons defying research was in 1944 located at 27 Pine Street, New York City.

> Dear Mrs. Beyrle:
>
> Reference is made to payment of the six months' death gratuity made to you in the amount of $861.60 on 12 October 1944 in the case of your son, Technician Fourth Class Joseph R. Beyrle.
>
> Information received from the Adjutant General is to the effect that your aforementioned son is a prisoner of war, and that previous notification of his death was in error. . . .
>
> Therefore it is respectfully requested that you make refund to this office in the amount of $861.60, by personal check or money order drawn in favor of the Treasurer of the United States, using the enclosed envelope which requires no postage.

The Beyrles were never so happy writing a check as when they dutifully made refund to the secretary of the treasury, Mr. Morgenthau, better known to Joe, after the interrogators' indictment, as an archvillain in the global Jewish conspiracy to rule the world in league with the Bolsheviks.

THERE WAS A MUSKEGON youngster named Ed Albers, a sophomore at Saint Jean's when Joe was a senior at Saint Joseph's. They were athletic rivals, especially in basketball, where people would remark on their similar physiques. As teenagers of the Catholic community they hung out in the same social group, often at the Hubb Recreation Center, an approved pool hall.

Ed's dad had the curious distinction of having been the first American POW to be captured by the Bolsheviks when a regiment of U.S. infantry was sent to Archangel as part of an interventionary force in the Russian civil war. He was treated pretty well, as his captors were eager to win over proletarians in America. The draft soon blew Ed into uniform. His dad was stoic, only wishing at the bus station that he could go in Ed's stead. "Be a good soldier" were his parting words before another Greyhound took another Muskegon boy off to Fort Custer, which would later become a camp for German POWs.

From there Ed went to the San Diego County coast, where he was trained as a 40mm antiaircraft gunner bound for the Pacific. Week after week there was nothing to his duties except digging gun emplacements in ground so hard that shovels constantly struck sparks. One day Ed entered the company orderly room to ask for Merthiolate for blisters that had popped on his callused hands. On the bulletin board next to duty rosters he saw a newly tacked poster. It showed an exultant paratrooper—tommy gun cradled in one arm, the other gripping his parachute riser—descending from a Venetian blue sky. The poster was captioned JUMP INTO THE FIGHT! Ed was more than ready to jump out of an antiaircraft pit. The army quickly obliged, and within days of volunteering for the Airborne he was on a train to Fort Benning, Georgia, for parachute training.

On June 1, 1944, he embarked on the *Queen Elizabeth*, one among seventeen thousand troopers, quadruple the ship's peacetime capacity, so the swimming pools had been drained and filled with stacks of bunks, a desirable location for being airy. Ed was not so lucky; his assigned bunk was way down on R Deck, the most remote bowel of the ship, formerly quarters of busboys, the last living area below the waterline and the depth at which U-boat torpedos were aimed. So Ed moved his sleeping bag to the promenade deck, even though it was a kaleidoscope of crap and poker games, but he had to leave his duffel bag on R Deck, where unbeknownst to him it was rifled.

In mid-Atlantic, weaving along the main deck, he heard, "Hey, Albers!" It was a buddy from antiaircraft training on the other ocean.

"Tim! Whaddya doin' here?"

"Manning this forty-millimeter."

"You still in the army?" Tim was in dungarees.

"Yeah, but I'm workin' for the navy. This is the ninth time I've crossed the pond."

"Any action?"

"Nope. But I'm ready to shoot a U-boat if it surfaces!"

Outrunning any U-boat by a factor of three, the *Queen Elizabeth* zigged and zagged at thirty-five knots, speed, rather than a convoy, her protection, and steamed into Liverpool on June 5, the originally scheduled D Day. Before she moored, a scow came alongside to take off priority cargo—less than a tenth of the passengers—fifteen hundred paratroopers. Arbitrarily, half were assigned to the 82nd (Ed's bunk mate became Major General Gavin's jeep driver), half to the 101st.

The 506th rookies pitched pup tents on a cow pasture near Ramsbury, where they were all temporarily assigned to Second Battalion under Lieutenant Tanin, the "rear detachment" commander.* All other Currahees were fighting and dying in Normandy. Out on the pasture Lieutenant Tanin was like a personal trainer, a brutal one pushing the rookies to get in shape as never before. He formed them up and announced they were reinforcements rather than replacements; in other words, they would be going in shortly to tip the battle rather than replace casualties from it. For at that point in the second week of June there were

---

* Tanin was killed two days after jumping into the Netherlands.

only estimates of casualties as Screaming Eagles literally kept coming out of the woods after scattered drops. So as the war for Western civilization raged two hundred miles away, Ed and his cohort did calisthenics by day, pulled guard by night, and kept their powder very dry.

England bubbled with news and rumors as the Allied foothold strengthened and expanded during the ides of June. For the reinforcements it was a singular sensation to be part of a team winning world-class laurels but not to have met their teammates. That began to change as the wounded and escaped POWs like Brown and Harwick returned to England before the rest of the division. The reinforcements (a term soon to be dropped) felt like freshman pledges to a fraternity whose seniors suddenly appeared for the first time, then as suddenly disappeared to carouse off campus. They looked at one another, the faces of veterans and those who had not yet seen the elephant, then quickly parted as the vets took London passes to forget, the rookies to wonder and aspire. David Webster, he who had pleaded that D Night never arrive, described them in reflection as half of a symbiosis: "And so we went forward together, one regiment, filled up with replacements, the dead as fine and strong a part of us as the living men, so fresh and new, who had come to take their place."

In their introduction there was a provisional schism expressed in how the vets called themselves "originals," those who had been Currahees since Toccoa. With some wariness they began training with the replacements, who by and large were physically heftier and showed more stamina, facts from which originals excused themselves by reason of lingering exhaustion from Normandy. The predominant attitude developed among originals was that these new guys hadn't shown them yet but looked like they could.

No other regiment in Overlord had lost a larger percentage of officers than the 506th. As the bulk of Currahees dribbled back around the Fourth of July—more than three weeks after General Taylor had promised, before D day, that they would be relieved—Sink was intent on reestablishing his chain of command. Regenerate the regiment, integrate our replacements, and revive Currahee standards, he directed. Eyewash and horseshit, this amounted to for the troopers, including battalion guard mounts.

There had not been such formality since Toccoa. Mounting the guard fell to Sergeant Engelbrecht of Third Battalion, to which Albers had been assigned. Engelbrecht ordered Ed to fall out in class-A uniform, and though only a private he was to be corporal of the guard. Ed went to his duffel bag, unopened since the *Queen Elizabeth*. The contents had been stirred, and his two dress shirts were missing. With trepidation he reported the loss to Engelbrecht, who swore like a trooper, a paratrooper. Gruffly he directed Ed toward the I Company supply room.

"Turn out in a nice pressed shirt, Albers."

Luteran, the supply sergeant, was uneasy. The only source for such items of uniform was the duffel bags of Blues who had not made it back from Normandy. There were several hundred, stacked in bins marked KIA, MIA, POW. No one but duly designated officers was authorized to open these bags, which regulations required be sorted through for personal effects to be returned to next of kin.

"Make it snappy," Luteran muttered, trying to remember which of the casualties was about Albers's size. He retrieved a bag, flung it on the counter for Ed to open. "This guy's shirt might be a little big," said the supply sergeant, glancing at the door. "Try it." At the top of the bag was a dress shirt neatly folded, if not pressed. Ed held it up by the sleeves to drape on his body. "Good enough," he heard Luteran pronounce, but Ed's attention was on the name stenciled inside the collar.

"Did you know 'Buy-early,' Sarge?" he asked with wide eyes.

"Sure did. Company radio operator. How did you know how to say his name right?"

"Where was he from?"

"Someplace in Michigan."

CHAPTER TEN

ANGELS DON'T SPEAK GERMAN

THE BLOW OF A RIFLE BUTT CAME FROM OVER JOE'S RIGHT shoulder. Behind him the guard must have raised his weapon high, awaiting a signal to strike. He did with a cross-body sweep like the paddling lunge of a canoe racer—down, back, and deep.

The indentation of Joe's skull fracture is like a heel print, tapering upward parallel to the angle of the blow. He fell backward off the high chair, sustaining a secondary concussion upon hitting the floor. That much has been established by forensic surgery; what happened during his coma can only be inferred. Among the scores of POWs interrogated in the château, Joe by then must have been labeled a waste of time, or why else club him with such finality? So his overall resistance strategy succeeded, his paymaster secrets remained secure. Indeed, within a week of being bludgeoned, all FFI territory in which he'd jumped was liberated.

Unconquered but unconscious, Joe presented something of a problem for the interrogators. There on the floor, bleeding slightly from nose and ears, was this stinking, low-rank prisoner about to die. He had a previous wound, but it could hardly be blamed for his death. To avoid an investigation, the interrogators would have moved him into medical channels at once, perhaps citing serious infection of his butt as the reason. They no doubt hoped that hobnailed bootprints on his torso would go unnoticed in a German field hospital, rife with horrific wounds.

Joe had been kicked viciously while he was down, while he was comatose. Permanent damage resulted from scar tissue that pressures the top of the sciatic nerve. On occasion it has caused him to black out. The skull fracture remains sensitive to barometric changes, especially with high humidity, another reason why Joe lives in Muskegon with its cool lake breezes.

FOR ABOUT A WEEK he was in and out of consciousness, hearing things the way music can be heard, not with the ears but in the mind. At the same time Joe visualized things that didn't relate to what was heard. Body sensations were the last to check in, not preferable to delusions that made him feel as if he were in the afterlife. The transition to reality came when he focused on two white figures hovering over him, talking about him. It was then he knew this wasn't heaven because angels don't speak German.

Coming back was very much coming down. There was the body pain, pulsing headaches, but mostly a woozy feeling like the worst case of flu times ten. Joe realized he was back when his senses became continuous and connected, as when he perceived that one of the "angels" was a doctor, the other a male nurse. An interpreter came over and asked him how he was. Sore all over, was his response, especially where my ribs were kicked in.

Joe was sat up to take pills. During his unconsciousness he'd been washed down and put in a hospital smock. The ever-efficient Germans had laundered his underwear and tattered uniform—nothing left of it except jump pants and khaki shirt—which was labeled with his name and left on a chair by his bed. The ward was crowded. Every time an orderly came around he asked if Joe could get up. Foolishly Joe did as soon as his legs could support him. A doctor watched him totter around, then told Joe to get dressed. Shortly afterward he was returned to a stable by the château.

It would have been entirely natural to fear more interrogation, but Joe's reasoning faculties had not been impaired: he was sure that he now had a medical entry in the punctilious German records, so it looked as though he wouldn't be put through life-threatening interrogation again (unless perhaps Greta reappeared). Rommel's question to the prisoner with a head wound—"Are you receiving medical treatment?"—was an encouragement for Joe. He was beginning to learn that humane treatment was sometimes employed by the Wehrmacht under certain circumstances. Joe made the best of that possibility, seeming slightly loony, drooling when appropriate, mumbling when guards could hear him. Eventually a couple of other wounded POWs were shoved into his stall.

"Tell them what happened to you, Beyrle!" the guard yelled. Though Joe craved companionship, he continued to act like a dazed dunce even with his stable mates. They didn't want to talk about their interrogations and asked Joe nothing about his. They were reinterrogated; he was not.

The Allied advance was approaching the château, and the Wehrmacht evacuated POWs in the bow wave of retreat. One evening they were loaded onto trucks for Alençon, then on to Chartres—so said the ones unwounded and alert. Joe listened to them appreciatively. He had been acting demented for the krauts, but now it seemed impossible to drop the role with his countrymen, who apparently were as convinced as his captors that a screw had been knocked loose in Joe's head. It had, not to be rethreaded for several weeks, during which time he was pretty much like a drunken spectator of his life.

The drive to Alençon took all night. The destination did not register with Joe as the region he knew from paymaster jumps. He was disgorged into a huge warehouse with hundreds of other prisoners, most from Starvation Hill, including a Currahee, George Rosie, who shared many POW experiences with Joe, although they were never to meet till after the war. Rosie's memories are of rain that soaked and resoaked. The French blamed the monsoon on all the combat dust and gunpowder in the air, the same as in World War I, when it rained for months.

The German commandant of Alençon decreed that if one man escaped from the warehouse, ten of his fellows would be shot in reprisal. That night POWs huddled to discuss the seriousness of such a threat. Unacquainted with Geneva Conventions that absolutely banned reprisals, they dispersed from the huddle with no consensus. Rosie felt that the commandant was full of typical kraut bluff and bluster. If he had a chance to escape, he'd take it. That was the Currahee way. The next day he was put on a work detail to dig up dud bombs, told to dig down in a crater till they found a bomb, then the Germans would haul it out with a winch or detonate in place. The craters were on city streets. Guards provided picks and shovels, then went behind buildings, which they could peek around to see if the prisoners were working. They were, digging very softly and slowly. When the guards weren't looking, they broke tool handles. After his first sabotage Rosie strolled up to a guard and said, Sorry, Fritz, but we can't dig anymore. The guards provided more handles, with advice as to where they would be shoved if they were broken again. Even so, Rosie never dug down far enough to uncover a bomb. But the detail on another street did, and a huge explosion rocked the block. It jarred Joe back in the warehouse where he was splinting handles like those Rosie had sabotaged.

The warehouse had been used to store coal, so the POWs were covered with a black dusty film. The straw on the cement floor was full of fleas and lice, and soon so were the prisoners. There was barely room for everyone to lie down at night. Turning over started a chain reaction. Scuttlebutt was that, as soon as the krauts repaired the railroad, POWs would be shipped to Germany. Furthermore, they'd go through Paris, the ultimate tourist destination. From the way railroads were being bombed, Rosie figured the line to Germany would be repaired shortly after Christ's reappearance, but sure enough, the Paris part came true.

The August 1944 triumphal march of the American infantry down the Champs Elysées became one of the most famous and photographed events of World War II. Earlier that month American troops had made another march on the streets of Paris, this time for Nazi cameras. Joe and Rosie were part of that spectacle of humiliation. Filthy and famished, they were trucked into Paris. The Germans must have wanted them that way because at other times they could make prisoners look presentable, as they were for Rommel or for a visit by the International Red Cross.

Rosie remembers standing in formation till "the Huns' Hollywood got everything ready." He was confused. For whom was this film being shot? France was being liberated a mile a minute, so there didn't seem much use in convincing the French they were better off under Hitler. Slowly it became apparent that there was another purpose: to show Americans as a contemptible presence in Europe. The miserable POWs surely looked the part.

Loudspeakers announced the start of a parade of murderers and rapists paroled from U.S. prisons to attack Franco-German civilization.

French collaborators took up a chorus of hisses and jeers, then began to throw garbage at POWs shuffling by, some of whom were so hungry they caught and ate it.

Joe's height made him stand out, a magnet for abuse. Aftereffects of his six-day coma had turned him into a zombie in this zombie jamboree. Rosie was on an edge of the column closest to the collaborators, a number of whom took pleasure in tripping the wounded on canes. There was also a Nazi whore drunk enough to run up and spit. She got to Rosie's buddy, Jim Bradley, and started to spit in his face when he blew a huge honker into hers. Rosie muttered, "Boy, are we going to catch hell now!" But a guard pushed her back into the crowd and nodded at Bradley approvingly.

For Joe, with his brains full of static, the Paris march was incomprehensible. Not until years later, when he watched POWs exhibited on TV in Hanoi and, later, the American body dragged down a street in Somalia, did his victimization by the Nazis reveal its intent. POWs were not just military captives for such enemies, they were a propaganda resource.

The office buildings on the route were used by German bureaucrats, who hung out the windows as a sound truck, working up the crowd, preceded the show. Movie and still cameramen were positioned on pedestals at various points. It made Joe think of how the press publicized the Currahee march from Atlanta to Fort Benning. Physically he felt about the same at the end of both marches; the first had been 142 miles, the second about 2.

Lights, camera, action, mostly for French civilians whose jobs depended on the German occupation. They shouted on cue, some pelted the POWs, but most were just grim, no doubt aware that the next American soldiers they'd see in Paris would be carrying weapons and riding tanks. Something revived in Joe when a trooper started singing the 82nd's march, which begins, "We're all American and proud to be . . ." Joe tried to stand tall, march like a soldier, and stare down spectators. Rosie remembers it as a surreal spectacle. There were the Germans at the windows, cursing without much gusto. He had crossed the ocean to rid France of them, but there were the French spitting on him.

At the end of the shameful parade a thousand prisoners bound for Germany squatted at the squalid station till trains sent on higher-priority cargo. After some twelve hours without food or water, boxcars arrived: "forty-or-eight" boxcars, famous from World War I—they could hold forty humans or eight horses. One such boxcar is on permanent display at the Holocaust Memorial Museum in Washington, D.C.

The German filmmakers had a final scene to shoot. They kept some cameramen around to photograph a guard light up, take a couple of puffs, then throw the cigarette on the ground in front of POWs. Smokers like Rosie hadn't had a drag for weeks. They'd scramble on the ground for the butt. To increase mortification, guards started dropping butts, then ground them with a boot while POWs clawed to save them.* This got to be too much for Jim Bradley, who was gaining a reputation for guts personified. He whispered to Rosie: next time they throw a butt on the ground, step on it first—and anyone's fingers who tries to get it. This they did while cursed by fellow POWs and cameramen wanting more shots of Americans groveling for smokes.

Overloaded fifty to a boxcar, without food, with only one bottle of water and a can for waste, the POWs were bolted behind sliding doors. In humid heat the train languished in a railroad yard hour after hour. They tried to arrange themselves so everyone could sit down, but there wasn't nearly enough room; about ten in each car had to stand. Rank was as nothing in their situation. When it was agreed that a couple of hours had passed, ten seated men would change places with standees.

Under way at last, Joe's train lurched along, causing some air to pass through cracks between the car's slats. Someone thanked God for that small mercy, and a prayer for His protection was answered by forty-nine murmured amens. They didn't know one another, but when a man started crying there was someone beside him with the comfort of feelings as intimately shared as they were impossible to express. There was little age or perspective in that stifling mass of bodies, no motto to sustain them. All they knew for sure after the Paris march was how wantonly evil the creatures of Hitler were. The American army had tried to warn them how evil but lacked the capability to tell how much. In the case of

---

* This film was shown in Germany for the secondary purpose of depicting the U.S. Army as a despicable rabble that could not stand up to soldiers with the sterling discipline of the Wehrmacht.

the Nazis, the shibboleth of demonizing the enemy could be faulted not for falsity but only for inadequacy.

Thoughts turned to buddies fighting at that moment in France. They had grown to know the Nazis too and remembered Brays, Vanderpools, Harrisons, and Wolvertons, what they meant, why and how they'd been killed. These buddies were not forgetting the prisoners, who seemed to receive a telepathic message in the boxcar, which steeled their resolve to survive—because the war would be won, it had to be. The 101st had returned to England by the time Joe was in the boxcar. After the war they said how hard it was to think about those who'd been left behind in France. He was to have that feeling when visiting Gettysburg with its photos of Confederate dead all over the battlefields. Lee's army had had to march away and leave them.

THE TRAIN TO GERMANY bumped and banged along for about as many hours as it was shunted to sidings. That was the routine for a claustrophobic week: herk, jerk, and halt. Guards were on top of the boxcars. Prisoners yelled for water when the train stopped but never got a response though they could hear guards scramble down if there were sounds of aircraft. They also got down at each stop, went off and watched with their weapons pointed at the cars. They were watched in turn through the slats.

The prisoners were so packed that those sitting had to fold their knees into their faces. Being trussed that way became too much for two troopers near Joe who started talking with him about escape. At a corner of the boxcar was a rectangular grille, about eight feet up. Slowly making their way to the corner they positioned themselves to remove it. Joe was the tallest, so he went to work first. The grille was sturdy metal mesh embedded in wood. More discouraging than that was its size, only a couple of feet in diagonal. With his build, Joe couldn't possibly get through.

Undeterred he pushed and pulled on it for two days and nights. Prisoners watched like a silent chorus; some offered to help but couldn't because only one could work at a time, so the grille was recognized as a project for the pair who would use it. There was a quiet cheer from the others when the heavy mesh finally came loose. Now it was for the pair to decide at what time and by what method to attempt to get out, a one-time only experiment. They'd have to be boosted, then held horizontal while trying to wriggle through the hole.

Joe recommended that the attempt be at night to have the longest period of darkness for getting away. Surprisingly the Germans had not taken a head count in Paris, so if anyone could depart undetected, there'd never be a search for him. The big question was whether to go out facedown or faceup. The guard was judged to be sitting at about the middle of the roof. Along the side of the boxcar was an eave. The escapee would have to grab it to pull himself through the hole. If the eave didn't break, he'd then have to push away from the car so as not to be run over, a lesser problem because the train never went faster than ten miles per hour.

The first trooper decided to go out faceup. That way he could grab the eave without reversing his hands, somehow extract his feet, push off with them, do a half twist, and land rolling forward. The second trooper would be boosted up so he could see what happened to the first. He would go out facedown, if faceup didn't work for his buddy. They hugged each other while Joe hugged them both.

Lifted by four POWs, up went the first trooper on his back. He had to gyrate his shoulder into the diagonal of the hole, then his head disappeared. The train rocked along slowly. The decapitated man crossed his arms tight to his torso. His hands gestured to push him out, even if to his death. Both arms couldn't make it. He dragged one forward. The wood frame, full of splinters, drew blood, but he was going to get that arm through even if it meant leaving all the skin behind. The arm ground through. A silent cheer, as everyone listened for any movement by the guard on the roof. Total quiet reigned over fifty men packed head to head.

With one arm out, he had an easier time with the other. He was still being held—the two-thirds of him still in the car—horizontal. He must have gripped the eave because he started easing the rest of his body through. He was disappearing. Joe's recollection of that scene reminds him of the Assumption of the Virgin Mary.

The second trooper's head was right beside the first one's hips. When the feet went out, the second trooper demanded to be boosted up the next second. His buddy was gone, and he couldn't wait to join him. Just then the train built up speed as if *Gott mit uns* was coming true for the Germans, but Joe saw it another way: not more danger for the escapees but a sign that they could speed away to freedom. And Jumpin' Joe had counseled them, reminded them how to do a good PLF, and that it would be an easy one because the train was doing less than fifteen miles per hour.

The second trooper's feet went out the grille hole. Men had ears to the wood when he dropped but didn't hear anything. Joe crossed himself and prayed for the two of them, pleaded for God to protect them. For the first time since his head had been bashed in at the château, his compulsion to escape revived. There were other reasons he can't quite identify, but the major ones were Jack Brown going over the wall on Starvation Hill and the two troopers jumping from the train. Joe never stopped comparing what they did to what might be a similar gamble for him. If others were getting away—though quite likely they had been killed or recaptured—then he was lacking something more than luck. That infuriated him. To have been recaptured was an ignominy that could only be mitigated by escape.

THERE WERE TWO FEWER in the boxcar now. Places were reshuffled, and it was Joe's turn to be crammed next to "Stinky." Off and on during their POW time, they'd run across each other. He got his nickname because of the strafing outside St.-Lô more than a month before. He dove for the nearest cover, and it turned out to be a French four-holer. He came out looking like a soaked chimney sweep, and the way he smelled was so bad that in the Paris march no one would go near him, not even the hecklers. Now Stinky was back-to-back with Joe, sitting on the floor of the boxcar knees to face, both of them wrapped in a stench strong enough to cause pain. Stinky whispered that he wanted to tear off his skin, that he had been prevented from trying. After the war Joe heard he became a compulsive bather.

AT DAWN AFTER the escape, the guard on Joe's boxcar shouted, *"Jabos!"* They sounded like P-47s. No one inside knew if the cars were marked POW. They weren't.* The first pass reached out ahead of the train as it chugged on. Would there be a return pass? Yes, because brakes shrieked, the boxcar jolted to a halt, and the guard climbed down, his rifle clattering against the slats. POWs cringed as antiaircraft machine guns fired from the train. Joe's car was two or three down from the locomotive, the *Jabos'* target, and they hit it. He heard steam blowing out of the perforated boiler like a huge whistle. Prisoners piled on one another, their only protection the men they could burrow under.

The third pass, with armor-piercing 50-calibers the size and weight of poker tips, destroyed the locomotive. Pulling off, one *Jabo* stitched the nearest boxcars with a burst. The pilot just kept his finger on the trigger a second too long—erupting the flesh of a score of his countrymen.

Joe has a lot of trouble telling about this, as if it shouldn't have happened—God to whom he'd prayed shouldn't have allowed it to happen, and Joe shouldn't have had to witness it, as if to be witness was all but as horrible as being victim.

Pulp and bone particles dripped from his face, mixed with the unique taste of someone else's blood. Blood that for a lifetime till the previous minute had been contained and circulating in veins and arteries. Blood, now a cloudburst of stickiness, hovering like a pause in a water show. Blood spurting, then flowing, finally just seeping, spreading, soaking as if to quench the screams and gurgles of the dying, those dying in extended torture, all in the space of a boxcar.

The living, many crying to die, couldn't move except to grapple against one another. Those shot through the entrails vomited, starting a slithery chain reaction among men gone thrashing mad with pain. The unwounded tried to slide the wounded around to take care of the worst off. The worst off didn't scream as much as the ones with guts torn out or cheeks blown off. Joe struggles to exorcise the memory deeply dredged.

---

* Wehrmacht intelligence warned the German high command that boxcars marked POW might become targets for paratrooper raids that could easily stop a train and liberate its prisoners, a good idea but one never contemplated by Allied Airborne planners.

"Euthanasia is against my religion, but if I'd had enough will to do it, I could have strangled those sufferers and I think they'd have blessed me with their last breath."

The 50-calibers had blown huge rips in the boxcar's side, blasting jagged splinters of wood everywhere. Slats became splints and grimy T-shirts bandages, sopping in seconds, handed off to be wrung out, then wrapped on again. A shredded artery pumping blood was just clamped by hand. Till the man died, someone else would take over as a manual tourniquet.

Three, four, five men died from loss of blood during the next twenty-four hours, a calendar for Joe watching them pale whiter and whiter, weaker and weaker. An American son, husband, brother, name. Some wailing so much the survivors were glad to see them go. The dead, and pieces of them, were piled in one corner. By everyone else standing, a bit of room was made for the dozen wounded still living. Nothing else could be done for their awful pain, nothing at all. For the unwounded it was like watching relatives being executed in a torture chamber. Joe stood hour after hour, rocking and holding the man beside him, watching and hearing others struggle and die, each in his own individual way. The stench from ruptured bowels became so overpowering that the un-wounded passed out standing up. When that happened Joe felt a new heavy weight and propped himself to support it.

The guards never unbolted the boxcar till it reached Germany four nights later on a Stygian night setting a scene from Auschwitz as flood-lights shone on the train and a wide semicircle of SS troops guarded the unloading, while German shepherds snarled, barked, and lunged on their leashes.

The POWs in Joe's boxcar were uncowed. They ignored the order to form into ranks, instead performing a duty to their countrymen. First the wounded were passed out, then the dead—with dignity that silenced even the SS. Joe had been an altar boy, and lifting mutilated bodies, he felt, was like raising the bread and wine.

A fellow pallbearer thought similarly: "Here's *our* offering, you Goddamned krauts, *your* curse. If you get back half of what you did to us, you'll get off easy."

CHAPTER ELEVEN

THE STALAGS

WHEN THEIR TRAIN HAD RUMBLED THROUGH FIELDS DENSE with concrete antitank barriers, the POWs knew they were crossing the Siegfried Line into Germany. Joe arrived outside Limburg, noted for its cheese, at a camp with STALAG XII-A arching over the gate. It was one in a prison archipelago created five years before when Hitler had invaded Poland. From now on POWs would be "krieges," *Kriegsgefangener.* Hardly any of them remained in the same stalag for the rest of the war.

Unlike concentration camps, designed for slow or rapid extermination, stalags were essentially bins to store captured soldiers.* By 1944, with the outcome of the war threateningly uncertain, treatment of krieges was a concern of the Wehrmacht high command, whose nightmares included answering to nations who had sent their men to war under the Geneva Conventions. So despite hard labor, severe hardships, and sporadic cruelty, the lot of krieges was surpassingly better than that of other prisoners of the Third Reich. In contrast to France, there would be scant interrogation in stalags. A kriege might never again be questioned by the Germans unless his current conduct ran afoul of camp regulations. He could nearly hibernate, as many did, like the protagonist in *Slaughterhouse-Five* by kriege Kurt Vonnegut.

Each kriege was assigned a prison partner called a "mucker" (British

---

* Except for selected POWs, inmates of concentration camps were all civilians; these camps were run by the plainclothes branch of the SS. Stalags were run by the Wehrmacht or the Luftwaffe.

terminology), a mate with whom to muck it through captivity. Why the Germans in 1940 set up such a buddy system is unclear, probably as a device to apply pressure vicariously through the mucker of a truculent kriege. That worked sometimes, but far more often muckers helped each other cope. In Korea and Vietnam when the captors paired prisoners, it was to divide the POW chain of command or insinuate potential informers with suspected resisters. Propaganda to the outside world was the principal aim of the Communists, brainwashing the means.

But in stalags such propaganda was a low priority because the world, by this time, had been immutably fixed in its division between the Allies and the Axis (Switzerland maintaining an amoral appearance), so there were no important outsiders to win over. And for the very practical reason that they held more than three million POWs at one time or another, stalag commandants could devote few resources to brainwashing. What effort there was came from the propaganda ministry run by the notorious Joseph Goebbels. He wore a uniform but was not in the Wehrmacht.

Krieges were constantly exposed to Goebbels's pronouncements and publications, but that was about as far as Joe's stalag commandants went after hearts and minds. Far more important was a tacit understanding that the relative positions of captors and captives would be resolved by the outcome of the war as it plunged toward conclusion. Winner take all, and if Hitler won, the losers would lose all. That much was clear from what krieges saw of the hideous treatment of Soviet prisoners, millions of whom, when the Wehrmacht overran most of European Russia, were simply enclosed in barbed wire to die of starvation and exposure. Russian prisoners later in the war fared even worse.

Churchill opined that "the Germans are either at your throat or at your feet." As the Allies closed in on Hitler's frontier, stalag guards treated Western krieges like fellow soldiers. But when British armor failed to seize a bridge too far at Arnhem, camp authorities celebrated victory through new restrictions on kriege life. Into the winter when General Bradley breached the Siegfried Line, these same restrictions relaxed noticeably. Then with Hitler's initial success in the Battle of the Bulge, more and worse restrictions were imposed.

A dynamic of the war watched constantly by krieges and their guards was the strategic bombardment of Germany, the attempt to deliver body blows on Hitler's industry. It meant American bombers by day, British by night, nearly every day and every night. In 1944 the targets were usually away from stalags, though frequent thunder resounded across the land. Fighters from the depleted Luftwaffe rose to meet Allied armadas, but aerial combat was at altitudes too high to see more than contrails and casualties. A plumed spiral of smoke ejecting parachutes was a bomber; a meteor could be either a German or American fighter, but nearby bombs were a rarity. Stalags had been openly identified by the Germans and the locations circled on maps of Allied pilots, making a stalag one of the safest places from air attack, yet a place from which krieges were often ghoulish spectators. Joe grew to dread seeing a formation of B-24s attacked by the Luftwaffe. A similar flight of B-17s (Flying Fortresses) usually battled through intact, but when Liberators were hit by fire they soon disintegrated and, after the first fighter pass chewed up a B-24, a couple of the crew would "hit the silk." They used a rip cord to open their chutes and steered them down. Suddenly above them the Liberator blew apart and there were a half-dozen more canopies clustered up there. From his jumping experience, Joe was pretty sure that the B-24's explosion had blown open the chutes. He could tell they were not being steered because random wind drifted the canopies like confetti of death. He mumbled something about bodies descending, souls ascending. His mucker looked at him with approval—Joe's head was coming back together.

WHEN JOE REACHED STALAG XII-A, he was among some thirty thousand Americans who had been captured so far, more than half of them airmen like the crews who jumped from their B-24s. Joe and fellow Airborne men presented a typological problem for the German bureaucracy: in Hitler's military organization, paratroopers were part of his air force, but in America they were in the army, so how should they be categorized in the stalag system? Unluckily for the Airborne, custody went to the Wehrmacht. Luftwaffe stalags were considered upscale by comparison. The floodlights and police dogs awaiting Joe's train were a statement by the commandant that Stalag XII-A would be no country club.

Glazed by blood from the ghastly boxcar, survivors were searched one by one and stripped as if a gas chamber would be their next stop. It was, but for delousing. The Germans had developed a deathly fear of typhus, "the Jews' revenge," they called it, carried by lice that swept through every concentration camp. The lice didn't care if they fed on prisoners or guards, so after fumigation Joe got a shower with industrial-strength lye soap. Their skin scrubbed clean for the first time in months, the POWs welcomed the caustic even when it brought out rashes and boils nearly unnoticed before. While a guard watched to retrieve the razor (one for every five men), new krieges had the painful luxury of a shave.

In a demonstration of German efficiency, their clothes were laundered and hundreds of odd-lot uniforms unerringly returned in bundles marked with the men's names. XII-A was big, with a fluctuating population of between five and ten thousand prisoners. Joe's group marched several miles through the encampment, then up a small hill to four circus tents. Inside, the ground was lined with straw, clean straw. It was dawn, but they slept for twelve hours, interrupted only when names were called out alphabetically to start processing.

Processing meant being registered, photographed, vaccinated, and given a POW number stamped on a dog tag. Joe's number was XII-A 80213. Thus identified, the new krieges were allowed to write a postcard (censored, of course) to their families, a Geneva Conventions requirement. Messages that complained about anything had to be rewritten; rejection a second time meant no message went out, so Joe mentioned neither of his wounds in the first postcard, which reached his parents within days after they had mourned at his funeral mass. He had no inkling that the death of the line crosser had been reported as his own, nor that the postcard fulfilled Sister Angelique's prediction from gospel.

Though the Beyrles knew his handwriting like their own, they compared it with everything they could find that he'd ever written, including his last essay retrieved from student records at Saint Joseph's. Without doubt now it was true that their son was alive in Germany, a fact they assumed known by the army when Major Reidy called Mr. Beyrle from the Pentagon. However, Joe's postcard went through Red Cross channels in Switzerland to enter the U.S. Postal Service like any other piece of international mail, bypassing army cognizance. That was the reason for

Secretary Stimson's letter in November awarding Joe a posthumous Purple Heart. Even after the medal was retracted, some bureau of the army continued to carry Joe as KIA rather than POW. That error would have stunning consequences.

Stunned was how Joe felt during his early days at Stalag XII-A. His head reeled from cranial aftershocks that blacked him out without warning. When he revived it was like trying to remember what had happened while drunk. Except for these frightening interludes there was only the continuum of monotony. Little of significance ever changed in the drab listlessness of the camp. It took energy and initiative, largely drained from Joe since his concussion, to sustain interest in anything. What interest there was—the personalities and outlooks of fellow krieges—was overpowered by the constant gnaw of hunger. Everyone knew what was foremost, even if not expressed, in everyone's mind: food. When would the next scanty ration appear? What could be traded for a little more?

Joe took courage from watching those in worse shape than he. What was happening at XII-A was triage: the worst off, because of wounds or extreme depression, were removed to die. Other lives ebbed away through malnourishment, but most were felled by diarrhea brought in by each new wave of prisoners with diseases contracted where they had been captured, locations as far apart as Italy and Scandinavia. When disease broke out, quarantines were common, a measure for which captor-captive cooperation was the best.

Krieges were also segregated by nationality and rank. New arrivals milled around in every sort of uniform—American, British, and Canadian—while the Germans methodically sorted them out. In the U.S. Army, Joe was a technician fourth-class, the equivalent of a buck sergeant. By the Geneva Conventions protocol, sergeants didn't have to do manual labor, which meant that if he were to die a prisoner, it would not be because the Germans worked him to death, as could be the fate of privates and corporals.* A stripe of rank made that difference.

XII-A was also a Red Cross reception station. For bona fide IRC

---

* The Japanese, also signatories of the Geneva Conventions, made no effort whatever to observe them, and worked POWs of all ranks, often to death. Consequently

representatives Joe was now willing to name his prewar occupation: butcher, he said, a white lie. That's what his uncle did, and Joe thought it might help him get a job around the stalag kitchen, where he could scrounge scraps of meat as during the Depression.

Each day went by in idle talk while krieges waited for the daily ration of black bread, mostly sawdust. Everyone ate very slowly to prolong the sensation. In the British compound was a group of Gurkhas who received little sun-dried bananas in their Red Cross parcels. Joe found Gurkhas to be the kindest people in the world, willing to toss bananas over the fence to new krieges even before the Americans had anything to barter. The nutritious fruit was gummy, with the taste and color of licorice.

Hunger was relentless, but Joe dreamed of more than a full stomach. Gintjee (the diarist from Starvation Hill), by contrast, visualized éclairs days after someone mentioned them. There were krieges like that who took masochistic pleasure in describing meals to one another. For Joe the worst of stalag existence—hunger excluded—was the knowledge that he was in the bowels of Germany, a dismal world away from the joy-filled liberation back in France. He had served that purpose, risking his life as if it were no more than a poker chip, but what had he accomplished? Not much that his reassembling mind could appreciate.

It was a month before he began to recover physically and mentally, about the time of his transfer to Stalag IV-B, where there were chaplains of several nationalities who conducted moving services inspired by the Psalms. Not since Wolverton's pre–D Night invocation had Joe felt such power from combined prayer, and with it the addition of diverse perspectives of God and His ways. These sermons pointed in ramiform directions: resignation or at least acceptance; hope of ultimate deliverance; strength from spiritual unity. Abstractions abounded, the soul a focus, but Joe was more intent on revivifing his body.

"The best thing I could do for my soul was to get in shape," Joe recalls. "The first thing was my butt wound. It was infected and draining.

---

30 percent of their American POWs died in captivity compared with only 2 percent of krieges. Joe is a member of the Barbed Wire Club (ex-POWs), and reflects that but for their incomparable Nazi partners in the Axis, the Japs would rank number one as the most evil of all fascist empires.

A British doctor [captured by Rommel in North Africa] cleaned it up and removed the last bit of shrapnel. He gave it to me and I still have it, the only thing I carried all the way from Normandy to Muskegon."

In an Allied stalag, the margin of survival usually depended on IRC parcels. They came in four brands: American, British, Canadian, and Australian, put together in those countries for their men. If there weren't enough American parcels, the Germans substituted Australian or any other kind that came in, creating an international bazaar for essential trading and dealing, with the additional benefit of being a great time-passer.

There was supposed to be a parcel for each man, but that never happened, and in a well-provisioned stalag the norm was one parcel for four krieges. Through inter-Allied swapping—also with guards who wanted U.S. cigarettes as much as gold—Rosie found he could have some oat gruel for breakfast, a scrap of bread and a cup of swill for lunch. The Germans considered lunch the main meal, sufficient for compliance with the Geneva Conventions, so nothing else was required the rest of the day, and krieges were on their own.

That's when barter became overridingly important, and gambling a game of life or death. A stalag was like Las Vegas, with croupiers everywhere. Food items were chips, and everyone played by trading ruthlessly, disregarding the weak for whom a bad trade or bet was worse than worthless—it could drop him to third in the triage of survival. For American krieges, the ultimate dinner was a three-ounce can of Spam and a cracker from an IRC parcel. Parcels also included powdered milk and a bit of rock-hard chocolate, tragic ingredients for a few men who craved to reexperience indulgence even at risk of life.

Like a pharaonic scribe, Gintjee recorded the death of such a man who traded his all for a half-pound each of powdered milk and chocolate. It all blew out in acute diarrhea, then his life squirted and dribbled away as he paled and cut a wide hole from the seat of his pants. His mucker was criticized, but he had done all he could to dissuade the dead man, whose name and face faded in memory, his mucker to be paired with another kriege orphan.

On their way to other stalags, three forgotten muckers moved in and out of Joe's ken at XII-A. Since his traumatic coma he had found it impossible to consistently interact with anyone (probably why Joe never connected with Rosie). As his mind reassembled, he became appraising and observant, seeking signs from other men that the future could hold more than staying alive and waiting. Naturally he gravitated toward Airborne krieges, in whom that spirit could be expected. What Joe found was not the previous Airborne spirit but a steadfast casualness that was more mature for the situation, for the long term. "We're inside here," an 82nd sergeant said with a sigh, gesturing to the barbed wire. "The war's way out there."

Adjusting to permanent kriege life, the troopers' precombat training lapsed. Many had stayed with name, rank, and serial number during interrogations in France, but now they relaxed, knowing that nothing they knew would be of any use to the Germans. So when asked by the Red Cross (with Germans listening) about their previous occupations, krieges were wise guys, coming up with titles like "professional assassin." That went over well with the Germans, so it was used often. So was "gangster." Another good response was "student." For reasons believed only by Goebbels, it was thought a student could be taught the virtues of national socialism. Jim Bradley's answer was "cowboy," though he had never ridden a horse. That was just written down as if cowboy were a common profession in the States. A New Yorker said "rumrunner." He was closely questioned about what that meant and had to explain Prohibition and speakeasies. The next trooper wanted no questions, so he answered "pimp." The Germans laughed and slapped him on the back. After that "pimp" was the favorite item on a kriege's résumé. But it must have been difficult for the commandant to report to Berlin that the American Airborne was actually a flying prostitution ring. The occupation Rosie gave was "golf pro," because once he had shot a ninety.

One day his and Joe's names were called off among four hundred others. They were deloused once again and marched to a rail spur, where their boots were removed before the POWs were loaded into boxcars. Inside were bread and water for three days. The train included flatbeds for Tiger tanks, so Joe was glad to start off at night, when there was less chance of strafing. The train stopped in the morning to dump out latrine cans and take on more water. Next evening the krieges arrived in Mühlberg (directly south of Berlin), got their boots back, and marched off to Stalag IV-B, the best-run camp Rosie ever saw. The barracks were wooden huts furnished with triple-decker slat bunks and two thin blankets. Each new arrival received twelve precious cigarettes from Red Cross parcels, beginning a game like Monopoly where every player starts with the same amount of play money for trade and investment. Cigarettes were the ultimate currency for everything. Rosie was too much of a smoker to accumulate many. Joe, unaddicted, aspired to be a banker.

IV-B was like an international convention of NCOs, for all the inmates were sergeants. Guards boasted that this was the oldest, indeed the original stalag. Most of them were pretty old too, veterans of World War I. The camp was divided into nationalities with the most senior Allied sergeant controlling the POW side of it. Joe never figured out if "senior" meant rank, prison time, or a combination. Anyway, the Commonwealth NCO corps ran things. For four years they'd interacted with the camp authorities, and there was mutual respect. The Americans felt like kids entering junior high, not knowing teachers or schoolmates, grimly accepting new-guy status and making the best of it.

Rosie admired the organizational skill of the Germans, but they had nothing on the British when it came to setting up a prison. There was a formal ceremony at IV-B where the senior NCO of the arriving Americans was received by his Commonwealth counterpart amid salutes and handshakes. The Americans were shown to their huts by British hosts, who the next day held a briefing complete with map and charts. The camp worked this way, said a former announcer for the BBC, to begin a description of the POW organization.

It was headed by "the Man of Confidence," or MOC. A Canadian sergeant major, he had been elected by the inmates. Whatever needed to be brought up with the Germans, he was the man to do it, the man in whom fellow prisoners had to have confidence—a confidence that was to undergo more tests than before. Americans proved much more vocal with their complaints than krieges of other nationalities and created many new problems for the MOC, whose interest in what he called stable "kriege-kraut relations" equaled that of the commandant. To Joe, Man of Confidence sounded like a Mafia title, and there was a considerable resemblance. Things went on aboveboard and underground. There seemed to be understandings between the British and Germans that he couldn't understand. They'd been friends and foes for centuries. At his age it was too much to understand. Joe knew himself, defined himself, as a soldier, intent to fit in but only to find a way to get out.

Eventually the British divulged their sub-rosa infrastructure, which included an escape committee. Any escape plans had to be approved by the committee, or they wouldn't be supported. It seemed a dormant issue. From what Joe could discern, he was the only one thinking about escaping into eastern Germany. As a new guy, Joe was being checked out. Week by week he learned a lot talking with Canadian krieges who'd been in the stalag system for years. His respect for them and the questions Joe asked impressed them that he might be an escape candidate. It was nothing solid or specific, but to Joe it was encouraging to be under consideration to enter a pool of potentials. Slowly the Germans seemed to be taking his measure too, now that he was in a small camp. Stalag authorities knew it took a long period to organize an escape. One of the ways they prevented that was to move krieges from camp to camp so a plan would fall apart when key men were transferred at random. It made sense too to move potential escapees to where they would be the problem of another commandant.

Yet there was one escape plan with which the Germans would cooperate. If a kriege could accumulate sixty cartons of American cigarettes—in Joe's experience that never happened—he'd go to the escape committee with his wealth. They'd provide him a tutor to learn basic German. His cigarettes would be left in trust with the escape committee, which would give him a civilian ID card provided by cooperating Germans in IV-B. From them he would later receive civilian clothes, a picnic basket of sandwiches, and a train ticket to the Swiss border with appropriate papers. There would also be advice on where to cross. The last step would be his assignment to a work detail in Mühlberg where the guards would arrange for him to change clothes near the *Bahnhof*. He would have a railway schedule and, with luck, a train within an hour; with more luck he'd make connections to trains that wouldn't be strafed during a four-hundred-mile ride to the border. Getting into Switzerland would be his problem, but if successful, he was to send a postcard to the Man of Confidence, who would then pay off with cigarettes the German accomplices. They'd have received some of the cartons up front for the train ticket and papers, but the basic deal was no postcard, no payoff.

The "Basel Express" was far beyond Joe's means. With experienced krieges he wasn't yet a gambler superior enough to win many cigarettes, and by just saving them it would take years to squirrel away sixty cartons. It did cross his mind to steal them from certain krieges who collaborated with the Germans without approval from the MOC.

However, Joe had no direct dealings with collaborators because they disgusted him to the point of depression. Collaborators were pretty well identified, so no one had to be with them unless he wanted to. He didn't know the most notorious, Master Sergeant Keating, who accepted favors from guards at the expense of his fellows. A big paratrooper, Keating got extra food from the krauts so that he was the strongest kriege in camp. His instructions were to taunt prisoners to get in the ring with him, that he was *Fallschirmjäger* Max Schmeling, champion of the Reich. Guards had to force most krieges to fight him, but not Jim Bradley, who was willing to take a beating if he could get in one nose-flattening punch. It cost him four rounds of vicious punishment before he did, till Keating snorted gobbets of blood as krieges roared for more. Guards halted the bout while their gladiator recovered, then pounded Bradley into the ground like a pile driver.

Of course Keating and other collaborators rose to the attention of the Man of Confidence, whose charter was to take the broadest view in considering the prisoners' best interests. Assuredly he had the cigarette wealth to take the Basel Express but didn't, a precursor of John McCain, who refused early release from the Hanoi Hilton. Based on the MOC's proven unselfishness, speculation was that Keating had to kick back some of his extra food to the kriege community, split with the MOC, who could use it for rainy days, of which there were many when *Jabos* strafed everything the Germans tried to move on the ground. That included carts hauling cabbage to the stalags, lowest of all transportation priorities.

The Man of Confidence had a staff, some in the open but more not, like the escape committee, concealed from both krieges and krauts. That way he had more real power. Accordingly he wouldn't summon Keating but instead would send someone to his mucker to explain alternatives, which were to kick back or have an accident (for which there would be plenty of volunteers). It would be safe to communicate such an indirect threat because the commandant valued cooperation with the MOC more than any other kriege relationship. On the other hand, it was for the MOC to accommodate the commandant's interests, one of which was to provide amusement for the guards through one-sided boxing matches.

Keating was situationally a borderline case, in contrast with even more blatant collaborators. A few appeared in XII-A after Joe left. They were complete turncoats with swastikas, working openly and informing for the Germans, who housed them outside the stalag and the reach of even MOC enforcers. Krieges would have bid up a cigarette auction to a Basel Express level for the chance to disembowel these turncoats. After the war they were subject to court-martial, but no one Joe knows of brought charges. It wasn't to save the traitors but to save their families from shame.

CHAPTER TWELVE

IV-B

THOUGH THEY LOST AN AVERAGE OF 20 PERCENT OF THEIR BODY weight, krieges nevertheless regained some strength as compared with prestalag captivity, probably because they were now settled into a system resembling that of their own army, and the long haul was the road to survival. "IV-B or not to be," one of them put it. Rosie and his mucker, Jim Bradley, would walk the perimeter to the Canadian, Dutch, and French compounds, divided by double twelve-foot-high barbed wire fences but open to international conversation. The only compound totally off-limits was the Russians', as if Germany denied their very existence. Each side of the perimeter was about a quarter mile. Joe paced it off repeatedly. Though IV-B was no less depressing than XII-A, here in IV-B he detected an air of latent verve among a few krieges drifting with the others, passing on rumors, looking to trade, exchanging survival tips. The most important were about new guards.

The worst news was that a Waffen SS had been detailed as camp guard because he'd been wounded and could pull only light duty.* If

---

* Waffen (armed) SS were all-Nazi units, usually division-size, tactically integrated with the Wehrmacht, which was otherwise made up of conscripts rather than party members. These units were Hitler's elite, getting the best equipment and replacements but also the least rest and suffering the most casualties. They were under the general command of Himmler, who parceled them out to Wehrmacht field armies according to Hitler's wishes. Stalin developed an equivalent of the Waffen SS, his Guards divisions, comprising chiefly fervent Communists. When the two elites clashed there was always a battle royal, as if a personal match between Hitler and Stalin.

he had been wounded on the Eastern Front, he'd take it out on the Russians—though nothing more could be done to them than what could already be seen. It was the Americans' turn in the barrel if a new guard had been wounded on the Western Front. At IV-B there was a postwar plan for the SS: to be loaded on the longest troop train in history and sent east (subject to *jabo* strafing) to wherever Stalin requested. That's what the krieges would petition Eisenhower to do with the SS.

With a settled population, krieges of different nationalities met and talked throughout the day. If Rosie took up with someone who didn't interest Bradley, Bradley'd go off and find someone who did. Then they'd get back together and both have something to discuss. Talk, barter, and gambling were the great time-passers. If a kriege was punished with solitary confinement, the worst of it was not bread and water but the loss of conversation.

Like George Rosie, Tom Gintjee had stalag experiences nearly identical to Joe's, but so far as he can remember they never met. Gintjee of the 82nd Airborne had been captured on D+1, strafed in the convoy to St.-Lô, and starved on Starvation Hill, and he had survived the death train to Limburg. At XII-A he presented a puzzlement for the Germans, for he was Japanese-American, one of very few the War Department had allowed to serve as individual soldiers outside the 442nd ("Go for Broke") Regimental Combat Team, which would win great laurels in Italy and France. Almost all other Nisei were employed as translators in the Pacific. The Germans made some effort to convert Gintjee to the cause of their Axis partners but soon shrugged him off as too scrawny. Besides, the Japanese were allies of convenience, not of the master race, as the Germans made clear to him.

Gintjee was an engraver, cartoonist, and diarist, leaving a vividly written, wryly illustrated journal much read by the postwar kriege community. He dated each entry D+_____, beginning with his capture, ending with D+320. Gintjee was the Pepys of IV-B, as stalag existence forced him to be by its unmitigable hours, days, and weeks of nervous boredom on which he reflected in the introduction to his unpublished memoir, *Don't Fence Me In*—the title taken from a Bing Crosby hit of the times.

Where Joe was restless, Gintjee was resigned to "the slow process of developing into an old kriege, a life expressly pointed to that day when [he'd] be freed and what was so important in prison life became suddenly useless. . . . [His] captivity was an utter waste, . . . a period of nothing, except for being sorely exposed to fellow krieges reduced to what was produced by their background and breeding." He likened himself to a newborn, learning, "There are three elements—air, water, food—and that only air is unrationed by the Germans. He must learn self and mental discipline, constantly exercise them in order to continue . . . things the Army, for all its hard training, never tried to teach. Being a prisoner was not something they ever wanted him to be.

"Maybe a lesson will be gained from this and I hope I'm wrong in doubting it. As long as there are wars, another face will appear where mine is gone. In the place I vacate will be another prisoner. I hope he fares as well as possible."

Like small slices of the IV-B pie were compounds holding French and Italian soldiers, who wore little silver stars on their caps and walked around freely—"not prisoners the way we are"—Gintjee noted, in extreme contrast with the mostly invisible Russians, the undead.*

"It's downright sadistic the way the Nasties [Nazis] slap them around. If we show emotion when the Russians are beaten we're punished too. I think that's why the Russians are beaten where we can see it. But the Nasties also beat them just because they like to do it."

And because the wretched prisoners were the only Russians the Germans could beat any longer. The crushing success of Red Army offensives in the second half of 1944 were little known in IV-B, but from BBC broadcasts, heard on a secret kriege receiver, it was common knowledge that the Reich was being constricted on two sides.

Gintjee recorded: "They fell us out in formation for an SS general. Of course he was hours late and that's how long we stood in the cold. Maybe he thought we didn't know how the war was going. He had this leer while he went up and down our ranks and nodded to himself as if he knew a secret. He looked straight into my eyes. His eyes were like a dead fish and I felt a cold hand on my spine. What was God thinking, what was He drinking, when He created creatures like this?"

---

* Originally Axis partners, the Italians surrendered in September 1943. Except for reliable Fascist units in Liguria, their army was rounded up by the Germans and made nominal POWs.

This SS general announced that lenient treatment of Western prisoners had improved their health to the point where they could now enjoy athletics. Thus boxing gloves were provided, this time for matches between nationalities. There were few volunteers. Anyone who could hold up his gloves for three rounds usually won. Once again the camp champion was Keating, though he was thoroughly booed whenever he fought.

Rosie remembers: "Keating was just a Nazi in an American uniform. He was a big help in their effort to divide us [by nationalities]. Brits and Scots played soccer against each other. That was also supposed to split them but the games become very popular for the bored guards to watch. How about another spectator sport? we asked, and got permission to put up two hoops and soon the krauts liked watching basketball too. They'd never seen it before. There were three American teams. Mine was called the Clipped Wings because four of us were Screaming Eagles. There was also a Canadian and a Polish team. The Poles didn't know anything about the game—couldn't even shoot a layup—but they sure learned how to play basketball like a demolition derby, and that's what the krauts liked to see. The Poles went after a rebound like it was a food parcel."

In the strange world of stalags, the strangest relationship was that between Poles and Germans. The earliest Polish POWs (1939) were long gone, gone to their deaths from the firing squads of Nazi *Einsatzgruppen,* because Hitler regarded Poles as nothing more than Slavs, same as the Russians, an undetectable notch above Jews, and they were all programmed and sped to extermination.* But the twenty thousand or so Polish soldiers who somehow managed to reach Great Britain had there been formed into units under the aegis of the British, and wearing British uniforms, they acquitted themselves magnificently in North Africa,

---

* *Einsatzgruppen* (special action groups) were mass killing teams who began the Holocaust by shooting Eastern European civilians in droves—but not nearly fast enough for Himmler. Besides inefficiency there was a morale problem reported by *Einsatzgruppen* commanders: some of their men were not sleeping well after machine-gunning civilians all day. Thus the search for alternatives began, leading to poison gas in centralized facilities rather than bullets in the field as the final solution.

Italy, and Normandy. To these latter Polish prisoners stalag authorities accorded Geneva Conventions respect, nearly equal to that of other Allied krieges.

Rosie recalls: "To beat the hard-rebounding Poles, I recruited Pat Bogle for our team. He, Bradley, and I became a mucker trio. That worked real well because Bogle and I were smokers and Bradley wasn't and could barter his cigarettes for food. Bogle and my contribution was to star in the basketball league so our team won the championship prize of three packs each. I guess that made us professional athletes!

"Basketball also got me promoted. When I was captured my rank was PFC. Joe says IV-B was all NCOs, but there were EM there too. They were sent out on work details to farms, factories, and road repair. That meant digging up bombs the way we did at Alençon. The only reason you'd want to leave camp on a detail like that is if you were trying to escape. Otherwise you'd come back every night so worn out you couldn't get up next morning. Some guys were literally worked to death that way."

The Man of Confidence at IV-B, Sergeant McKenzie, kept all kriege records. He also played on the Canadian basketball team with a few Americans who had joined the Canadian army before Pearl Harbor and were captured at Dieppe. McKenzie wanted to keep the league active because he was winning a lot of bets on games. That way he became a cigarette millionaire. He could have bought his way to Switzerland if he'd wanted to, but he stayed because of his responsibilities.

"Enlisted men had to pull work details, but NCOs didn't," Rosie says. "That's according to the Geneva Convention. So—to keep me in camp and on the basketball court—McKenzie changed my records to read 'corporal.' I may have been the only American to have been promoted in a stalag!"

With no athletic ability, Gintjee's distraction was recording routine:

Days start at 0630 to the sound of a British bugler, and we fall out for roll call, followed by police call to clean up the area. The Nasties like to watch that. Some kriege will bend over to pick up trash and suddenly he hasn't the strength to straighten up. This really appeals to the German sense of humor. . . .

The air raid siren sounded and I wasn't fast enough getting into my hut. That got me a hobnail boot in the ass which is so bony that it probably hurt him as much as me. . . .

I was wondering what's wrong with me. Everyone else in the hut has the squirts. Finally I got them too. Made me feel normal. . . .

The crafty Brits built a crystal radio receiver tuned to BBC. The Nasties know it but can't find it because it's moved around the camp, sometimes in the wooden leg of an amputee. We get an oral summary of world news from the British compound. This is a real life line for our morale though the way BBC tells the news we have to wonder if the U.S. is in the war.

An inflexible curfew was enforced each night at dark. Anyone found outside the huts, the Germans announced, would be shot. There was also "warning wire" three feet from the barbed wire. Crossing into this zone was a capital offense. Krieges queried the MOC as to whether the shooting policy was for real. He replied that anyone who wanted to could be the test case, and he'd see that he got a postwar posthumous decoration for bravery.

Meanwhile, British uniforms were issued to everyone in rags. Gintjee stayed with his tattered jumpsuit, though the hole in his pants grew larger. What he was losing through his bowel did not concern him as much as petty theft in his hut, mostly from the tiny bread ration some krieges stashed to eat just before they lay down for the night, when without distraction thoughts focused on food and hunger prevented sleep.

"This is a cardinal crime because bread means rest. The less you have of one the more you need the other. The Nasties are curious about how we'll handle the problem. We're pretty sure the thieves are Americans. The Man of Confidence got wind of this and told us there had never been that problem with Commonwealth krieges. I'm sorry to say that he's probably right. He also says if we catch the thief he can make his death look accidental. Muckers are now sleeping in shifts so the hut is never empty."

Gintjee was detailed for "camp fatigue" with thirty-four other EM. Tools were piled on the athletics field: shovels, rakes, and two pairs of pliers. He was able to grab the pliers and spend the day pulling nails from crates while fellow krieges shoveled and raked. They thought one job would be to level the field because of a big mound in the middle that spoiled soccer games (played with a patched-up bladder). That didn't happen. They learned that the mound was a mass grave for Russians and the Nasties didn't want them dug up. There was a second cemetery, begun with a test of the curfew policy. One night Gintjee heard a single shot. It killed a Dutchman who went outside his hut to pee.

Entry 108 began with the exclamation: "A God sent issue of fifty cigarettes per man!" Krieges took this as confirmation of news that the invasion of southern France had linked up with the Normandy invasion, so Nasty was nicer. A British chaplain immediately went around asking for each man to donate ten smokes to the Russian compound, where they were dying by the hundreds from typhus. From what he saw, they looked no more than twelve years old, and all maimed in some way: a twisted hand, a nose on the side of the face, legs that stuck out to the side at 45 degrees, a missing ear, a toothless mouth. The chaplain ended his appeal for cigarettes with the confession that it was difficult to consider these victims of atrocity as fellow humans, and even more so the monsters who had done it. Without complaint, nearly all the Western krieges donated ten precious cigarettes to be tossed over the fence. "For every Keating," Gintjee scribbled, "there are a hundred guys who take pity on those worse off."

After morning roll call Gintjee made it a habit to wander over to the Polish compound and admire one of the most ingenious contraptions in camp, a little stove made from German cocoa cans, with cups and saucers fashioned out of the tin in Red Cross parcels. The Poles auctioned them for souvenirs but had few sales till Gintjee made a deal to monogram them with solder, resulting in a hugely profitable collaboration. Something to *take home* from a stalag revived hope that home was out there, waiting and attainable. How far, how long, only the outcome of the war would reveal, but a souvenir from IV-B suggested inevitability.

Gintjee's mucker was John Marshall, whose souvenirs were buttons from uniforms. His ambition, pursued daily, was to acquire at least one button from every country represented in camp, including Germany and nations most krieges didn't know were even in the war, like Serbia and Albania. Slowly—one thing available in abundance was time—Marshall sewed them on his coat, like the weavers in a myth Gintjee tried to re-call. In time Marshall became a camp celebrity. Krieges and even guards stopped him at all the compounds, studied his button collection, and sometimes donated or proposed trades. The buttons became too much for his coat, bulging his pockets and the bags he carried like some vaga-bond. His trove grew to hundreds of buttons, and the collecting kept him occupied and engaged. But a message came down from the Man of Confidence to Gintjee: was his mucker collecting buttons or losing his marbles?

There were krieges at IV-B who had slipped into that second cate-gory, most famously the RAF sergeant who had to be escorted at all times by another kriege or he'd head for the wire. At different times both Joe and Gintjee had that job, coveted because the Scotsman's tale was fasci-nating. He should have been in a Luftwaffe stalag, so he said, but since he was the very first kriege to be captured in the war, IV-B's commandant wouldn't approve a transfer. McKenzie asked him to negotiate with the IRC to have the original kriege exchanged in Switzerland for some Ger-man psycho prisoner held in England, but again the commandant re-fused. The Scotsman was so confident of his immunity that he claimed the guards wouldn't shoot him even if he went for the wire. That's why he had to be accompanied by volunteers like Joe and Gintjee.

"The benevolent krauts," wrote Gintjee, began distributing a quatro newspaper named *OK Kid!* The editorial policy, of course, was propa-ganda, but the effect was informative and an entertaining distraction. "They couldn't have imagined what a pastime it was for us to read be-tween the lines and guess what might really be going on in the world. We have to do it through articles like 'What the Atlantic Charter Really Means' (a Jewish conspiracy), and 'Formosa Victory' to show how the Japs were winning the war in the Pacific."

A favorite was the Goebbels editorial saying democracy may be okay for some people but Europe has always preferred dictatorships like the Bourbons, Hapsburgs, and—no surprise—Hitler. The only disturb-ing feature of *OK Kid!* was Keatingesque essays by krieges about life in American slums. Readers were divided by these accounts. "Why not?" one of Joe's muckers shrugged, "if it gets you a parcel. We all know it's bullshit." McKenzie felt otherwise, and anyone in IV-B who contributed material felt his wrath. Gintjee recounted:

The British love plays, especially comedies and musicals. No tragedies, thanks, there's enough of that here. The "theater" charged a two-cigarette admission till the Americans arrived. Most of us had never seen a play except maybe in a high school auditorium, so it took the boredom of a stalag to raise a little interest. To get us more involved the Man of Confidence ordered that the first play be free.

I'll never forget it. The cast was in civilian clothes though they were *streng verboten* in camp as a possible aid to escape. It was a variety show with an MC who came out, casually lit a cigarette then dropped it to go into his spiel. "My God," he cried, "this is only a play!" and scrambled to retrieve the butt. But the audience was ahead of him and grabbed it. That was the biggest laugh I had in prison.

The Americans' greatest influence in IV-B was gambling, which for krieges of other nationalities there had been scant interest previously. With energetic ingenuity and imagination, crap tables and roulette wheels were improvised. Gintjee felt gambling was an appeal to the spirit that tomorrow we may die or next month be liberated, so what the hell, it's only cigarettes—let's get some excitement in our lives, win or lose in an egalitarian contest. That became a campwide attitude expressed in raffles, numbers rackets, and gruesome betting on how many American bombers would be shot down the next day.

Gintjee also made observations as an economist. When there was a bonus issue of cigarettes from the IRC it did not make everyone happy. Creditors with tobacco fortunes saw their net worth reduced when debtors paid off in devalued smokes. The British especially grumbled about such volatility and how widespread gambling upset the equilibrium that had sustained them before the Americans arrived. What if McKenzie became a debtor to Keating? It was a question hard to answer.

Marshall invited a French Legionnaire to our hut to hustle him for a button. This Algerian was a recruiter for the Legion, so before he donated his button we had to hear his pitch. Travel, freedom, adventure and amour would all be ours. He almost had me convinced to join up after the war (they didn't have any

Japanese!), but then I asked him about the pay. Two cents per day. I said I hoped he enjoyed riding camels but I'll just smoke 'em, thanks just the same. . . .

Looks like the Allies are on the Siegfried Line. The Brits are giving odds that Montgomery will be here in a month. They're so confident that they'll accept IOU's. I bet twelve cigarettes at three to one, and will happily lose. . . .

Now and then the Brits pull practical jokes on the krauts and get away with it. There's this half-wit guard walking the perimeter and he's really bucking for corporal. After a rain he spots a bit of commo wire sticking out of the ground. He pulls on it and up comes some more wire. He yells to the sergeant of the guard—he found it!—the top priority contraband in Stalag IV-B—the Brits' secret radio antenna. Guards gather around and pull up wire that leads all over the camp, and sure enough it ends at the British compound. They yank up the last stretch of wire. It's threaded through a pile of rusty cans at the bottom of a latrine! . . .

Much colder weather at roll call this morning. Men in the hut next door did not fall out. It has been quarantined for diphtheria. No other cases yet. . . .

Klug is the top poker player in camp. He's so good Marshall and I asked him to invest for us. Sure, he said, for a percentage of the winnings but we take the losses. We won a thousand postwar dollars but then Klug hit a bad streak and we're down $1,500. Creditors are concerned about our health and want us to move away from the diphtheria hut. It's nice to know that people care. . . .

A new sergeant of the guard, an asshole wounded in France. Big shakedown and inspection of the hut found some cartoons I'd been drawing of the krauts. That got me dragged into the commandant's office, an *oberst*. He only "reprimanded" me, and my sentence was three days in solitary with bread and water. Not much change in my diet, colonel!

Gintjee and his mucker of button fame were probably known to Joe but lost in his slow-healing head, as are most memories from XII-A and IV-B except for his twenty-first birthday, celebrated with a sugared lump of dough baked on the hut stove, a cigarette for a candle. The Germans had a present for him too, a few weeks later, when "Beyrle" was read out at roll call for transport to another stalag. Hundreds of Americans were joining him (but neither Rosie nor Gintjee), many unhappy to leave the tolerable routine of IV-B, but not Joe, who felt bridled by a chain of command that seemed reluctant to bring a rash Yank into their escape plans, if there were any.* They reminded him of the pilot of his Lysander, war-weary, war-wise, and willing to wait for war's end. Joe had been a .400 hitter in high school, but oh for two against the Germans. He wanted another at bat, and not with a cricket paddle.

Joe hadn't found a really kindred kriege (his IV-B muckers had been shuffled several times), and it was accepted practice not to ask personal questions because they could ignite short tempers and end in fights, which burned up scarce energy and satisfied only the authorities, who never ceased trying to turn krieges against one another. Nonetheless IV-B had been an education for Joe, thanks mostly to what he'd learned from two Rangers who'd been captured at Dieppe in the summer of 1942. They were the senior American krieges but didn't transfer with the others because the Germans had permanently classified them as Canadian. Joe can't remember their names. Names didn't matter much; men went by monikers like King Corporal and Hockey Shorts. Joe's was Spud because he was always scrounging potato peels.

The two crease-faced, stubbly Rangers did a lot to clear his head and bring it to the most practical level, the only one that could sustain any other level. Their patient instruction reminded him of Saint Joseph's basketball coach, who first showed him which foot to pivot on, what pass to look for, which teammate was in the best position. Fundamentals, essentials:

Save some food from every meal, no matter how much is available from the IRC or won by gambling. Tomorrow there could be none.
Don't expect to learn about a successful escape. The krauts

---

* As best as research can determine, in 1944 there were three one-man escapes from IV-B. At least two were successful, a tribute to British patience and their meticulous planning.

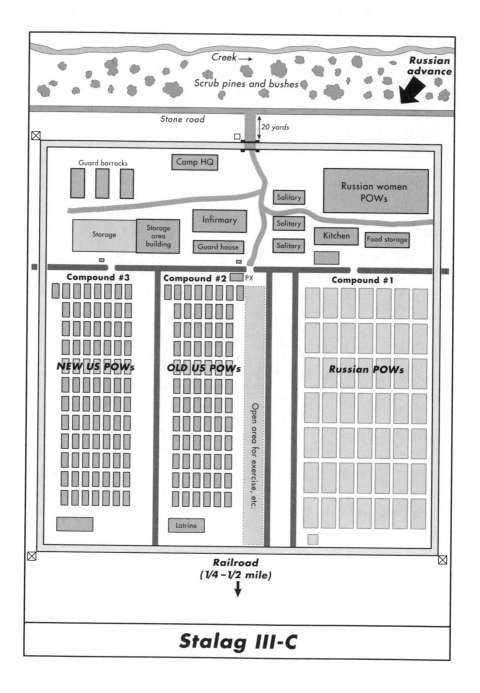

Creek →

Russian advance

Scrub pines and bushes

Stone road

20 yards

Guard barracks

Camp HQ

Russian women POWs

Solitary

Storage

Storage area building

Infirmary

Solitary

Guard house

Kitchen

Food storage

Solitary

Compound #3

Compound #2

PX

Compound #1

NEW US POWs

OLD US POWs

Open area for exercise, etc.

Russian POWs

Latrine

Railroad
(1/4 – 1/2 mile)
↓

Stalag III-C

won't want to admit it and the escape committee doesn't want
to be flooded with proposals.

No matter how tired you are, exercise. The energy you put out
actually adds to overall strength even when it tires you out.
Like stashed food, you'll need that deep strength when you get
sick, as everyone does sooner or later. Exercise makes it later.

If your legs swell, it means you may be getting beriberi, so
trade for anything that has protein.

The MOC has a net of informers, so be careful about what you
say and to whom. It could be worse to be on the wrong side of
the MOC than to piss off the krauts, sort of like the choice
between being fingered by the police or the Mafia. The
enforcers can get at you in ways the cops can't.

At XII-A and IV-B Joe was never made by the MOC mafia but now,
from what the two Rangers had taught him, he felt ready to step up in
an American camp. Early in the afternoon his name was called again and
he was sent to a table where kriege dog tags were checked against POW
records that had begun at XII-A. For the first time Joe saw his mug shot,
now on the cover of this book.

Ditty bags were inspected for contraband, then there was a personal
pat-down, which did not uncover Joe's shiv (won in craps), a sharpened
fragment from a truck shock, an all-purpose tool used mostly for opening Red Cross cans. He had tucked the shiv into a jump boot that stunk
so much the Germans wouldn't examine it. The transfer began with a
two-mile march to boxcars at a siding. The krieges groaned to see them,
"forty-or-eights" again, likely to invite air attack.

But Allied fighters had not been seen much lately because they were
concentrating above the Netherlands, as Joe would soon learn. A guard
noticed his jump boots and asked which Airborne division he'd been
in. When he answered the 101st, the guard said they had jumped again.
Joe's buddies were back in the war for the first time since Normandy,
on a date famous in Screaming Eagle history—September 17, 1944—the
same day as his funeral mass in Muskegon and also the day in 1943
when he landed in England. September 17 is the only day of the year
when Joe reads his horoscope.

CHAPTER THIRTEEN

MARKET-GARDEN

BY SEPTEMBER 17, 1944, ED ALBERS FELT FULLY INTEGRATED into Joe's old company, what was left of I Company after Normandy. Duber was still around, and though his crossbow was never fired in France, he continued to practice. One day he took aim at a royal oak that shaded the bus stop in Ramsbury. The bolt shattered bark, shaking the tree as well as the folks waiting for a bus. This time Duber was identified, for there were no other crossbowmen of any nationality in the county. His weapon was confiscated, the only instance Albers can remember of Duber being punished for anything. A prewar army man, thirty-eight years old when he became Airborne, Duber had the guile to disappear for a whole day undetected. Albers wondered how he had done in Normandy. The originals said fine: Duber dodged and defied the Germans as easily as he had his officers.

Third Battalion officers now included the recently promoted CO, Major Shettle, who had saved the day on D+1 by seizing and holding the Douve bridges with fewer than a hundred men. Commanding I Company was Captain Fred Anderson, a platoon leader in Normandy. His family, like Wolverton's, resided in Charlotte, North Carolina. That state was overrepresented in the Airborne, probably because it had been born there and the first wave of volunteeers were local. The Anderson and Wolverton families didn't know each other, but at war's end Anderson paid a call of respect to Wolverton's widow, a visit that led to their marriage.

Albers's platoon sergeant was the redoubtable Alex Engelbrecht from Syracuse, New York. Like the Beyrle family, his had spoken German at home, and he reveled in pouring profanities on SS POWs in their vernacular. Albers's squad leader was Ted Dziepak, a Polish-American from Perth Amboy, New Jersey. Not that there was ever much question, but Dziepak didn't have to be told what he was fighting for.

Fighting spirit was quiescent among the Screaming Eagles during the latter days of summer. The pre–D Day "can't wait to drop on the Wehrmacht" attitude had been replaced by memories from the invasion. New men like Albers soon comprehended from the veterans that Airborne recruiting posters delivered one message, combat quite another. Consequently, the troopers would get ready but were not raring to jump back into the fight. This was a temperament that somewhat discomfited hard-charging commanders like Sink, but they understood and in various degrees felt it themselves.

So the 101st cheered on Patton's Third Army as it drove across France, overrunning one planned Airborne objective after another. Sixteen division-size drops were planned, several to reach the stage where jumpers went into their marshaling area only hours from enplaning, but each time Patton beat them to the drop zones. The Screaming Eagles were like pinch hitters watching the regular lineup run up the score: Go, team! We're ready if needed but won't be disappointed if you keep circling the bases.

While the troopers waited to return to action, decorations for feats in Normandy came down. Three Blues received the Distinguished Service Cross, second only to the Medal of Honor for extraordinary heroism: Captain Shettle, Donald Zahn and George Montilio. The latter two crossed the Douve under fire and held off a company-size counterattack. There was a glitch in Zahn's paperwork: his medal had not yet been fully processed before the ceremony at which General Omar Bradley presented the decorations. As soon as Montilio received his DSC he took it off, refusing to wear it till Zahn got one, which he consequently did, along with a battlefield commission. Montilio was promoted to sergeant, but in late April 1945 he became one of the last Screaming Eagles to be killed in action.

The third Currahee to win the DSC was Private Lee Rogers, a tree-topper from Aberdeen, Washington, who would become famous as "Ike's corporal." With the 506th formed up on Wiltshire County's most impressive parade ground, Rogers's feat was read out by Sink's adjutant. Even in reserved official language the citation was awesome: how the private, after his leaders were killed, had rallied a few men, leading them to destroy a machine-gun nest and a score of *Fallschirmjägers*.

Eisenhower listened with eyes that began to glisten, attached the medal on Rogers's jacket, then shook his hand more slowly than he had those of the other heroes. As Rogers returned to ranks, Ike turned to General Taylor and asked softly why such an intrepid leader was no more than a buck private. Would Taylor permit the supreme Allied commander to promote Rogers and do it on the spot? Taylor's answer was of course affirmative, so Rogers marched away from the parade ground with the DSC and two more stripes than he had worn.

Sink, never one to shun publicity for his Currahees, pinned new chevrons on Rogers in front of the press. Soon pictures appeared in *Yank* and *Stars & Stripes* as well as stateside newspapers, especially in the Pacific Northwest. Rogers's fame, alas, then plummeted to infamy. A superb performer in combat, he was equally inept in garrison and soon took leave of it without authorization to celebrate his uniquely bestowed rank. He did so in London pubs, where praise and pints went to his head. Leg MPs returned him to regimental control—disheveled, disreputable, and reeking of Guinness.

Sink was away when Rogers was hauled in. Lieutenant Colonel Charles Chase, the deputy commander, took one sniff and look at yesterday's hero, then demoted Rogers to buck private as summarily as Ike had promoted him. When Chase briefed the CO on this outcome, Sink pushed back his hat, lit a cigarette, and exhaled with exasperation.

"Charley, you can't bust Ike's own corporal!"

To which Chase replied with dignity, "Sir, I wasn't aware that General Eisenhower intended for the rank to be hereditary."

Taylor related Rogers's volatile rise and fall to Ike, who reddened with laughter, promising to never again intervene in promotions. Rogers, perhaps sobered by his vicissitudes, jumped back into the fight to rise from buck private to buck sergeant, a rank he earned and kept in what Screaming Eagles remembered as Holland.

THE NAME GIVEN TO the second of the 101st's three great rendezvous with destiny was a misnomer. Holland is not the province of the Netherlands the Screaming Eagles dropped on as part of history's biggest airborne operation—that province is actually North Brabant. Holland is up around Amsterdam and Rotterdam, north of the Rhine and near its mouth.* The objective of benignly named Operation Market-Garden was to establish a bridgehead on the north bank, not at its estuary but at the industrial city of Arnhem, where there was a bridge, one that would become known as "too far."

Blue chips were again on the table, almost as much so as on D Day. A mighty Airborne formation had been assembled, the largest of all time, named the First Allied Airborne Army and consisting of the U.S. 101st, 82nd, and 17th Airborne Divisions, the British 1st ("Red Devils") and 6th Airborne Divisions, plus an air-transported infantry division, along with the Polish Parachute Brigade. Despite a huge airlift capability, not all those units could be dropped on the enemy at one time; there simply were not enough transports in the world.

Ironically and increasingly, Eisenhower was fast running out of manpower on the ground while at the same time holding this vastly potent force of elite warriors ready to alight into the fight. There had been nowhere for them to attack while Patton galloped across France, but then his and all five Allied armies dashed like impotent waves against the breakwater of the Siegfried Line, the most formidable fortification in the world. It was a stalemate, and perhaps even trench warfare loomed unless Eisenhower came up with a good idea for how to commit the First Allied Airborne Army, ideally to vertically envelop the Siegfried Line.

The man whose idea prevailed was Field Marshal Bernard Montgomery of Alamein. He did so over the customary fury of his inveterate rival, General George Patton, for if Monty got the First Allied Airborne Army, with it would go resources craved elsewhere, everywhere along the Western Front. Nevertheless, Ike turned to Montgomery, asking for a plan that featured imagination and daring, even though they were not characteristic of the field marshal's generalship.

---

* The misnomer can only be attributed to Americans' typically poor knowledge of foreign geography. To them, the Netherlands meant Holland with wooden shoes and windmills. The error was never corrected, not even on a stone memorial at Arlington Cemetery or the 101st's monument at Fort Campbell, Kentucky. This is a source of polite annoyance for the Dutch where the 101st jumped, one of whom told the author, "If we had liberated New Jersey during World War II, what would you think if we had called it New Hampshire?"

An imaginatively daring plan was indeed produced. An "airborne carpet" was the Market half of it, landings to secure vital portions of the highway running from Monty's front lines on the Belgian border to Arnhem. The Garden half called for a powerful British armor corps to thrust up the corridor created by the Airborne and pile into the Arnhem bridgehead over the Rhine, flank the Siegfried Line, and open Germany's guts. The air-land jab was to strike with such surprise that Rundstedt would not have time to shift reinforcements into the Netherlands, apparently the least threatened sector of the Western Front.

Sounded good. Intelligence estimates were that the Germans had no more than a hundred tanks in all the Netherlands. Then by unhappy happenstance the 9th and 10th SS Panzer Divisions, Rundstedt's best, began regrouping and refitting around Arnhem after desperate fighting in France. Their addition to the equation was detected by Ike's code breakers and the ominous information passed along to Montgomery with a strong inference that changes to Market-Garden plans were called for, changes that represented only a theoretical possibility of compromising "Ultra" intercepts, the basis for the Allied ability to read the Wehrmacht's radio messages coded by Enigma machines. Perhaps that remote possibility—even after the war Montgomery never revealed his reasons—is why he kept such utterly vital information to himself, though nothing is more important to Airborne planners than the presence of enemy tanks. Tanks are to paratroopers as dogs are to cats, as cats are to mice.

AFTER SO MANY CANCELLATIONS and postponements I Company finally had a firm objective to study in detail. Originals were pleased by aerial photos showing expansive, perfectly flat drop zones, heartened that the drop would be in daylight. If only the fornicating pilots would fly straight and turn on the green light at jump speed, Blues would do the rest. This was the big-time test for rookies like Albers who now made up nearly half of the regiment. They looked to the originals but in order to show them. Albers was tired of hearing about Toccoa, what *real* Airborne training had been like. The purpose of training is performance. Let's go out and we'll show you how we perform.

The Currahee yearbook put the mission this way, probably paraphrasing Sink, who recalled that this was September and football season had begun back in the States:

Take cities and bridges and you have the road. Fold the hostiles (Sink's terms for the Germans) back from that road—the Eindhoven-Arnhem road—and there's a touchdown pass thrown across the Rhine. You're running interference for the British ball carrier. It's the big game, the biggest of the season. The Airborne Associates (a derisive term for the 82nd, whose shoulder patch is AA) are to our north and so are the British 1st Airborne and the Polish Parachute Brigade. The whole world is in the grandstands. Go to it, throw your blocks, get that ball carrier into the end zone.

With such an exhortation Currahees put on their game faces, but there was no camouflage this time, no Mohawks, no war dance. Just get on with the job—it may be the last one. Such was the thinking in the 101st, but there was something providentially added for the Blues as they waited for transportation to the marshaling area. A truck rolled up, and two troopers alighted. They were Jim Sheeran and Bernie Rainwater of I Company, captured in Normandy, paraded by the Nazis in Paris, but successful escapees who pried open the grille of their forty-or-eight and subsequently reached Patton's forces. Now here they were, hours before the 101st's takeoff for Market.

There was no hesitation for Sheeran. Just give him a weapon; he was ready to jump back into the fight—even though he and Rainwater were entitled to thirty days' leave in the States before their status was resolved. Through a curious interpretation of the Geneva Conventions, that status presented a poison pill for any escaped POW who went on to fight against former captors. If recaptured by the Germans, both could be legally executed as spies because they presumably had seen German installations and deployments the way a spy would. So U.S. Army policy was that if a POW escaped from the Germans, in the unlikely event he wanted to go back to war, it would have to be against the Japanese!

Raised not far from Toccoa, Rainwater was a Currahee through and through, more so than any other man in the regiment by reason of his Cherokee blood. His escape with Sheeran had been stupefying. Sheeran spoke French and was costumed by the FFI as a Frenchman. Rainwater had to impersonate an Algerian, a mute retarded Algerian, in Sheeran's charge. By hair-raising, hairbreadth evasions they came out of France together, and together they rejoined the Blues.

In Normandy they had been in Anderson's platoon. Now I Company's commander, Anderson, exhorted, C'mon, Bernie, you're not gonna get captured again. I guarantee it, guarantee it, Goddammit. Listen, I'll make you the company runner (courier between company HQ and the platoon leaders). Before you could be captured they'd have to get me first. You think that's gonna happen? Hell no, no way—not in Item Company. So you're with us, okay?

Not quite. As further persuasion the two celebrities were taken to battalion HQ, where Sheeran was promoted to buck sergeant and made a squad leader on the spot. Now, how 'bout you, Bernie? Major Shettle put the question, an amazing question to which no sane civilian would have replied affirmatively. Rainwater's buddies like Engelbrecht and Dziepak offered an answer: come with us. He did. He was a Currahee. Albers was in awe, not so much at the time but months later after reflecting on what was to come on Dutch and Belgian battlefields. Sheeran and Rainwater didn't have to be burned in those crucibles—as heroes already they could have gone home, probably for the rest of the war—but an irresistible magnetism, overcoming the longing for family in America, drew them back to their army family. It was a tribute to both families.

At midmorning on the beautifully sunny Sunday of September 17, the 101st, less sleep-deprived than before D Night, took off for its part in Operation Market-Garden. So vast was this aerial armada that while the first troopers spilled out over the Netherlands the last had not departed from England. Captain Anderson, leading a stick that included Albers and Sheeran, was not about to tolerate a repetition of Normandy's unimaginable dispersion. Drawing his .45, he entered the C-47's cockpit, piloted by a gum-chewing Long Islander who looked fresh out of high school. If you miss the DZ, Anderson advised, twirling his pistol, someone on this plane is going to come back and find you.

The pilot was nonplussed. "Captain," he said, hardly glancing at the weapon, "we're going to put your whole company on a DZ the size of a football field."

"Make it within the twenty-yard lines."

This rendezvous with destiny was in full daylight. Albers gazed down on Montgomery's assembling formations in Belgium, poised and timed to crash north on Hell's Highway, pennants snapping in the wind, as armor troops waved to parachute and glider legions passing low overhead. At no other time in the war was there such a coordinated armor-airborne assault. The Germans executed plans to delay the British through a series of canals and torpid rivers, barriers to the Rhine some sixty miles north. What the Wehrmacht was not ready for was a vertical invasion to span those barriers by capturing existing bridges intact, and that is what made the saga of Market-Garden a story of bridges held and lost, captured and recaptured.

Anderson was impatient to inform the krauts that Screaming Eagle wrath was upon them again. He staggered to the howling door of the C-47, shook his fist, and screamed imprecations on the enemy below— whose response was flak bursts that drove him back to his bucket seat. Flak was ignored by the pilots and no evasive action was taken as the transports flew straight, true, and in formation.

Fulfilling the promise of Anderson's pilot, the brunt of the 506th dropped on a rectangular DZ about a half mile long by a quarter mile wide. Jump altitude was 600 feet, exit speed a mild 150 knots. The sky blossomed with multicolored parachutes, white for troopers, a whole spectrum designating loads like a howitzer or medical supplies. Dribbling German tracers added more color. Albers saw jumpers tuck their knees to present less of a target. A good idea—why hadn't someone told him that in England? Eyes wide open before his chute opened, he saw a chunk of metal flapping from the tail of his C-47, the only sign of damage. There had been fear that the Luftwaffe would take to the sky, but not a single German fighter plane contested the 101st's jump. With his leg bag full of machine-gun ammo and his gas-mask case full of candy, Albers landed surely and popped open the harness with a quick-release device (developed from a lesson learned in Normandy where jumpers used knives to cut open their harnesses—and in the dark and haste sometimes cut off their thumbs).

The DZ swarmed with troopers assembling like chicks in a rookery, distinguishing their mother's call within a cacophony. Originals glanced at one another and nodded: hey, this plan is working, hell, better than any training exercise. That too was General Taylor's impression, for the drop of 6,800 Screaming Eagles produced only 2 percent casualties and an amazingly low 5 percent loss of equipment (better than jumps in England). His regiments set off for their objectives with confidence from evidence that this landing was the antithesis of Normandy.

Not that there was no mixture of units. Ed Manley of the 502nd found himself on the 506th's drop zone in a unique predicament. His legs were knee-deep in soft earth, while his canopy hovered overhead like an umbrella. Because of rare air currents it would not deflate, so there he stood suspended as the DZ emptied. Finally an artillery concussion knocked over his chute and he collapsed just as Taylor came striding by, map cases in hand.

"Don't you have a job today, trooper?" he asked Manley, still sprawled on the ground.

"General, the first sergeant said if I made it down okay, I could take the rest of the day off."

Taylor and his staff were staggering with laughter as they caught up with Sink, whose first task was to speed about a mile south, through the neatly tended Zonsche Forest, to the little town of Zon, where a bridge spans the Wilhelmina Canal, a placid, banked waterway so narrow that barges passing in opposite directions almost scrape each other. This was the essential first crossing for British armor to meet the Market-Garden schedule. Sink was on the edge of the DZ to start the timetable tolling. As soon as each squad assembled he shoved it south. "Minutes count, men!" he shouted after them. "Minutes count!" For originals like Engelbrecht and Dziepak, memories went back to the Atlanta–Fort Benning forced march and its purpose of getting to an objective first with the most.

They reached it while the Germans were still pulling up their pants. Sink's Second and Third Battalions surged through and around Zon, which was defended by an 88 emplacement located for antiaircraft purposes. Another 88, its tube lowered for ground action, zeroed in on First Battalion. Starting the battle was the dry cough of the high-velocity flat-trajectory 88, a familiar sound for Normandy vets. The war was on again after a two-month leave, and this time it was a lot better: they were all together following the drop, with the Dutch underground surfacing like dragon's teeth. A man with an orange armband appeared beside Shettle and offered to guide his attack around the most threatening German position. Away they went on the double. At a corner the Dutchman halted to advise that the target was just beyond the next bend. Fine, said Shettle; lead on. For closer guidance there were the Dutch at high windows, pointing with their hands and holding up fingers to indicate the number of Germans ahead. The Blues felt like a posse about to close in on outlaws.

Albers remembers the Dutch as bird dogs on a duck hunt. After they got the troopers in position, all there was to do was look down the sights and cut loose. It wasn't a duck shoot—the ducks shot back—but that was okay; let 'em. For Albers it was dangerous fun, shooting it out against *Deutschen* the Dutch hated, and doing what he had been trained to do. That was satisfying, gratifying, realizing that those in charge knew some practical applications of training. For the originals it was all business, but they understood how Albers was feeling.

Aided immeasurably by the Dutch, within fifteen minutes the Currahees destroyed both 88s, killed thirteen Germans, captured forty-one, and rushed the Zon bridge—only to have it blow up in their faces. No army planned better than the Wehrmacht; the bridge had been prewired in the event of a British surge from Belgium just fifteen miles away.

That surge was coming, the Garden armor scheduled to meet the Market airborne near Eindhoven, the major city in the southern part of the Netherlands. The 101st had a plan to accomplish that even if the Zon bridge was blown. An engineer company that had jumped with the Currahees went to work and within an hour fashioned a footbridge that could bear a few men at a time. Taylor radioed the British to put a folding bridge among the first vehicles in their column. German planning could be thwarted by farsighted counterplans. And improvisations. "General Taylor," Sink proposed, his helmet askew, "we're going to sweep east and west on the canal and look for barges." Two big barges side by side would create excellent pontoons for a formidable bridge. But no barges were found floating. Allied air strikes had sunk them all.

During the night of September 17, 101st engineers labored as Sink dribbled all his Currahees over the footbridge. Third Battalion was the last across, sprawling in irrigation ditches as they watched a fireglow of shells in dark skies. The dawn, they were warned, would start a regimental attack on Eindhoven. Remembering Carentan, originals were glum about the next day's prospects. Eindhoven was a city, a big city (population 100,000), its every building a potential fortress for defenders. World War II's costliest battles were fought within cities. Albers was advised to get some extra grenades, the weapon of choice in urban fighting.

But he and innumerable Screaming Eagles were saved from that because of German planning, which rightly assumed that the Dutch would rise up in their cities and draw major elements of the Wehrmacht into an urban quagmire (as occurred in the Warsaw uprising). General Student, the major commander opposing the 101st, therefore kept his scant forces out of Eindhoven, kept them hovering to cut Hell's Highway in the countryside. Sink's orders for September 18 were don't spend any time killing hostiles, just get through Eindhoven and link up with the Brits. That's our job; don't forget it for a second.

What Albers remembers is how much the Dutch wanted to get rid of the Germans.* The Eindhoveners came out of houses and fell on their knees in prayer and thanks. He was darting across a street when a barrage of mortars bracketed his squad. Suddenly men with orange armbands tackled him and covered him with their bodies. When the shelling stopped they let him up. He asked what the hell they were doing. In broken English one of them said Albers was a soldier fighting the Germans. Protecting him was the best way to help get rid of them.

Dutch collaborators and Nazi sympathizers were also brought to reckoning, run out of town with their heads crudely and cruelly shaved, run north where their marks of shame would be further reviled by liberated countrymen. Eindhoven was the first Dutch city to be freed, and jubilation became a serious problem for Sink as he tried to set up defenses and send out patrols to contact the British. Liberation joy was expressed in the downing of limitless quantities of schnapps and excellent beer as well as in showers of apples—at first ducked by troopers because they looked like hand grenades. Where German resistance had hardly slowed Sink's troops, Dutch gratitude and hospitality did.

The Germans' surprise had been utter. Whatever its local setbacks,

---

* The author attended the fiftieth-anniversary celebrations of "Remember September," marking the liberation of the southern Netherlands. In 1994 commerce with neighboring Germany was brisk and cordial, but for the week of September 17 not a single German license plate could be seen on Hell's Highway.

Market-Garden was on track though twenty-four hours behind schedule because of coordination glitches between American and British forces such as planned radio frequencies that did not mesh. The sound of tanks, usually dreaded by paratroopers, was that of British armor rumbling north incessantly. Albers heard it during his shift on an outpost, and when he returned for another shift after two hours' sleep the sound had not changed. It carried up through Zon, on to St. Oedenrode, then Veghel, to pass into 82nd territory. The 101st's first mission, to open the corridor, had been accomplished. Now came the second: to protect it from counterattacks as the Germans shook off their surprise. A brigade of panzer grenadiers, recently arrived from Poland, nearly overran the 101st's division CP. Currahees from Eindhoven were called north to help beat them back.

I Company was similarly detached to meet a threat from the German border less than thirty miles away. "The krauts have set up a roadblock," Captain Anderson told his platoon leaders. "We're going to eliminate it." It was difficult to assemble I Company for this mission, as so many were in the embrace of Eindhoven's ardent gratitude. Albers had never seen the originals so pissed, especially Duber, who had met a woman he called "the countess," and was about to be married by a judge from the underground. All of I Company was pissed. No firefights or even fire could be heard, but loading on full packs and extra ammo, they obeyed orders to march out of the festive city into the night. Then behind them Eindhoven lit up like flashbulbs. The Luftwaffe had slipped through, to kill thousands of civilians in a raid of terror and retaliation for Dutch joy. Duber's countess was among the missing.

GENERAL TAYLOR COMPARED the 101st's mission to the U.S. cavalry defending a railroad in Indian country. Except that the division had no horses. Between villages and bridges the Screaming Eagles rushed in "brown leather personnel carriers," clashing with parties of Indians who probed gaps in a fifty-mile periphery, defended by about a hundred troopers per mile. At first the Currahees encountered mostly rear-echelon Germans with little combat ability. This was one of the assumptions of the Market plan—that against ferocious paratroopers, logistical personnel of the Wehrmacht would not last long. September 17–19 was pretty much a rout for Currahees. The British ball carrier looked to be heading directly for the end zone.

A battalion of Red Devils had seized the key Arnhem bridge but were encircled in house-to-house, hand-to-hand combat. They would be succored only if British armor could drive on to the bridgehead, the final and vital objective of Market-Garden. In tactical command to prevent his linkup was Army Group B commanded by Field Marshal Walther Model, as ardent a Lutheran as he was a Nazi, called "Der Führer's fireman" for his genius in improvisation while plugging huge holes in the Eastern Front during 1942–1943. He was the man for the job in the Netherlands if the job could be done. To help him, Rundstedt pushed every resource on the Western Front to Army Group B. The campaign then boiled down to which side brought in the most reinforcements first.

The advantage seemed to be with the Allies, who when not grounded by days of extraordinarily bad weather could deliver soldiers and supplies by parachute and glider. The Luftwaffe tried to intervene but was held off by swarms of fighter planes. Defending transports, however, diverted *Jabos* from overwhelming attacks against ground targets of the kind they had experienced in Normandy. This allowed Model to maneuver forces to cut the corridor. He moved them by foot, bicycle, horse, rail, boat, truck—anything that could move—wherever he could, preventing British armor from reaching Arnhem before he wiped out the Red Devils. Any German in uniform or who could fit in one was Model's soldier: Luftwaffe ground crews, naval cadets, NCO academy students; even customs agents, Dutch Nazis, and convalescents closed in on the corridor like filings to a bar magnet. They were winnowed by gales of ground fire but sufficiently occupied the 101st and 82nd so that regular Wehrmacht units could concentrate and find openings into Hell's Highway.

Model's deputy, Kurt Student, a *Fallschirmjäger* general, understood the 101st's difficulties. Obviously American artillery that had dominated battlefields in Normandy could not be centralized enough to provide coverage all around the division's perimeter in the Netherlands. He had an additional advantage: a glider had been shot down near his headquarters. Smoldering in the wreckage was a set of plans for how the

101st was to accomplish its mission, so Student had as clear a picture of Market-Garden as Taylor did.

Student's first panzer raid nearly killed Taylor in his CP at Zon. Tiger tanks rolled south, and orange bunting began to disappear in Eindhoven. By September 20, intelligence from the Dutch underground was not so helpful now that the Germans were in constant motion. Even with best guesses about Student's likely objectives, Taylor could not position a reserve force where it could respond to any threatened area. And his reserve was reduced to the division musical band because all four of his regiments were fully engaged and scattered. Never would the Screaming Eagles have to march so far to fight so much.

Urged on by Model, Student struck at Veghel, a small town just north of a significant canal. If the bridge was recaptured or destroyed, the Garden column would halt. Recognizing a major threat, Taylor rushed the entire 506th twenty-two miles north to Uden; Sink and Second Battalion reached Uden, but before the rest of the regiment arrived, panzers attacked from the east and *Fallschirmjägers* from the west, squarely cutting the corridor. They were dislodged after a brawl of twenty-four hours. Prisoners were taken on both sides. Colonel Sink and Colonel von der Heydte, commanding the 6th Parachute Regiment, wryly realized that they were up against each other as they had been in Normandy, so hereafter there would be a heavyweight fight. The ground was flat, silhouettes high, trees and barns prized for observation. Both regiments were good at this sort of whirligig warfare, circling in and around each other while British armor on the corridor awaited the outcome.

As the bushwhacking swirled, after five hours of marching to Veghel, Albers's platoon was in a low crawl through waterlogged meadows, their objective a farmhouse with an overlook of Hell's Highway. He tried the door. It was locked, with no sound from inside except pigs squalling, a good sign to Dziepak: either no one was home, or the Dutch were still there because krauts would have turned those pigs into bratwurst. Kick in the door, ordered Lieutenant Green, a nonoriginal.* Dziepak was

---

* Survivors of the farmhouse fight cannot remember the lieutenant's name, a common lapse after searing combat and the passage of years. What Albers remembers is that "Green" had been a track star at the University of Southern California, one who would never run again.

right, his squad doubly happy because great blocks of aging cheese hung in the kitchen.

There was little time for gorging. From the second floor Green could see burning skeletons of British vehicles. Growling from the west came six German half-tracks. Two disgorged troops then turned south on the road, weaving between wrecks. Green reported this on the radio, while a platoon of *Fallschirmjägers* warily advanced to check out the farmhouse. Green had bad news: no artillery was available; it's just us and them. Dziepak smiled as he set up a machine gun and a surprise for the approaching Germans. He identified the leader, pointed him out to the best marksman in the squad, a rookie who started to lean his rifle on the windowsill before Dziepak jerked him back.

Germans noticed the movement and went to ground as Dziepak's machine gun followed them with fire. Shell casings spurted and rattled around the upstairs room, soon faintly gray with gunsmoke. Outnumbered by the attackers, his squad had protection and a height advantage in the farmhouse, so the firefight devolved into a standoff. Ammo then became Green's main concern. The nearest resupply was a half mile away. "If you ain't got a kraut in your sights, don't shoot," Dziepak announced, as if his men needed the reminder.

German bullets had been ineffective, but now their mortars ranged in. A scream, and a fragment was buried in Green's thigh. He had to be evacuated and more ammo brought up. The farmhouse fortress kept the *Fallschirmjägers* at bay while Albers, Dziepak, and Green went out the back door but were spotted. All hit the dirt, the wounded lieutenant dragged by his arms till they finally reached a shallow irrigation ditch.

Behind them the firefight intensified, and by wounding Green the Germans had taken out three men, a situation that caused Dziepak to rejoin his embattled squad. By himself Albers would have to drag Green back the rest of the way. Dziepak's rump disappeared in the grass. Albers looked at Green to explain, but the lieutenant's face was pale and distorted as a Halloween mask. A heavy man, heavy and strong, Green wrapped his arms around Albers's waist while with a swimming motion Albers slowly pulled him across the next field.

Green's arms weakened, and his leg became so bloated that it rose like some grotesque balloon. At a dip in the field Albers loosed the tourniquet, let blood flow till Green blanched silver-white, then retight-

"Jumpin' Joe,"
Camp Mackall,
North Carolina,
1943. As an expert
parachutist, he
should have had
his legs together.
(Joe Beyrle)

Joe in front of his tar
paper barracks (built
by the Civilian
Conservation Corps)
at Camp Toccoa,
Georgia, 1942.
(Joe Beyrle)

Top deck of the HMS *Samaria* as it crossed the Atlantic in September 1943. (U.S. Army)

Joe's cohort in I Company, England, 1944. His best buddies, Orv Vanderpool *(top, second from left)* and Jack Bray *(bottom, second from left)*, were killed in the same plane on D Night. Two others in this group also died during the war. (Joe Beyrle)

Sergeant Barron Duber, I Company's master scrounger of illicit fish, game, and brandy. (Joe Beyrle)

Currahees, faces blackened with charcoal, about to take off on D Night. Draped over his reserve chute, the trooper on the right has a coiled rope to help him descend if he lands in a tree. (U.S. Army)

The church in St. Côme-du-Mont where Joe landed on D Night. He slid down the long pitch *(center left)* into the small cemetery. The top of the steeple, used by Germans for observation and anti-aircraft fire, was subsequently destroyed by American shelling.
(Joe Beyrle)

Highway 13 in St. Côme-du-Mont, where Joe flung grenades at a group of Germans on D Day.
(Joe Beyrle)

Paratroopers advancing in Normandy.
(U.S. Army)

Exhausted Screaming Eagles take a break by a hedgerow on D+2.
(Jack Schaffer)

Joe with JoAnne, his wife, at the monument in Normandy where he was "buried" in 1944. (Joe Beyrle)

The obituary photo of Joe that appeared in the *Muskegon Chronicle*, September 1944. *(Muskegon Chronicle)*

A Nazi propaganda photo that humiliated American POWs in Paris,
July 1944. Joe is second from the right.

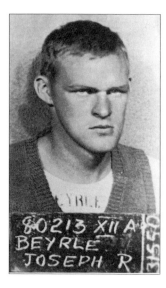

The Germans' mug shot of
Joe, with his kriege number,
when he was first registered
at Stalag XII-A.

Typical items in an
American Red Cross
parcel for POWs.
(American Red Cross)

A kriege barters with a German guard. This remarkable picture was taken by Angelo Spinelli, a captured combat photographer who was able to smuggle a camera into Stalag III-B.
(Angelo Spinelli)

Ed Albers in 1943.
(Ed Albers)

In England, apprehensive Screaming Eagles listen to a briefing for Operation Market-Garden. (U.S. Army)

At a departure airfield for the Market-Garden jump, troopers get a last-minute briefing on what to expect. Censors scratched out Screaming Eagle shoulder patches. (U.S. Army)

Currahees board a C-47 to jump into the Netherlands for Market-Garden. (U.S. Army)

Charlie Eckman *(right)*, who was wounded seventeen
times, spars with Denver Madden, who was killed
during Market-Garden. (Charlie Eckman)

American wounded in a makeshift aid station, Bastogne, Belgium.
(U.S. Army)

The cold, the ruins, the dead of Bastogne. (U.S. Army)

Currahees, upon liberating the Landsberg concentration camp,
approach some of the victims. (U.S. Army)

Russian soldiers receiving mail from home, an event that Joe never witnessed and that was probably staged for this photo. The soldier on the right holds a submachine gun like the one issued to Joe. (Novosti)

Waffen SS troops, exhausted from fighting the Red Army. (Imperial War Museum)

Russian troops during house-to-house fighting in Kustrin on the Oder River. The soldier on the left has a flamethrower.
(Novosti)

Saint Joseph's convent in Warsaw, where Joe found refuge in 1945. He took this photo in 1989, and found the statue of Saint Joseph still pock-marked from World War II.
(Joe Beyrle)

The basement of the convent, where the sisters treated his many wounds.
(Joe Beyrle)

Joe with two
Polish sisters
in 1989. (Joe
Beyrle)

Liberated
krieges,
April 1945.
(U.S. Army)

Ex-krieges of the 101st
Airborne were served
chow in April 1945 at
Fort Sheridan, Illinois,
by German POWs,
some of whom had SS
tattoos. The result was
an international melee
in which several
Germans were killed
with steak knives and
cafeteria trays. Joe is
the third man from the
right.
(Daily News)

Joe embraced
by his parents in
Muskegon,
May 1945.
(Muskegon Chronicle)

Joe *(left)* and
brother Bill with
their mother,
shortly after V-E
Day. Bill un-
wittingly covered
Joe for two
clandestine jumps
into France.
(Joe Beyrle)

Joe in a convalescent hospital in the summer of 1945. His recuperation from his wartime traumas was erratic.
(Joe Beyrle)

Joe in Normandy for the thirtieth anniversary of D Day.
(Joe Beyrle)

In the White House Rose Garden, Joe presents
Russian president Boris Yeltsin with a D Night
cricket. (JoAnne Beyrle)

The Beyrle family, 1994. *Seated, left to right:* Kathy, Victoria, Jocelyn,
Caroline, John, Alison, and Amanda Schugars. *Standing, left to right:*
Christopher, Joe II, Joe III, Joe, JoAnne, Eric Schugars,
Julie Schugars, and Jack Schugars. (Reflection Studio)

ened it. Albers wallowed on with Green draped on his back. They formed a profile so high that a bullet singed Green just as they reached a drainage ditch. Both men collapsed, one at the end of his strength, the other near the end of his life.

Like angels two medics appeared. While one gave Green first aid, the second dodged away under fire to return with a litter under each arm, assuming both blood-soaked infantrymen had been gravely wounded. Green went off on a litter, out of the war, never to return. After checking Albers, the medics, needed elsewhere, scurried off. He loaded himself with bandoliers and a machine-gun belt. He had crawled back to safety; now he would have to sprint back into danger. Bullets kicked up around him during the chest-heaving run. He burst into the farmhouse as his squad came down the stairs equally winded as incoming mortars exploded on the roof. Thatch ignited and timbers crashed while Dziepak distributed the ammo Albers had delivered. ("Why didn't ya get some grenades, Ed?") Before the Germans completely surrounded the house, Dziepak's squad shot their way out, herding pigs as they retreated.

THUS ENDED A SUCCESSFUL German snip of the corridor, one to be reversed in a matter of hours, but too late for the Red Devils who expired around Arnhem, still waiting for Montgomery's tanks. Between the Waal and the Rhine, Screaming Eagles were now deployed on a large wedge of land they called the Island, where many of their grimmest Dutch memories were imprinted during seventy-two days, an American record for continuous contact with the Germans.

Albers remembers the Island as a dreary wetland, so sunken that dikes ringed it to hold off two rivers. Across the Rhine the Germans had observation posts overlooking every movement. "So they just plunked us all the time with artillery. That's how General Taylor got hit in the butt. The worst part was trying to keep dry. Dig a foxhole and it filled with water before you put down the shovel. We lost more guys to trench foot than enemy fire. Sort of like World War I."

The 101st's losses from all causes had been crippling since September 17. Sink was the last regimental commander to have jumped in Normandy. The other two had been either killed or permanently evacuated with wounds. The 506th had lost a third of its officers and a quarter of the enlisted men. Albers's rifle squad had but one rifleman, him. There were plenty of mortars but no one left to load and fire them. No Airborne replacements; Ike's priority was for leg infantrymen, as his manpower pipeline from the States was running dry.

"I remember what the British we relieved said about the Island," Albers says: " 'Quiet as a bloomin' churchyard, mate. The only thing you'll die from is boredom.' For a while that was right. My squad had an OP in a jam factory near Dodewaard. We ate jam, sweetened our coffee with it till we were sick of jam and just used it for trades. Arnhem Annie was the krauts' propaganda broadcaster. Her favorite saying was, 'You can listen to our music but you can't dance in our streets.' She'd play good swing and in between tunes ask us to come on over and surrender. We'd be treated well. Just bring a toothbrush, overcoat, blanket, and sit out the rest of the war.

"Some nights we'd paddle across the river in little rubber boats. One of these patrols left a toothbrush, overcoat, and blanket on the kraut side, with a note that they'd tried to surrender to Annie but she wasn't around. They also mentioned how much fun it would be to make contact with her, and offered a standing invitation for her to cross the river. Just wave panties instead of a white flag."

In the foggy predawn of October 5 the Germans paddled across themselves, a full regiment swarming over the dikes. The surprise attack was preceded by the heaviest enemy artillery concentration that even Dziepak had ever experienced. Incoming flew over like flocks of birds. The jam factory had been zeroed in on. Civilians were huddled under big skylights that shattered into thousands of shards, cutting faces as if there had been a huge knife fight.

"There were lots of puddles from the drizzle," Albers remembers. "I watched them turn red from the civilians' blood till Dziepak jacked me up. 'Get on the machine gun!' I started feeding in belts. The krauts were coming out of the fog—no targets till they were big enough to hear. They came on like Pickett's charge, but we were on the second floor where they couldn't get at us. Every burst seemed to take down a half dozen. As soon as the shell casings stopped bouncing, you could hear more krauts screaming and moaning out there. Dziepak was worried that when the fog lifted they could swing around the factory and we'd be cut off, same as almost happened at the farmhouse back at Veghel. What, me worry? That was the squad leader's job to worry. What we were doing was holding them off. Someone said every kraut we kill here we won't have to kill in Germany."

When the fog lifted, Second Battalion counterattacked in a scene from nineteenth-century war when foes stood, rushed, and fired at each other without cover. That didn't last long on the Island. Infantry on both sides grabbed mud when artillery found them. A windmill became crucial, a place from where artillery could be directed. Neither side could hold the windmill.

Albers changed machine-gun barrels as they began to glow red. Darkness set in with both sides blazing away extravagantly and insatiably devouring ammo as fast as it could be brought up. To develop a more thickly defended line, I Company was ordered to withdraw a thousand yards from the jam factory. Dziepak's squad nearly revolted. They had ruled from their roost and would not likely get another nearly as strong.

"We were saying, geez, we're slaughtering 'em. Why pull back?"

Because Sink wanted a free-fire zone for *Jabos* to trample on German reinforcements. Thus deprived of nourishment, the Germans' attack withered. As the Currahee yearbook related, "[It had been] the hottest action this side of hell. . . . Dusk settled its dark cloak, but the savage battle went on lit by fires from gutted houses. . . . The next morning was still as the krauts left their dead and dying among ruined buildings and lying along a railroad track. Our price was heavy, theirs ruinous."

Albers recalls, "After that we finally were pulled off the Island. The next night in Nijmegen we were taking our first shower in weeks when what looked like a meteorite in reverse took off from across the Rhine. What the hell was that? Next day another launched, a long white streamer like skywriting. Those were the first V-2 missiles headed for England.

"So, when we left, Arnhem Annie was bragging how Hitler's secret weapons were going to change the war. We didn't know, didn't worry either, and celebrated leaving by throwing grenades into our old water-filled foxholes and cheering the fountains. Don't know what the Brits who relieved us thought about that. Maybe that we were as tired of the war as they were.

"We knew what the Dutch thought about us as we trucked on Hell's Highway for the last time. When they saw the Screaming Eagle on our shoulders they came out as they had in Eindhoven, hundreds of them, just as full of joy as the first time. They kept yelling, 'Seventeen September! Seventeen September!' "*

The destination of the 101st was Camp Mourmelon, a former artillery garrison twenty miles from Eisenhower's headquarters at Reims. Since Caesar's time Mourmelon had been a military encampment and battlefield, still pocked by craters and scored with crumbling trenches from World War I. Most recently it had been a tank depot for the Germans, who left the barracks in graffitied tatters.

No matter: a roof overhead was luxurious compared with a chilled water-filled foxhole on the Island. Besides, passes were the order of the day, the first in nearly three months. Unleashed, Screaming Eagles took Reims by storm, frolicking and forgetting while swinging from crystal chandeliers as substitute for parachute risers, doing PLFs from balconies onto feather beds. Drinking as if the dead were there with them, despising those who had not seen the elephant and smashed its tusks.

In early December General Taylor departed for Washington to represent the 18th Airborne Corps at a conference called by General Marshall concerning structural changes in Airborne divisions based upon their combat experience in Europe and the Pacific. The 101st's assistant commander went off to England for a critique of Market-Garden, leav-

---

* As did Robert Postma fifty-five years later, recalling that day when the 101st departed from his homeland: "I was eleven years old at the time of our liberation. We had been under Nazi occupation for almost five years. Our beautiful little country lay in wreck and ruin till 17 September, the day the sky filled with hundreds of planes. From the place I was watching I could see gliders coming down and paratroopers from the 101st Airborne Division landing just north of Eindhoven, my home. Soon there was incessant gunfire and explosions. To me the Screaming Eagles were like ferocious gods from heaven. That has remained the greatest moment of my life: when I knew we were free, free to live, free to breathe the air. It meant the terror was over, the pain of cold and hunger would cease. It meant that we could laugh again. It meant that all the cherished things of life that were lost would gradually return to us. It meant that once again we could live as a people with dignity and respect."

ing the Screaming Eagles to rest and recuperate under Brigadier General Anthony McAuliffe, who headed division artillery. The departure of the top of the chain of command raised no comment: the Western Front was quiet, the Germans seeming content to man the Siegfried Line while their hands were full of Russians on the Eastern Front. The prospective contest closest to combat was a football game between the 506th and 502nd on Christmas Day. Before then those troopers not on pass lazed about as the scent of a thousand turkeys from home wafted over mess halls.

Ed Albers was alone on duty in I Company's orderly room at 3:00 A.M. on December 17 when the phone rang. Uh-oh; at that hour it must be MPs holding some trooper who had closed a Reims bar with a smoke grenade. Instead it was Captain Anderson, ordering the cooks to produce breakfast in an hour.

"What's up, sir?"

"The krauts have broken through somewhere. That's all I know, but the division's been alerted to move."

General McAuliffe knew little more. His orders from Reims were just to motor march toward Luxembourg, Tony. Flatbed trucks are en route to pick up the 101st. You'll be with either 18th or 8th Corps, we haven't decided yet. You probably won't see any action, and we're sorry if this spoils the holidays.

A peppery but self-commanded man, McAuliffe rose from his chair, muttering profanity, as he received those instructions on the phone. He gathered himself to point out to Ike's staffer that the 101st didn't have winter gear or even much ammo. "I've got companies that haven't received new weapons for the ones disabled on the Island. I've got hundreds of replacements who haven't even been assigned."

We know, we regret, but just get moving and report to General Middleton. Things will sort out, sir, and you'll probably be back in Mourmelon by Christmas. Ike's looking forward to seeing that football game (he was a punter at West Point). What did you call it—the Champagne Bowl?

There was a total of forty players on the two football squads. In the next month seven would be killed and seventeen wounded around the Belgian town of Bastogne.

CHAPTER FOURTEEN

A DOG AND A MOLE

STILL WEARING ITEMS OF JOE'S UNIFORM, ALBERS WAS PUT IN FOR the Silver Star for saving Lieutenant Green at Veghel. In the meantime Joe was in a boxcar with trembling memories of the train across France. Now a homemade compass gave a depressing answer to the krieges' question of where they were going—east, deeper into Germany, farther from the liberation that seemed possible after initial good news from Market-Garden. They had just left a stalag that might soon be liberated, en route to one that obviously wouldn't.

As the suffocating miles rattled by, Joe's disappointment reached despair. The news of September 17—Market-Garden—had been like a call from the Screaming Eagles: we're coming! Then the echo faded. If luck were a lady, Joe had been her unnoticed suitor. Yes, he was still living after several events that could have killed him and nearly did, but merely being alive produced little gratitude at his age. It came over him that he'd have to change his luck by will alone. So Joe began eyeing the boxcar grille. The two troopers on the train from Paris could have been crushed on the rail bed for all he knew, but the memory of them disappearing into the night air was still an almost religious vision.

He maneuvered under the grille, pulled out his shiv, and started prying. Other prisoners helped. They pried, dug, pushed, and wrenched, but the German boxcar was better built than the French forty-or-eight. For two days and nights they worked on it, then tried the wallboards but found them inches thick with a metal plate in the middle. Joe gave up when his shiv broke, a time mark of prudence in his mental recovery from the blow that had put him in a coma for six days and distorted memory the way sunspots short-circuit the electromagnetic field. He was able to reconstruct his thoughts for a period thereafter, able to reflect that breaking the shiv probably saved his young life.

"Even if I'd gotten out, I was in the heart of Nazi Germany—not France—with no real plan to get away. I pushed my luck. Lady Luck doesn't like that. After the war I read a perfect description: luck equals opportunity plus preparation. I sure wasn't prepared."

Mostly at night, skirting air raids on Berlin, the train rumbled on, its occasional toots low, grim, and authoritative, as if saying, Make way for Hitler's *Reichsbahn*. Joe awoke feeling a different pulse from the rails, a new sound that came from a bridge over a good-size river. The best guess was the Oder, that the train had crossed the prewar frontier into Poland.

"Anything in Germany at that time was nothing compared to what had happened in Poland," Joe says. "Now we were in it. One of the college guys on the train said, 'All hope abandon, ye who enter here.' "

AFTER THE FALL of the Berlin Wall, it became possible for Joe to search for Stalag III-C, the destination of that train. During the cold-war years he had retraced his journey through France: St. Côme-du-Mont, Starvation Hill, Alençon, the Paris railyard, visits therapeutic and resolving of memories. In 1992, when Joe crossed the Oder for the fourth time, John, his son in the State Department, was driving a rattletrap rental car. Joe had a detailed Polish map but only a vague idea of where III-C had been. As he had since V-E Day, Joe wore a small compass on his watch strap. It didn't help. With growing discouragement, father and son crisscrossed miles of unbroken pine forest. Saint Christopher never adopted me, Joe joked wanly.

Then on a dirt road they came upon a farmer trudging east. Fluent in German as well as Russian, John hailed him with *wie gehts?* There was a slight but not too friendly response, so John tried a Russian salutation.

Stalag III-C? Da, the farmer knew where it had been, and since he was headed that way, he'd gladly accept a ride. Joe moved to the backseat and peppered him with questions for John to translate. The farmer was impressed that Joe had been a III-C kriege, and was now the first American to return. But there had been French, he explained, and for good reason, as the visitors would see. He was a boy at that time . . . life had been extremely hard . . . he'd lost his parents, their farm confiscated when this part of Poland was annexed by the Reich. The Russians gave it back. They were hard masters but nothing like the Germans.

The dirt road became stone, huge flagstones pressed flush with the earth, stones scarred and marred by deep gouges, which, though anciently weathered, were so evident that Joe asked to stop and examine them. The farmer nodded; yes, down this road had come the first Russian armor, each cannon overlapping the hull of the tank ahead. No rubber treads, just the metal cleats clattering like tractors from hell. Stop, please. In twilight the farmer pointed to a low silhouette in the forest, a cairn. They got out to look, for this was all that remained of III-C, all that had not been reclaimed by the state-planted pine forest. The eerie cairn was a memorial to seven thousand French POWs who had been wiped out by a typhus epidemic in 1941–1942 when the stalag opened.

There was one other artifact. Where everywhere else the forest floor was flat, there was a field of wavy earth beneath the trees. Before years of gentle erosion the waves had been mounds, the mass grave for twenty thousand or more Russian POWs—the farmer could only guess how many. Most died, he supposed, from starvation, for even farmers went hungry during the winter of 1944–1945, the hardest winter anyone could remember, the winter he'd lost his parents.

The three walked while Joe tried to orient the present with his memories, then returned to the car where he sat for long minutes hunched with hands clasped between legs. What happened to the railroad track? he asked suddenly. They had not walked far enough, replied the farmer. Darkness was deepening, but Joe wanted to see it. They found it, the single track overgrown with weeds higher than the rusty rails, weeds so strong they had pierced a rotted platform.

JOE'S TRAIN HAD DISGORGED its first load of Americans on the platform at III-C, half the size of IV-B, whence they'd come. There was no forest then; the surrounding land was farmed, luckily for the new arrivals because local potatoes became their sustenance. Back in Germany everything had to be trucked to stalags or brought in by rail. The more the Anglo-Americans ruled the skies, the harder it was for the Germans to transport anything. But *Jabos* didn't strafe across the Oder. By Allied agreement, they left it to the Soviet air force, which at that time was out of range and not nearly so strong as the RAF and AAF. So in a way Joe never expected, III-C's location near the city of Kustrin was a blessing.

"If ten thousand Russians starved to death at III-C," Joe says, "it wasn't because there was nothing to eat but because the krauts wouldn't feed them. That farmer's parents died when the Wehrmacht took their produce and livestock. Guards told us that all Slavs were to be exterminated. Starving them to death was the most efficient way to do it. When the guards said that, they just looked at us as if we should understand. The farmer's parents understood. They let themselves die while they gave him all their food so he could survive. It was that simple.

"I read that right after the war the U.S. government asked Hollywood to reconstruct the Germans. Please don't make any more movies about nasty Nazis; don't always make the Germans the villains. We need American public opinion to support the new Germany as an ally against the USSR."

The British felt similarly, that the looming threat from Stalin was justification to sweep the evil of Hitler under the rug. After V-E Day Montgomery said, "Uplifting and enlightening films are needed at once. . . . He who controls the cinema controls Germany."

FROM MEMORY JOE CAN diagram the layout of III-C: railroad track on one side, stone road on the other, with a creek beside it. Within a double fence of barbed wire, German buildings fronted on the road, separating several rows of American huts enclosed in another barbed-wire fence. The Russian compound, also set off by a fence, adjoined. Joe was among the first Americans transferred to III-C. More arrived after Market-Garden, and a flood after the Battle of the Bulge, but the Germans kept them in separate compounds so they could not learn the ropes from the old guys. Eventually the total number of Americans reached two thousand.

In setting up their compound they followed military organization, forming squads, platoons, and companies. Senior NCOs formed the chain of command; the lowest-ranking were hut commanders (six huts to a company), the highest being Master Sergeant Coleman from the 82nd Airborne. Joe never met him. Coleman and his small staff lived outside the compound by the stalag headquarters. That created some resentment at first, but they had to live where the Germans told them to, so if they were better off than other krieges, that was just an example of an old army acronym, RHIP—rank hath its priviliges.

There was another chain of influence, if not command, a democratically capitalist one headed by BTOs—big-time operators. They gained that status by being the shrewdest barterers or biggest winners at gambling. A big loser had nothing to pay off his debts except personal service, so he became what the British back at IV-B called a dog robber or batman.

"I don't know where *batman* came from," Joe says, "but it wasn't the comic book. You might see a BTO private with a staff-sergeant batman who made his bunk, stood in for him at roll call, swept his hut, brought him chow—did anything else the BTO wanted. Now and then those roles would reverse after a big crap game. Coleman's chain of command had a lot of respect for the BTOs, more so than vice versa.

"Our first concern at III-C was the winter coming on. A smart thing I did was throw my ditty bag on the top bunk of a three-decker. There was a small stove in the middle of the hut, and I knew the heat would rise. Also no one would climb over me and drop straw. I think it was at that point I considered myself an old kriege.

"I did all right in crap games but wasn't a BTO and, looking back, actually didn't want to be. BTOs pretty much lived in the present, accepted it, made the best of it, enjoyed the status. It could be very different from what they'd been in the army. I understood their point of view: if you had to be a POW, be a BTO. But for me escaping was all that mattered, so I used my hoard of cigarettes to get on the escape committee."

Word evidently reached Coleman about Joe's efforts to break out of the boxcar. His application for the five-member escape committee was readily accepted. Three of them had to approve any escape plan before it went up to Coleman for the final go-ahead and support from the supply committee. During Joe's first month only three proposals were presented, two for tunnels—the classic British way—and one jail break. None was approved, indeed not a single vote cast in favor of any. Tunnels, the committee felt, were too slow, especially with the ground starting to freeze. Using force (jail break) needed enough "nonescapees" who would risk their lives to support it. To get a few escapees outside the wire required a full-scale riot inside. Lives were sure to be lost and everyone else punished. None of the committee thought krieges would sacrifice the way they had on D Day. Back then their attitude was save the world; now it was save yourself.

"When the Market and Bulge POWs came in we heard their slogan, 'Win the war in '44.' We told them that here it was 'Stay alive till '45.' "

Proposals were also rejected for want of an escape strategy when loose in Poland, the inherent problem with III-C. No one had a solution, just as Joe had not when he tried to pry his way out of the boxcar. Nor was there any precedent because no one in institutional memory had ever escaped from III-C. After a while proposals stopped coming in and the escape committee was dormant, but their deliberations had keened Joe's thinking about the potential and pitfalls of an escape. Just as important, he had identified two men who looked like good escape confederates. Their names, as Joe remembers them, were Brewer and Quinn. He transferred to their hut, though that meant giving up his top bunk.

One of the first essentials for an escape was getting to know the Germans and their routines. The guard shifts were eight hours, one of which was at night when krieges couldn't leave their huts, but shifts rotated, so if Joe wanted to focus on a particular guard, he could talk with him every couple of days. Starting a conversation was no problem. Guards liked to practice English. Word was that several were planning their own escape, to get away from the Red Army and be captured by the Americans. Using his German name and a cigarette, Joe could get along with almost any guard who wasn't SS. The rule was, don't mess with the SS. Don't even try to talk to them, or you might get a smashed mouth. Besides the guards, there was a "ferret" in his compound, Sergeant Schultz, the only German Joe ever got to know. Their introduction was through a warning.

The pitiful Russians were herded around like sheep, taken out to labor details before dawn and returned after dark, worked to death while being starved to death. Schultz advised Joe about a new guard—don't go near the fence when he's on duty. One afternoon the Americans saw him in action. The Russians had been hauling garbage from camp headquarters when a whistle blew, the signal to get back to their compound or be lashed there with bullwhips.

"One skinny little kid tried to scoop up potato peels from the bottom of a garbage pail and fell behind," Joe recounts. "The master racist Schultz warned me about was a dog trainer—police dogs. He yelled something, let a German shepherd loose, and it sprang right for the jugular. The dog threw the poor kid's head back and forth till the neck was cut through and his head came out like a wine cork. The new guard had a belly laugh, and the kriege next to me threw up. He was sick all day."

Schultz's job as a ferret was to roam around the compound during the day, observe what was going on, and chat with krieges. He had been a World War I POW himself. He made a daily report to the commandant, so the Americans knew why he was there but didn't mind. Schultz was a shrewd psychologist for offering tips like the one about the sadistic guard, both for its apparent generosity and the chilling reminder of the penalty for disobedience. Schultz was a Bavarian, which provided an entrée to speak with Joe about possible common ancestors. His wife lived with him in a cottage just outside the camp. They had two sons, one serving in Italy, the other last seen in France. He hadn't heard from either in months.

Joe hadn't received a single letter either. Schultz said he'd look into it and shortly advised that some mail had arrived at XII-A or IV-B (the return address Joe had used on postcards) but for some reason was sent back to the Red Cross. Schultz gave him an extra postcard and offered the hope that with a permanent III-C address he'd get a Christmas package. Schultz had gone outside channels to help Joe, who showed appreciation by giving him some Red Cross chocolate. So it wouldn't be seen as a bribe, Joe gave it to him to give to his wife.

Curfew rules were the same as at previous stalags, but power generators were scarce at III-C, causing frequent outages, so it was hard to keep the fence floodlit throughout a night. Schultz enforced the curfew, however, which was broken usually when diarrhea forced visits to the latrine. He solved the problem by putting a can in each hut. To prevent other curfew violations he loosed a pack of police dogs in the compound at night. If a hut door was closed, there was no problem, just the sound of them sniffing and growling as they roamed around. Brewer and Quinn decided to make friends with them. It took many nights of "Here, boy, nice doggy," but then they could open the door when it was dark and watch the brutes think about entering. The biggest, a huge Belgian shepherd, was the one Brewer wanted.

They argued some about that. Quinn and Joe said let's take any that'll come in, but Brewer pushed them aside and kept calling for the Belgian shepherd. Because only Brewer was willing to give up a Red Cross biscuit, he got his pick, one he named Heinz. At last Heinz trotted in, looked around, pissed on the stove, wagged his tail, and almost let Brewer pet him. They planned for the next evening. Quinn smuggled in a small coal shovel, and Joe gathered some kindling during the day. But that night was not Heinz's shift.

"We were sure disappointed, though Brewer didn't give up and spent most of the night calling quietly for the dog. Before I went to sleep I told him he'd have to improve his German because Heinz didn't understand English."

Early the next evening Heinz came around. Brewer stood well inside the hut and called him. Joe was beside the door ready to slam it. Quinn was on the other side with the coal shovel. Heinz never knew what hit him. Four feet spread like he'd walked on ice. Heinz was still warm when the krieges bled and skinned him. Fur, guts, and bones went down latrines. In a Red Cross can the rest was slivered and broiled. What came out was three jerky steaks for Brewer, two for Quinn and Joe, a half each for their hut mates. The testicles were offered to a West Virginian, but he was insulted, so Heinz's future went into a latrine too.

His meat was stringy and tasteless, even as hungry as they were. Heinz wasn't very filling either, and a full feeling was what krieges craved most of all. As the three dognappers ate they talked about future canine ranching. Was the risk to grab more dogs worth the skimpy reward? Besides, Schultz might notice that Heinz was AWOL, so better to lie low for a while.

"I said Schultz would think Heinz went off with some Polish pooch," Joe recalls. "Yeah, Quinn came back, but what about the next three or four missing males? I said when there's a bitch in heat, they go off in a pack. Okay, but why would they disappear one by one? I didn't have an answer for that. Then Brewer and Quinn got into it: every mutt removed was one less to guard the fences at night, so don't just think about dogs as food. I gave them each a cigarette because they were thinking about escape as much as I was.

"Schultz . . . What did he look like? About fifty years old but looked more like seventy. Maybe six foot, thin but with a paunch. He wasn't a good poster boy for Goebbels. We watched his attitude closely after Heinz disappeared. He acted like nothing had happened. Still I felt he suspected that one hut had chowed down on canine fillets. He knew and we knew that we were not buddies. We were enemies whose job was to attack each other. It took a while before he counterattacked."

American krieges in III-C, especially Airborne, constantly pushed the limits of camp regulations. Whereas earlier the Germans hadn't been much good at uncovering transgressions, in October 1944 it seemed that no one could get away with anything. Now far too many clandestine meetings were being busted, even those arranged by BTOs, whose security measures were the best. Guards had to be bribed and they could squeal, but the law of averages wasn't working. Men were being thrown into solitary on bread and water. With everyone's health so borderline this was more than punishment—it was life-threatening.

The secondary duty of the escape committee was to prevent penetration by the Germans. Ferrets were open penetrators, pretty easy to neutralize, but it became clear that Schultz was also running something covert and effective against the Americans. The escape/security committee had a long talk about what could be going on. Krieges who looked like they might be collaborating were the first suspects. Coleman put out the word to rough them up. If they continued to be palsy with the krauts, beat them up. This was done, but the busts and punishments continued as before.

The committee then had to consider that there might be moles in the compound. A Ranger at IV-B had warned that the krauts' best opportunity for mole planting occurred during transfers between stalags. After

Joe persuaded the committee that this had happened between IV-B and III-C, they pondered countermeasures. The one approved was to create kriege groups from all regions in the United States, create them openly for an ostensibly benign purpose. With the commandant's acquiescence, Coleman announced that there would be regional meetings to disseminate local news from home. Bring any mail you got, and read it to your buddies.

By then hut commanders knew the home state of all their men. If someone didn't go to his regional meeting, he became a suspect. There were only a few like that, checked out thoroughly and found to be just lone wolves, men who chose to go through the kriege experience by themselves. They did so very well, and none turned out to be a security risk.

The regional group that uncovered the mole was from Ohio. It took days of innocuous but very specific questions put casually: "Hey, anyone from Senator Taft's hometown?" Like the needle on a gyrating compass, suspicion began to home on a man who said he was from Cleveland but didn't recognize the name Bob Feller. How about the mayor in 1942? No response. What high school did you go to? He had an answer for that, however, he didn't know any of the ice cream parlors in the neighborhood. What do you hear from home? Nothing. No mail? No. Why not? No parents? No girlfriend? They didn't write him. He had a Polish name, something like Websky, but couldn't say anything about the part of Poland his ancestors came from. This seemed like a pretty tough requirement to Joe, who couldn't have said much about Bavaria either.

After increasingly less friendly questioning, this Websky owned up. He'd lived in Cleveland for four years with an uncle from Lithuania before returning to East Prussia, where he was drafted into the Wehrmacht. He clerked on the Eastern Front for two years, then felt lucky, because of his American English fluency, to be pulled out in 1944 to serve as an intelligence staffer in France. It was quite possible that Websky had worked at the château where Joe had had his head bashed in, but he was not allowed to ask because Coleman designated a prosecutorial team to handle Websky's case and they provided him Fifth Amendment protection. However, he made the mistake of acting as his own counsel. His defense was that he couldn't turn down the mole job, he didn't have a choice, and if he didn't produce results, it was back to the Eastern Front, this time as an infantryman.

That was too bad, but the committee didn't have much choice either. His hut commander was briefed and provided a stand-in for Websky at roll calls after Coleman ordered a secret court-martial. Joe asked, how can we court-martial a guy who's in the enemy army? Coleman's answer was, you know what I mean—have a trial and make it fast. It was fast indeed, as a six-by-six hole was dug under a hut. What took inordinate time was the question of whether the hole would be Websky's execution site, grave, or both. He was given the choice of a shiv in the heart, a club on the head, or being strangled.

"He didn't choose, he just started praying out loud, going from English to German, whatever came to his head. One trooper volunteered to club him, two to strangle. We chose the strangler, who was less eager for the job. I didn't watch the execution because I volunteered to be on security when it happened. I didn't say so, but I would have liked to have clubbed him, the way I was clubbed in the château. Getting rid of a cockroach like Websky also made me feel better about a chance to escape."

There was a lively debate within the committee about how to dispose of the dead man. Joe was angry because the question should have been answered before Websky was executed. What's the problem? said Coleman's staff. Just leave him in the hole. The committee objected: dammit, when Schultz misses Websky, any fresh dirt in the compound will be dug up. We can't tamp down the earth enough to fool the krauts—they'd had a lot of experience in uncovering British tunnels.

Coleman sided with the committee, one of his most important decisions. Websky was dismembered and fed into latrines like Heinz. When the latrines were routinely emptied for use by farmers, the committee had a quiet party catered by extra rations from Coleman.

"Before long we knew that Schultz knew what had happened, but there was no reprisal. He had lost a dog and a mole, probably caught hell from the commandant, but he still showed respect for what we were doing."

THE COMING OF WINTER was on everyone's mind, more than anything besides food. Before it permanently froze, Russians had dug under the ground with scraps of wood tossed over the fence to them by Americans. Three or four feet down it was not quite so cold as on the wind-chilled surface. The Russians were digging their graves, but why freeze before dying? Unless you wanted to die, or felt that if you died today, you wouldn't have to die tomorrow. Across the wire Joe understood what the Russians were saying by digging: do what you can, do what you want to do. God understands. He'll call you when ready. God's always ready. This subliminal message struck Joe because it was transmitted by voices of what the world thought were godless Communists.

In that way the Russians, their incomprehensible longanimity and endurance, began to haunt him. For Joe this had a double effect, reinforcing his gratitude, as with the terribly wounded in the boxcar, to be relatively better off; and forging a bond with Nazi-haters even more inspired than he. A somewhat mediating figure for him at that time was Schultz, working for the Nazis yet not one of them.

Though Schultz seemed to overlook Websky's disappearance, the commandant did not. Several moles were inserted into the compound. They couldn't have been more obvious if swastikas had been painted on their foreheads. The only question they consistently answered correctly was that Roosevelt was president. What invariably slipped them up was the location of the Grand Canyon. They always said Colorado.

With their cover so flimsy it wasn't healthy for new moles to stay in camp long and soon they were transferred, probably to other stalags, where they'd try again. Joe admits to taking part in a farewell party for one of them. It's a GI tradition that when a barrack thief is discovered he's wrapped in a blanket so men can pound on him without being identified. Then the thief is bounced down the stairs of the barrack. There was only one floor in kriege huts, but compensatory punishment was found. It was Joe's only opportunity to do unto the Germans, at short range, as they had done unto him, a satisfying experience of revenge without guilt.

Schultz said nothing about the mole batteries, indicating his wish for things to return to normal, the waiting to see how the war would end. Joe wasn't about to wait. With two good men willing to break out with him he felt it was past time to put it to the touch again.

"My last pre-escape conversation with Schultz went like this: I felt a little bad about Websky though he'd caused a lot of pain and grief and deserved to be where he was. Schultz took me aside and suggested we say a rosary together for Websky. Why? I asked. His answer was that it could be possible for all of us to find a way to escape more horrors from this war, one way or another. How each of us do it is between us and God. That's not a bargain, that's a proposal. We never know if God will accept it. That's why we pray, he said.

"My young mind was stunned to hear that. I had mixed my prayers for personal survival with prayers for the end of Germany. For sure the second was more important to the world than the first. Several miracles caused me to survive, and Germany was crushed. My prayers were answered in one result. Schultz's were not, in fact just the opposite, but I think God listened to him as much as me."

CHAPTER FIFTEEN

BERLIN

T HE JOE OF OCTOBER 1944 SORT OF SCARES JOE TODAY. A LOT OF him in III-C was still a kid, a kid who had gone through a lot, taken a lot, and dished it out, but still a kid who saw just about every chance as a good one. What drove him hardest was neither the Nazi murderers nor the Russians murdered but rather what his mother had said when he left home for the induction center in Kalamazoo: "Never do anything to make your family ashamed." Joe felt they might be ashamed if he didn't escape, and sure they'd be proud if he did. He was quite wrong—all the Beyrles prayed for was that he survive the war.

Withal he was on the escape committee, one of five men whose combined age was barely a hundred, whom Coleman designated as his most mature and cautious judges of risk, of what could work and what probably wouldn't. For Joe the best way to learn more, to gauge the lay of the land, was to get outside the wire where the stone road and railroad intersected at III-C. For that purpose he volunteered for work details in the countryside.

On one such detail, hunger got the best of him. A farmer's horse-drawn wagon loaded with potatoes went by close enough that the krieges conspired to liberate a few spuds. The Americans tried a diversion. Several went up to the guards and created confusion while others plucked potatoes off the wagon and stuffed their pockets, shushing the farmer with cigarettes. This kind of misbehavior was not rare—such pilferage was one of the reasons men volunteered for work details—and usually was punished with no more than kicks and curses, but this time the senior guard was a good friend of a former mole who had been punished by the Americans.

He shouted, *Feuer!* ("Fire!"). One man was hit, fell under the wagon when the horse bolted, and died when his head was crushed by a wheel. Joe was about to catch a spud when a bullet entered his right shoulder. It passed through the muscle without striking bone, but with an impact harder than the shell fragment in Normandy. It seemed his arm was blown off—it was so completely numb that he was surprised to find it still attached. The pain came on like flame dissolving ice.

"What I had to do was conceal the blood because guards grabbed anyone who was wounded," Joe recalls. "Another guy who was hit ended up in solitary and died there. I packed some dirt to stop the bleeding and with good luck was marched back to the compound with the krieges who hadn't been caught. I could have got an Oscar for pretending I wasn't in pain because I sure was. A guy next to me saw that and started telling nonstop jokes. I think the guards thought my expression was because of how bad the jokes were. The POW chain of command did not approve of what we'd done. I wouldn't have either if I'd had Coleman's job. We'd got a man killed for just a few potatoes.

"A kriege medic came around to my hut and secretly patched up my shoulder so the krauts never knew. Schultz saw something was wrong with the way I couldn't use my arm, but he didn't try to find out about it. But he knew. I was trying to lift my arm when he came by and said, 'Too much crap shooting, Joe?' He punched it in a friendly way. I winced, got the message, and felt I owed him. The only way I had to do that was to stop harassing him."

Harassing Schultz had been an amusement. Each morning at roll-call formation there were hundreds of krieges milling around as Schultz and his guards counted heads. Joe was among those who would move down in back of the formation, pop up, and be recounted so the count was screwed up. Schultz usually took this sort of prank good-naturedly, more so than the krieges who wanted to get out of the cold and back to their huts, but after Schultz overlooked the shoulder wound, Joe convinced his fellow pranksters to lay off for a while.

Joe's injury set back the escape plan he had devised with Brewer and Quinn. While they waited for the wound to heal (it never did completely), two fortunate events occurred: American krieges were issued winter clothing, and Joe won seventy packs of cigarettes in crap games.

His jump boots were so worn and torn that the sole at the toe had separated from the shoe, leaving a big gap that soaked his feet whenever it rained and making the sole flap. So though it meant looking like a leg, Joe was glad to put on standard GI brogans delivered by the Red Cross, along with thick GI overcoats, wool socks, and trousers.* Those were the clothes he would wear for the rest of the war. The fact that they were American uniform items would save his life.

"With my right arm out of action, rolling dice with my left hand seemed to bring luck. Shorty had said always use my left hand—I should have remembered that before. Anyway, I wasn't going out on any more work details, so there was time to circulate around the compound to a lot of crap games. There were at least two big ones every day. The winners got together for playoffs that drew plenty of spectators, including Schultz sometimes. Even when I wasn't rolling I'd bet on the guy coming out. Those were the best odds, no side bets, and slowly my cigarette fortune grew. One afternoon I felt my hand was hot and doubled up for four straight passes. Quinn came over, then Brewer. I crapped once, then made two hard points and went seven-eleven twice more. The nicotine addicts looked at me like I was Rockefeller. Quinn took my winnings away before I was tempted to gamble for more. Brewer had been counting too. Sixty was the number of packs we felt was necessary to bribe our way out. We now had a ten-pack cushion."

Thus it was time to present their plan to the escape committee, from which of course Joe would be recused. It met in the shed where Red Cross parcels were distributed, known as the PX. The cover for the committee to be there was that it was Coleman's auditing group to make sure krieges got what was coming to them. The escape committee played that role well because honest distribution was of prime importance to everyone. They spent much more time counting parcels than they did hearing escape plans.

---

* Under the Geneva Conventions POWs were to remain in military uniforms throughout captivity (a provision violated most noticeably by North Vietnam). It was for their nation to supply new uniforms, through the IRC, when the original ones wore out. The United States did so readily, but impoverished nations like Albania had none to provide, so their prisoners got nothing.

On the day of a proposal, security was posted around the PX to warn of any guards who might come through the area. A rough wood table was cleared of Red Cross parcels, then the presenter laid out his plan. The committee hunched over on their elbows to hear what the low voice had to say. Now Joe was the presenter, but the other four members of the committee didn't treat him any differently.

"My plan was simple. We would offer one of the night guards twenty packs if he let us cut the wire while he was walking his post. Then we'd go through when his shift changed so he wouldn't be blamed. A train went by III-C every night. We'd hop on it like hoboes. No, we weren't sure where it was going, but since this is Poland, all railroads probably led to Warsaw. Warsaw was hundreds of miles east. East was where the Red Army was coming from. We'd noticed how fewer Russkies were being brought into III-C. That was a good sign they were winning.

"We'd leave the train when we figured it was close to the Eastern Front, then hole up and wait for the Russians to overrun our location. Along the way we'd have plenty of cigarettes to buy cooperation from anyone who could help us."

As he finished his pitch the power generator failed and they were sitting in the dark. Someone laughed and said that wasn't a good sign, but Joe said yes, it was, because the plan was to break out on a no-moon night in early November.

Out of the darkness came very sober questions: had Joe identified a guard to be bought? No, but there were a couple he'd chatted with and they had been corrupted before. One had even offered, for a high price, to slip Americans over to the next compound to have sex with their choice of Russian female POWs. Someone on the committee knew a better candidate. Joe was glad to leave bribery to him.

Faint light came back on, and the committee decided that the deal, if Coleman approved Joe's plan, should be ten packs' down payment, ten more after the three escapees were gone. How many days' worth of food was needed? All the supply committee could afford, Joe answered. The committee said don't expect more than a few potatoes, apples, and Red Cross biscuits. That should be enough because the three had saved up a bagful of Spam, cheese, and chocolate.

What about reprisals, Joe was asked. Reprisals? The commandant had never stated a reprisal policy because no one had ever escaped from III-C. Reprisals were a big kraut bluff, Joe argued, because a commandant, to hide it from his superiors, wouldn't want to announce an escape, much less advertise it through reprisals (which, it should be added, were condemned by the Geneva Conventions, which commandants were reviewing with increasing interest as the war turned hard against Germany).

Did Joe have any alternatives if he couldn't link up with the Russkies? No, he didn't, except that by turning north they'd eventually reach the Baltic Sea, where there might be a chance of getting over to Sweden, cigarettes for a sailboat. Did they need weapons? Joe wasn't prepared for that question. Sure, it would be great to be armed, ideally with Schmeissers, but firearms cost the highest bribe of all. There probably weren't enough cigarettes in all of III-C to buy a pistol. Joe said the three had shivs and were satisfied with that. It was nice though to hear the committee even mention the possibility of getting a firearm. They were sold on the plan, the first ever to win a single vote. "Okay, Joe," the chairman said, "we'll ask Coleman to approve."

The plan went into motion. Within a week a guard on the right shift had been bought, one so cooperative he offered advice that on moonless nights the commandant required extra security; however, with the recent cloudy weather every night was dark so the one picked was as good as any. Joe told the go-between to slip this guard another pack and ask him about the dogs and if he knew the night train's destination.

The answers came back that it would help if dogs were barking all night. That had already been taken into account. Sometimes they barked a lot, other times not much at all, but it seemed that the darker the night the more they barked. And it didn't matter much: krieges and dogs had become so familiar that they ignored each other. Nevertheless Joe took the guard's advice and asked that barking be aroused (perhaps by a small scuffle) around the huts on the far side of the compound from where the three would be going out. Coleman vetoed such a distraction because it meant bringing more krieges into the plan. Joe didn't argue— he expected to be through the wire before the dogs picked up a scent.

The erratic floodlights were more of a concern. The train went by between nine and eleven. The maximum electric load on the generators was at around six o'clock, so that's when they hoped to slip out, while the lights were dim. The bought guard would be on duty as the escapees were cutting wire, so the more light then the better. He wasn't much help about the destination of the train—it came up from Breslau, he knew, because there was a girl there whom he'd visited on a two-day pass. The camp also got some supplies from Breslau. Where the northbound train went from III-C he didn't know, but he assumed it was east because everything on wheels was being used to bring up war matériel to try to stop the Russians. He did mention that when the train came south it often contained transportees to a place called Auschwitz.

"We weren't going south, we'd never heard of Auschwitz, and the last possibility on our minds was leaving a kriege camp and ending up in a concentration camp," Joe says.

"But that happened to some POWs who had *H* [for Hebrew] on their American dog tags. Before D Night, Jewish troopers in the 101st were advised to change the *H* to *P* or *C,* and I think most of them did. Rosenfield in my battalion didn't. He said he'd lived a Jew and he would die one. He paid. The Nazis didn't treat his wounds when he was captured in Normandy. They sent him to Buchenwald, but luckily his convoy was ambushed by the FFI and he got away."

The last part of the plan was how to abort or postpone. A candle would be lit in a hut doorway if the bought guard had his shift changed. That meant not to go out and cut the wire. If something went wrong after it was cut, there was no turning back: they'd be escaping during the next guard's shift, and he definitely wasn't in on the deal. Word that came back through the escape committee was the bought guard and his relief were rivals for a local girl—indeed that the bought guard may have planned it so that the other guard would catch hell when the escape occurred on his watch.

"There were potential squealers and double-crossers on both sides. We were playing the odds like a crap game, the best odds we had. Quinn, Brewer, and I didn't talk about it much. For one thing, we couldn't let the other guys in our hut know we were up to something. They'd only know when we slipped out right after curfew. It's not that we didn't trust our hut mates, it was that we didn't want to have to trust them."

The wire cutters were two long shivs bolted together, strapped to

Quinn's thigh. One by one the three went to the door, watched, listened, and slipped out without looking at their hut mates. If anyone had asked why, the answer was the squirts. Indeed they sat in a latrine, pants down, in case a guard came upon them. It was the latrine where they'd stashed a board from the ceiling of an unused hut, a board to help them through the wire if necessary. Before total darkness, the three separated. If one was caught, the other two could head back to their hut. Back and forth individually they slunk from the shadow of one hut to another, giving one another an all-clear signal after each move. It reminded Joe of some night maneuver at Toccoa.

"I felt Colonel Sink was nodding," Joe recalled. "My parents and Sister Angelique were also watching and supporting in the background. The plan was working. We couldn't hear any barking except over at the Russian compound, where the most vicious dogs always patrolled. I had this feeling that Schultz had called them off from our compound, that maybe he was in on our escape plan or had wind of it."

When they reached the shadow of the last hut it was time to really put it to the touch ("sort of like a cherry jump"). Joe crawled under a trip wire and quickly out to the fence and began working on it with the cutter. There were four strands closest to the ground, three above them, two more above that, then a weave of barbed wire they could never cut. If they had to get through that tangle of wire, it would be with the ceiling board.

Joe was determined to sever the lowest four strands before letting Brewer take over. The wire was rusty but tough. The wire cutter was clean but not so tough. Pushing his hands together over and over put severe strain on his wounded shoulder.

"It must have taken me five minutes to cut that first strand, minutes as long as hours. I don't have flashbacks anymore, but when I did they were about that first strand. I could even feel pressure in the palms of my hands."

No one had a watch, so it seemed they couldn't do enough cutting before the guard shift changed. Joe's right shoulder began to tremble so much he could cut no more. He signaled back to Brewer, who crawled up and took over. His look said that Joe had stayed at it too long. Brewer had the third strand cut before Joe got back into the shadows. Brewer whistled for Quinn, who thrashed up and went after the next layer of wire. Joe was still panting when they gave him the okay sign: everything that needed to be cut had been cut. Unhurriedly his buddies molded candle wax to connect the cuts.

"That took forever. The wire kept popping out of the wax. They gave up, glanced over at me, and shrugged. Only about half of the wire had been reconnected with wax. When they crawled back they looked with me, and I said I couldn't see much difference from the rest of the wire except a little droop in the bottom strand. They appreciated that because I wouldn't tell them anything except the truth just to make them feel better. We'd agreed not to fake anything about what we saw or felt."

In the shadows, teeth clenched, they waited for the bought guard to stroll by across the fence. Yes, it was him; they could tell by his limp while he was still far away. The guard knew what to do—nothing—and did it well. When he came back he gave the signal, by pissing, that his shift was over in five minutes. Beyrle, Brewer, and Quinn were more than ready, but the bought guard had insisted that they not escape on his shift. He would linger as long as possible with the new guard, giving the escapees between two and three minutes to crawl through the cut, reseal it, and get into the woods alongside the rail track. The moment the bought guard buttoned his fly and turned his back, Joe crawled like a starved python, but he was third to the wire.

"We went through, through the fence, and resealed the wire with time to spare. It was the planning, the preparation, the 'execution' as they say in football, that got us out of Stalag III-C. So we were out, free to some degree. That was a thrill! It was like leaving home for the first time as a teenager. III-C was something to get away from, someplace to leave to be on your own. Old British krieges had told me to throttle back, wait it out, take what comes and live with it. Good advice, but not for us."

Outside the fence was a patch of scrub pine, the beginnings of the forest Joe would walk through in 1992. In 1944 he had about four hours to wait for a train, time for the three to grow closer in a suddenly transformed environment where hope and fear were in nearly equal balance. In a few hours they had gone from hut mates to soul mates. However, Joe recalled, "I should be able to say much more about them than I can, but I can't, I just can't, and don't know why. We were all Airborne and had been together for months, but I don't even remember their first names, their units, or where they were from. I'm not even certain if 'Quinn' is right. Something erased all that. There's an empty pit there in my mind."

They were like mountaineers brought together for the first time to conquer an unclimbed summit. In the compound they had not been a threesome. Brewer and Quinn were buddies, more so than Joe was a buddy with anyone. He respected them; they respected him. Their lives now depended on one another. That was enough of a level to work at—more could have been distracting.

This detachment, the interpersonal distance, contrasts with Joe today, who is an easily approachable and congenial fellow, the ideal seat mate on an airliner. Want to talk? He's a ready listener. Want him to talk? Joe is a broad-gauge conversationalist. Rather read? That's fine too. Joe reads slowly. He will not let himself misinterpret a term or miss a nuance. His World War II library fills most of the Beyrle basement and claimed a lot of his time while he painstakingly mined the background ore and lore of his experiences for this book.

But when it comes to what must have been a most intimate connection with Brewer and Quinn, they who went through the worst part of his life with him, the memory tape has been erased. Or so spotted that their pictures degenerated like Dorian Gray's.

AFTER SWEATING THROUGH the wire, the three were damp and cold in the woods, waiting for the train. In a soldierly way they reviewed what to do when it came along or didn't. Though the escape committee had arranged stand-ins for morning roll call, they knew that if the train wasn't running that night they'd have to start up the tracks on foot and hope to catch another one somewhere. If that happened, their odds of getting away approached zero, but to improve them they planned to split up if search dogs were heard. Maybe with different scents in different directions one could get away. Brewer spoke some German. Quinn said the two of them would stick together. That was okay by Joe. On potato details he'd picked up a little Polish, and ever since the escape plan was approved he'd spent time over by the Russian fence to learn some of their language.

The wait in the woods was like D Night in England: they had prepared in every way, and what happened next was up to God and fate. They exchanged addresses of parents, repeated them in the frosty darkness till each became a potential locator of the other's next of kin. Such thoughts Joe pushed away, saying let's get our dobbers up—we're about halfway home, we did the hardest part, breaking out of the stalag. A million Russkies were coming, and the krauts didn't have enough troops to look for three little Amis.

They imagined the sound long before they heard it. The locomotive didn't toot as it sometimes did; instead it huffed and puffed. That night the boiler was on overdrive to climb the slight grade where they were waiting. From the steam jets and slow progress, they guessed this train must be very long and loaded, easy to board. It went by at the speed of a fast walk, so they had their pick among the cars. First came the coalers, then flatbeds carrying Mark IV tanks. Almost at random, the escapees swung onto an unsealed boxcar. As they heaved open the sliding door, it seemed like a rolling jackpot.

It was half full of grain, no doubt for horses, the prime movers for Germans on the Eastern Front. So this train must be headed east, confirming a key assumption in the escape plan, and the grain was a bonus, something to munch while saving emergency rations. They had to munch slowly, removing husks like tiny pistachio shells. The grain was hard and tasteless, but if it kept horses going, it could do the same for fugitives.

In addition to emergency rations, the supply committee had provided a primitive compass but without luminous points, so Quinn had to push the boxcar door open in order to read it. After trundling along in a northeasterly direction, the train heaved to a halt at a junction. After some jolting detachments, switching and reattaching, it moved off again—southwest, Quinn murmured. Around midnight the tracks made a new sound, the same sound Joe had heard going over the Oder for the first time. Now he was recrossing it, slowly drawn back into Germany.

The train went along the southern edge of Berlin. Joe found the rail yard fifty years later, still big, bleak, and in the worst section of town. In

1944 it was heavily cratered, a junkyard of twisted track and derelict boxcars. Joe's train arrived before dawn, then their car detached and shunted to a siding.

"What if we'd hopped another car, one right by the tanks that were *sure* to be going to the Eastern Front?" Joe reflects. "We took the grain car out of instinct, I guess. It must have been wishful thinking. I've learned that when instinct is right, it usually comes as a surprise. The boxcar instinct was no surprise, it was 'Hey, let's grab this one—looks like the best one coming along.'"

Stupefied to silence, the three contemplated how their situation couldn't be worse: they were smack in the center of Hitler's Reich, its capital, at maximum distance from friendly forces, with huge German armies to get through in either direction. Joe had prayed so hard, kept his faith, but been rewarded with disaster. There was no answer but destiny to why they ended up in that boxcar, only the certainty that they couldn't stay in it till Berlin fell to the Allies.

Back in England they'd heard something about a German resistance movement, and as krieges they'd learned there had been an assassination attempt against Hitler in the summer. Their only hope now was to try to find Germans in the resistance. Yeah, said Quinn. How do we do that? Just walk down Main Street in Ami uniforms and yell, "Hey, anyone want to help us? We're going to win the war, you know!"

In the boxcar there was plenty of time to debate. Quinn counseled patience. He felt the car was sure to be picked up sometime and taken somewhere, and anywhere was better than here. Horse feed probably wasn't the Germans' highest priority, but eventually it was sure to be moved to where there were horses, and that meant out of Berlin.

Brewer and Joe didn't feel that way. They couldn't live on grain that made them itch and sneeze so much someone walking by could hear them. By a 2–1 vote it was decided that they would prowl around the forlorn rail yard, "check out the area." Quinn vehemently disapproved: Okay, he said, if this were Poland where everyone hates the Germans, but this is the capital of Germany, where everyone hates *us*. As if to emphasize his point, a flurry of bombs dropped on the city.

If bombers were going over, they might be targeting boxcars, Joe argued. Some bombs fell closer, and Quinn agreed to get out till the air raid was over. They slipped into a culvert and scanned the rail yard. It was huge, about five miles wide and three miles long. They roamed back and forth for two or three days, their bag of rations depleting. At some point they got into the sewer system, a miasmic maze promising to lead somewhere better but mocking them to try to find a way.

The vast yard showed few signs of life, no trains moving in or out, till late one afternoon they saw an old man shuffling between train cars, checking grease fittings of the journals. He proceeded slowly and after an hour sat down to gnaw on black bread and baloney. Joe urged that the yard man be approached directly, no matter what the hazard. The three were in American uniforms, very motley ones. Should they pretend to be refugees? No, said Quinn, that story wouldn't last. Go right up to him, Brewer whispered, and tell him who you are. They studied the yard man for another half hour. He was hunched in the cold, a gloomy figure slowly munching as if his mouth had insufficient saliva.

Joe came up behind, called him Kamerad, and asked for help. The man's jaw dropped and so did his sandwich when Joe told him he was an escaped POW. Go away—Kamerad didn't want to hear anything like that. Joe gave him three cigarettes, which he grabbed but repeated that he wouldn't continue talking for fear of being shot. By the Gestapo? Joe asked sympathetically. The man nodded.

Joe left it at that and silently watched Kamerad trudge away. The next morning they saw him in another part of the yard, again checking journals. Joe emerged and asked for food and water. Kamerad wore a dingy overcoat and wool cap with a visor shadowing his eyes. This time he was willing to talk a little. He was forty years old and not well, he said—dysentery, the cause of his medical discharge from the Wehrmacht. Water? He pointed to a leaky cistern. Food—*nein*, it is very scarce. Ami bombers . . . Joe gave him a pack of Lucky Strikes. Well, Kamerad would check with a friend who might be able to help. He left before dark, and Joe's unease increased because he'd not been able to see Kamerad's eyes as they'd talked.

The fugitives had another debate about what to do. They didn't think Kamerad would be much help, but he was all the hope there was for now. If he betrayed them, it would probably be soon, so they entered a switch shack to watch for police. What's our plan, Quinn asked, if the krauts close in? Joe said he'd make a break for it. That might attract the cops because Kamerad would have told them of only one Ami on the loose. Brewer disagreed—word would be out by now from III-C that there were three escapees. No, Joe informed him, the commandant wouldn't want that kind of bad publicity. Quinn grew angry; they had agreed not to bullshit one another, and now here was Joe trying to make them feel better, feel safer. But hell, if Joe was to be a decoy, he should rest up. He and Brewer took turns on watch that night. The morning brought another question, whether or not to consume the last rations. They did so with little debate, for from here on there was no doubt that they would have to barter cigarettes for food or die trying to steal some.

Kamerad returned the next evening and wandered around with some apparent confusion till Joe whistled at him from a culvert. Kamerad seemed relieved and said he'd take Joe to a friend who had some food, then lit a candle to see that Joe had enough cigarettes to complete the deal. Suddenly he realized Joe wasn't alone; two other American faces had been illuminated by the candle. He stepped back and became very upset. Joe told him they'd be generous with cigarettes and leave as soon as they got a supply of food. Kamerad was still shaky, but he led them away from the yard, over twisted tracks and past bombed-out buildings. It was the kind of wet-cold night that makes a person shrink in the fog. In the distance there were lonely sirens and occasional probing search-lights.

"If this was the way the master race was living, I felt there wasn't too much to worry about winning the war. That was my twenty-one-year-old attitude when I thought we'd found the anti-Nazi underground.

"Blackout was seriously enforced. We had to feel our way into a four-room house with thick walls, then Kamerad lit a couple more candles. On a table was Brötchen, sausage gristle, and some weak beer. After months without alcohol, it put us on our heels."

Kamerad left, saying he'd be back to collect the promised cigarettes. Quinn went to a window where he could watch anyone approaching the house. In the middle of the night Kamerad returned driving a wagon pulled by a very skinny horse. Joe told him where their boxcar was if he needed horse feed. The three climbed in and Kamerad draped a tarp over them. They took turns peeking out. The ride was slow, jarring, and took over an hour. They were crossing Berlin but never heard a voice or vehicle.

"FIFTY YEARS LATER I tried to locate the route, but nothing was familiar," Joe relates. "What I wanted to find was where the wagon had taken us. It was a solidly built three-story house in a residential area. I suppose bombs got it after our visit. Good riddance."

Kamerad left them in the basement. After a while an old woman came down the stairs with some black bread, cabbage, and a dark liquid she called coffee. She demanded that Joe confirm what she'd provided, then promised to be back for the cigarettes. They checked out the basement, looking for a way out if needed, but there was only one stairway and no windows. That made them so nervous they couldn't nap. In the evening three men came down the stairs, introduced themselves by their first names, and asked Joe to repeat the story he had told Kamerad. Upon examining the kriege dog tags, the Germans were convinced and said relax, they would help the escapees move west. Had anyone helped them so far? Only Kamerad, Joe replied. The three Germans looked at one another and nodded.

"In the next minute flashlights blinded us. Eight goons rushed down the stairs with guns we couldn't see. They didn't use them except as clubs because they wanted us alive. We struck back, slashed at them with shivs, and got in some good licks before we were knocked down and held down. The one I was fighting stank like nothing I'd ever smelled before. There were some awful odors in the stalags but nothing like his.

"If God created humans, he didn't have anything to do with the Gestapo," Joe says. "Or the Japs, Stalin, Pol Pot, Osama—creatures from hell. They're here on earth, but the world wants to deny it or forget it. After tying us up they beat us till they were tired and we were nearly senseless. For young guys like us that took a while. All the time, the goon who spoke English was shouting, 'Spies!' Brewer had stuck one in the gut with a shiv. He kept bellowing *Schlagen, schlagen!*—beat us some more—then he'd moan and cry like he was the only one hurt. They helped him up the stairs like some wounded hero.

"By then we could only grunt when we felt the blows. The leader must have realized we were being beaten to death. He stopped it. The next thing I remember is being hauled up the stairs in my underwear."

Joe's memory fades in and out here as it did after he'd been clubbed into his six-day coma, but reconstruction establishes that the escapees were loaded into two cars and driven deeper into Berlin, evidently to Gestapo headquarters on Prinz Albrecht Strasse.* He went to that address in 1992. It had been totally annihilated by bombs, but there's a gruesome sort of museum underground.

"The roof of the Gestapo building had bomb holes that went down three stories. We were pushed up a long flight of stairs. Looking back I can see how we were a pretty big deal for the goons, probably the only American infantry to be captured in Berlin. The goons were met by some officers in black uniforms who slapped them on the back. Did we go up or down from there? I can't remember, just cells with big locks that looked like tombs. Along the way the three of us were separated, each to a cell."

IN DESCRIBING HIS PREVIOUS experiences, Joe's narration had been measured and deliberative, even when uneven. The Gestapo hours came out shatteringly different, like the excision of a vital but cancerous organ. He was in inaccessible mental territory, dredging up a pain too deep to scar, a place he'd recoiled from revisiting, where his thoughts crossed a galactic space, expressed with a lag and voice change like that from a space capsule.

"I'm still lost in this part. I don't want to describe it because I refeel things. That's one of the things they did, dislocate my shoulders so when they stopped I'd refeel the pain just as bad when the bones went back into their sockets as when they came out. . . ."

Fifty-five years later Joe finds detachment, merciful disconnection, in metaphor. One is a slow night shift on a production line. Gestapo headquarters was a factory in hard times but still turning out a necessary product. Once the production line had dominated and terrorized the world; now it was just a domestic industry. The old hands missed the glory days from not so long ago. They went at Joe with a vengeance, for he represented the vengeance of the world on Germany.

---

* A source for this was a Nazi newspaper that trumpeted the capture of three "parachutist spies," alleging that they had jumped like pathfinders to guide bombers onto targets in Berlin. The Gestapo's vigilance, of course, was praised.

His doctors say Joe has a high pain tolerance, but if he'd known what was coming, he would rather have rolled under the wheels of the grain car and never regretted not being able to relate what happened in Berlin. The worst of it, as he sees it now, was not the agony at the time but what has been taken away forever, an element basic to being a man, a human.

"I'd resisted interrogation before, better than most. Under the Gestapo I was not being interrogated, just tortured, extremely tortured for the pleasure of the torturers. They kept accusing me of being a spy, parachuting from a B-17, but they knew that wasn't true because they had invented the story. They wanted a confession for their records but really couldn't have cared. After a while I didn't even shake my head.

"They used their boots, truncheons, whips, and things I won't remember. The physical senses are an electrical system. The goons knew from lots of practice how to extremely stress but not short it out. Pain built up, beyond where pain had ever gone."

Analogies are vastly inadequate, missing the indescribable, indispensable elements. They resemble a theme taken by jazz performers for branches, variations, and sequels, forcing departure from physical sensations to mental constructs. Yet it was all sensations, thoroughly, previously tested in satanic evaluations. What they did sensitized and amplified every nerve in the full spectrum of agonies, repeating like an endless kaleidoscope, professionally modulated by expert torturers with unreachable mentalities. Joe was a subject for them, a laboratory animal. What he felt, he screamed.

"Sometimes I heard myself scream, other times I was sort of watching myself scream. Many times I was that scream.

"My mug shot from XII-A shows me glowering. They knew I was tough and stubborn. They were looking for a weakness, something like my shoulder wound. I was stripped so they could see how it was healing. They reopened the wound and probed around. And they had a favorite shoulder torture. They hung me up backwards, hoisted and dropped me till the shoulders dislocated. Releasing the ropes brought equal pain in reverse. The combination blacked me out for the first time.

"When that happened I heard other voices screaming like mine. Most were in German but also other languages. Whether it was my imagination or other cells I heard, it was a chorus begging, calling out to God. The walls absorbed it.

"From then on I must have been screaming in and out of consciousness. They were good at noticing that, bringing you up to passing out, then backing off a little to bring you up again. When I thought they could do no more they always found other ways. I saw them like looking through the wrong end of a telescope—they were shrunken heads from South America. They were in no hurry because what were hours for me were just minutes for them.

"I felt exactly what they were doing, felt it but at the same time watched. It was a terrible zone. That's the end point of terror. You don't get through it; you survive it or you don't, and if you do, you wish you hadn't. I was witnessing while having my body twisted and destroyed. It was burning and freezing at the same time. I was broken down into coals. I survived but was never made whole. And I was one of their luckiest prisoners."

CHAPTER SIXTEEN

BASTOGNE

CRAMMED ONTO OPEN FLATBED TRUCKS THE 101ST MOVED OUT on the morning of December 18, though a third of its strength was not present for duty, most on leave in France.

"Where are we goin'?" asked Albers, slinging his hastily assembled gear aboard.

"Someplace called Bass-tog-nee," Dziepak yelled back over the roar of the idling convoy. It was dark but all headlights were on. Security was to be sacrificed for speed, an ominous omen for I Company. This wasn't going to be a goldbrick, backup reserve job. Something real bad was happening, as was evident when the convoy began bucking a tide of vehicles going the other way, their drivers' faces blanched with fright. Yes, they were just legs, but the Screaming Eagles had never before seen American troops racing headlong for the rear. At least it wasn't too cold, Albers reflected, and there was no snow.

As they trudged over the cobblestones of Bastogne (population 5,000), few civilian faces peeped from windows as dark and hollow as the absent eyes in a skull. The Belgians, like the Dutch, had rejoiced in September when American forces liberated them. The approaching barrages of Wehrmacht artillery now suggested what could be expected if Bastogne were reoccupied by the Nazis, a fear subsequently confirmed by SS *Einsatzgruppen* who brought pictures and addresses of suspected Allied collaborators identified during the four-year German occupation. The reprisal teams were never able to enter Bastogne but held public executions in outlying villages. This was terror's high-water mark on the

Western Front for the rest of the war. The tide had turned, as expressed by Geronimo lieutenant Bill Russo:

"I think the Germans had gotten so confident in their terror—you know, scare the shit out of everybody in Poland, the Low Countries, Russia. They got onto terrorizing this and terrorizing that. . . . Well, when they met us we didn't terrorize. That's when it all started going the other way, really."

SENT BY MCAULIFFE to the village of Noville, five miles northeast of Bastogne, Currahees bucked a reeling counterflow. Like panhandlers, they stuck out their hands for clips of ammo from panicked legs. "You'll never stop 'em, boys," an outbound officer said, shaking his head in despair. "But you want ammo? You really do? Sure, take it all—and good luck."

Troopers were glad to see the likes of him gone. Others in the retreat, often Keystone Kops, were willing to turn around and face the enemy. McAuliffe had them formed into a tough rabble he named Task Force SNAFU, a last-ditch reserve, and they fought well. His other supporting forces were Combat Command B from the 10th Armored Division, elements of the 9th Armored, and the 705th Tank Destroyer Battalion. Eventually there would be about ten thousand Screaming Eagles defending encircled Bastogne and nearly the same number of armor troops, the latter ensuring a reverse outcome from that of the British 1st Airborne Division encircled and destroyed at Arnhem.

"Encircled?" Albers recalls. "Well, that's what we were trained for. When we land behind enemy lines—that's what we always do—we're encircled. When we heard on the radio that the 101st was encircled at Bastogne, we said, So what? What's new? Someone in the 502nd said something that became famous: 'They got us surrounded, the poor bastards.'"

Lugging a machine gun, Albers followed Dziepak on the road to Noville, an ordinary country road in the Ardennes but one remembered by Currahees as overhung by a presence of gloom and high danger. Outside Bastogne they'd awoken under a light snow, the first of the winter. The squad had increased in strength since the Island—replacements had doubled its number to six. Dziepak had trouble remembering their names, so recently had they been assigned.

From the side of his mouth, as I Company huffed along, he gave them a fast course on how to kill and not be killed by the krauts. Those evergreens over there—it's like the biggest Christmas-tree farm you ever seen, right?—well, panzers won't want to go in there. We will. Hope we set up on that wood line. We can stop 'em if you know where the nearest bazooka man is. You might see a panzer before he does. You got to cover it with fire. Keep the crew buttoned up. You know how to shoot a bazooka? The three rookies nod but without confidence. Good. Where's the best place to hit a tank? In the engine, Sarge. That's right. So don't try to shoot 'em head-on. Wait and get 'em when they go by. Don't we need some ammo, Sarge? Dziepak nodded. Ammo was what worried him most.

Ahead boomed a crossfire of artillery, each side feeling out the other. Artillery, Albers remembered, did not often duel (because of range) but usually fired on enemy infantry. On the Bastogne-Houffalize road there was this exchange of locating fire, more unnerving for the Currahees because the krauts had many more and much heavier howitzers. Listen to the artillery, Dziepak instructed the cherries. It'll tell you what's comin' up.

Up ahead at Noville a brave band of tankers (Team Desobry) was holding off a regiment of the 2nd Panzer Division whose colonel had almost as difficult a decision attacking as Sink did defending: how many chips to play, how long to hold a hand? The German's question was whether to crash through, with significant losses, to Bastogne or obey orders and stop for nothing in the charge for the Meuse River. The panzer colonel opted to go for the critical hub of Bastogne (where seven roads and two rail lines converged) but faced a changed equation when First Battalion of the 506th reached Noville. Here their excellent commander, Lieutenant Colonel Laprade, was killed in action. Stepping up was Major Harwick, who had escaped with Joe into the Normandy marshes.

Hearing First Battalion's fight north of Noville, Blues were eager to join it but still lacked ammunition. Then, as if by providence, a pyramid of all calibers appeared on the road next to an abandoned jeep and trailer. Sink had it dumped there. Blues dipped in as if the pile were warm popcorn. They felt like King Arthur presented with Excalibur.

Because of a roll in the road, all they could see of Noville was a glow from where the village was burning, and they heard the sounds of a surging firefight. Hold up, came the order from Captain Anderson, who went ahead for a reconnaissance. I Company was thirsty and formed cupfuls of water from newly fallen snow as they awaited an order to attack. Attack in what direction? There were Germans everywhere, but they were equally confused. For three days *they* had been attacking, overcoming, overrunning, overtaking routed American troops. Now what was this? Amis coming toward them, not with white flags but with well-aimed weapons.

The Currahee yearbook described how it looked from the Amis' side:

> Our mortar shells, evenly spaced ahead, echoing off the low hills on either flank. Across the valley onto a wooded hill where the company halted. . . . From the woods into an open field. Across the field and a frozen marsh, over a stream, into more woods and up a hill. [Not much German fire up till then.] On the reverse side the enemy waited. What an enemy! Seven Tiger Royal tanks, the dreadnoughts of a panzer army.
>
> One Tiger was burning, smoke swirled up in a cone shaped column. Bullets, shrapnel ripped by us. Loud bursts of artillery and mortars vibrated the frozen earth. Machineguns chattered, ours and theirs. Men were being hit, men groaning, but orders were shouted. The last one was to withdraw! We'd never done that before in the face of the enemy! We obeyed in a pissed-off way, with the wounded limping or carried by their buddies. Some of the dead had to be left behind, and that was hard to accept. We'd be back to get them, no one doubted that, and we sure were—about six times! But in everyone's mind was a hated word—defeat—yes, it was defeat. Our first. Noville was lost. The wind blew the smoke of its burning back at us, the smell of defeat.

At a cost of a dozen officers and two hundred enlisted men, First Battalion had bought McAuliffe a precious forty-eight hours.

So began a swirl of attack and counterattack that would continue for a month on the Bastogne-Houffalize road. The 502nd dashed in on Sink's left flank to hold off the next German drive, coming from the north. McAuliffe's loop around Bastogne was completed by the 327th, who had the longest line to defend—over ten miles, half the division front, but mostly full of woods, to the point where the glider men tied in with the 501st. No supplies could enter on any of the seven roads, but now neither could the Wehrmacht, not without a helluva fight.

Pushed back to the hamlet (seven buildings) of Foy, the 506th regrouped and took stock. They with dogged tankers now prepared to defend against massive attacks that were sure to come. Anderson said he'd never heard so many panzers that he couldn't see: from the sound they must have stretched all the way back to Houffalize, ten miles north. Their engines wouldn't idle long. If the weather cleared, they'd have to get off the roads for fear of *Jabos*. If the weather cleared, the 101st could be resupplied by parachute. So the snow clouds were a German ally; however, the eerie pale ground fog was Sink's.

Currahee Don Burgett described it "like looking into a glass of skim milk." Another trooper marveled at how the fog went up and down like a theater curtain. When it lifted for a while, panzers poking toward Bastogne were exposed to close-range bazooka fire from Screaming Eagles who had heard them coming and even stalked them in the fog. American tanks, dug in to defilade, had the road zeroed in and could fire blind on preregistered choke points. To counter these tactics, the Germans had to bring up infantry to accompany their armor. There wasn't a lot of infantry in the Fifth Panzer Army, designed for blitzkrieg rather than slugging through woodsy hills where paratroopers could ambush them like Indians.

But in the impartial fog, Indians were infiltrated and ambushed too. Vehicles evacuating wounded were shot up by squads of Germans lurking along ditches they'd been ordered to follow into Bastogne. Each lift of the curtain revealed a new scene, tragic for one or both players; then it descended over an all-directional firefight that turned into a tableau, melting further into milky mist till even the huge, dark silhouettes of panzers disappeared and there was only the sound of tapering fire and the wounded screaming in two languages.

The aftermaths were bedlam, like one described by Burgett, who saw a trooper rolling on the ground in hand-to-hand combat. A second kraut rose in the fog to intervene. With his .45 Burgett hit him point-blank, whereupon another German turned his rifle and fired a round that cut Burgett's chin strap with such force that the buckle hit him in the eye, the impact knocking him down. The German cranked the bolt for a coup de grâce when troopers stormed into the scene. The German spun around. Burgett grabbed his rifle and shot him through the cheek.

"The bullet came out the other side and took his whole ear off. He dropped straight down in his foxhole. I threw him on the edge of it, laid my rifle across him, and used the kraut as a sandbag as I shot at two of his Kamerads."

One of them, carrying a Molotov cocktail, burst into flames; he staggered, his smoking uniform blending into the fog till the flame set off his ammo belt, a string of firecrackers that stopped his screams.

"Bielskis had fired the last burst from a belt of machine-gun ammo. He did something that he knew better . . . he raised up to his knees, opened the top of the gun, and started to put in a new belt. . . . A bullet struck him between the eyes. I saw smoke, vapor, something come out the back of his head. It seeped around his helmet as he stayed on his knees for about a count of three, then all of a sudden Bielskis just collapsed over the gun. He was a very, very good friend of mine."

In a slush of blood and snow, "we assembled in a group after assuring that all Germans around us were dead or soon would be. Everything just closed in on me. . . . The smell—I'll never forget the smell—burnt powder, raw iron, steaming blood, splintered bones where a leg used to be. . . . Commo wire and tree limbs down. . . ." Transformed to symbols of death and horrible sadness as penetrating as the icy fog. "I had to do something and took aim at this badly wounded kraut in a hole. Just then Phillips walked up. I looked at him and said, 'How come you're still alive?' He says, 'I was gonna ask you the same thing. Whaddaya doin'?'

" 'Just gonna kill this kraut.'

" 'Save your ammo,' and Phillips pushed my rifle away. Then a German officer who'd been shot in the leg crawled over from the left and surrendered to me. He must have thought I was a nice guy for not shooting that other kraut! A trooper walked up behind me, looked at the wounded officer, and said, 'Has he got a Luger?'

"I said, 'Nope,' so KA-BLAM! He shot the German—who thought I shot him, so he started cursing me as he died. What a joke! Me, Phillips, and this guy had to lean on each other we laughed so hard."*

Goethe was a Currahee, Ross Goethe from Nebraska, whose hatred for the Germans was more vicious than his buddies could understand. One very dark night his company was on line in a dense pine forest when he heard kraut scouts slipping toward them. In inky fog, Goethe felt a hand grip the rim of his foxhole. He ducked back before a bayonet swept from side to side like an antenna, checking to see if the hole was occupied. Goethe grabbed the wrist, yanked the German in, stabbed him repeatedly with the bayonet, then flung the dying man out in the direction whence he'd come. Nice work, said Goethe's platoon leader next morning, killing without firing your weapon and giving away your position. But finish him off next time, trooper. That kraut was gurgling all night.

THE FIRST SNOWS WERE followed by deepening cold, a more implacable killer than even the renowned German formations, which in turn came at Bastogne from all compass points. What stopped them was a centralized defense and their own chain of command, which never designated a single commander to coordinate an all-out assault on the 101st's oval perimeter. McAuliffe, however, could hoard small tank-infantry teams to rush like firemen to whichever regiment was receiving the attack of the day. Furthermore, within "the hole in the doughnut," as the press would call it, he could mass his artillery fire on any threatened sector; what had been a major problem in the Netherlands, concentration of artillery, was a trump card in Belgium. For the first six days in Bastogne, McAuliffe had precious few howitzer rounds, but he knew how to use them, and when "Divarty" spoke, the Germans listened and rethought their plans.

Exasperated, the attackers called upon their own artillery to end what had become a siege. On December 23, Lieutenant General Heinrich von Lüttwitz, a monocled Prussian who commanded the

---

* Though many times wounded, Don Burgett was one of the few who made it through Normandy, Holland, and Bastogne.

panzer corps controlling most of the surrounding forces, sent two officers toward American lines under a white flag. This wasn't particularly notable; brief local truces had been carried out previously, always for evacuation of wounded from between the lines. On these occasions Screaming Eagles were grateful to rise from frozen foxholes, stretch, yawn, and even shave without drawing sniper or mortar fire.

The Germans this time had a different request, though one, by their lights, with a humanitarian aura similar to succoring the wounded. The message, written on a captured American typewriter, was from Lüttwitz (identifying himself only as "the German Commander") and addressed to "the U.S.A. Commander of the encircled town of Bastogne." The 130-word text demanded surrender, otherwise "total annihilation" by more than a corps of German artillery. "All serious civilian losses caused by this artillery fire would not correspond with the well known American humanity." McAuliffe was granted two hours to "think it over" before this bombardment commenced.

McAuliffe was far too busy planning how to parry Lüttwitz's next thrust to devote two minutes, never mind two hours, to thinking over a reply. Upon being read the translation, his firsts words were "Aw, nuts." In 1944 that meant "Fuck off." No one on his staff could improve on "nuts," so that was the message sent back to the Germans, out to the world, and into history.*

The rumor spread around the 101st perimeter as quick as the cold: *the krauts* had recognized futility and offered to surrender. Albers was skeptical. Yeah, we're killing a lot more of them than they are of us, but there're some pretty good enemy troops out there, not the kind to surrender. I think they'll try again.

They did that night, preceded by the first Luftwaffe air raid, and the hardest of the 101st's thirty days of fighting in the Bulge was yet to come. Hard-bitten troopers brushed mud and snow off with the same

---

* It took three more days before General Taylor broke into Bastogne with Patton's tanks led by Lieutenant Colonel Creighton Abrams. Years later the author asked Taylor how he would have replied to Lüttwitz had he returned in time for the surrender ultimatum. Taylor's answer was that because this was an international communication he would have replied in French, the proper language of diplomacy, and would have said something like, "These are still the Ardennes, but this is no longer 1940."

sort of sardonic outlook that had allowed them to briefly consider that the krauts might be ready to surrender. If the Luftwaffe was aloft, C-47s could not be far behind.

That's exactly what was on McAuliffe's mind. Nuts was sangfroid, relished by his staff, who clapped like the audience in a nightclub when he announced his one-word reply; but they, like him, were best aware that though tactically the 101st was holding its own against 4–1 odds, logistically there was deep crisis. When surrender was refused, only two hundred howitzer rounds were available to support each of the four infantry regiments. Against a major coordinated attack, two hundred rounds could be expended in ten minutes. It had come down to this policy for artillery economy announced by G-3: only if there were "four hundred Germans in a one-hundred-yard area would howitzers be fired at them—but no more than two rounds."

Though there was a small resupply by parachute on December 23, the shortage of small arms and machine-gun ammo was only slightly less severe than for howitzers. Orders came down that the infantry positions now occupied were the last. The perimeter had been compressed to implosion, and there was nowhere to withdraw. "Defend in place" is the military euphemism for hold at all costs. It was the order of the day on Christmas Eve, when on the firing line friends shivered with cold and shook hands as if for the last time while darkness fell. With few rounds per man, the only way to produce firepower was to get it from the enemy. Dziepak reviewed the most desirable German weapons. Stay low during their attack, kill a kraut, grab his Schmeisser, and there's your ammo resupply. And, oh, yeah, before you fire a kraut weapon, yell "Friendly" or you might get return fire from your buddies.

Christmas Day produced a lull. Down in the foxholes men could hear their counterparts singing "Silent Night" in its original German. They also broadcast Bing Crosby's "White Christmas" on a loudspeaker. Listening were troopers in shallow foxholes lined with tree boughs. As body temperature melted the frozen pine branches, water penetrated clothing. Out went wet boughs while new were gathered in, preventing cold immersion but also preventing anyone from getting more than twenty minutes of sleep. With the Germans so close, snoring was a grave offense.

The big Christmas present came the next day, delivered by air as if by Santa. Riddled by copious flak, waves of C-47s bore in to drop cargo from five hundred feet, low enough to prevent chutes from drifting into German hands. Gliders coasted in with tons of ammo. Almost every Screaming Eagle could see the daylight drop. It was all they needed to keep the faith. Soon previously muted howitzers began to cough and roar like long unused cars. Companies of Germans had been seen roaming unconcerned around the perimeter outside small-arms range. Now there was abundant artillery to rain on their movements. Divarty's radios were swamped with calls for fire missions. One of them began, "It's like Forty-second and Broadway out there!"

December 26 was also the day Patton's 4th Armored Division made its breakthrough to Bastogne from the south. It was tough going over ice that sent tanks lurching off roads, and a third of them were lost to 88s and Tiger Royals dug in on every hill. Ralph Ingersoll described his first view of Bastogne:*

Riding through the Ardennes I wore woolen underwear, a woolen uniform, combat overalls, a sweater, a tanker field jacket, a muffler, a lined trenchcoat, two pairs of heavy woolen socks, combat boots with galoshes over them—and cannot remember ever being warm. There was a mean dampness in the air and a cutting wind that never seemed to stop.

On the edges of the town you could see, like a picture story in a book, where the German columns had broken through the perimeter defense and come right up to the edge of houses. You could see this from the burned-out panzers. They had come in one by one and been bazookaed. The trail of them was like a snake cut into little pieces, winding up the low plateau on which Bastogne stands. Here and there, black in the bright sun, were

---

* The press described the linkup of the 4th Armored and the 101st as a "relief" or "rescue" of the paratroopers. General McAuliffe took umbrage at such terms, declaring, "We resent any implication that we were rescued or needed rescue. . . . I know of no man inside Bastogne who ever doubted our ability to hold it." Not so with men on the perimeter, however, who had many reasons and more occasions to disagree with him.

little basketfuls of charred junk, all that's left when an aircraft hits the ground at three or four hundred miles an hour.

What Ingersoll saw was the history, recorded by Colonel Harper of the 327th in his after-action report: "All we commanders at Bastogne could do was put our men on what we considered the critical ground. When that was done the battle was delivered into their hands. Whether we were to win, even survive, was then up to the individual soldier. . . . He stayed, and froze, where he was put and often died rather than give an inch."

Even Hitler had something to say about the defenders of Bastogne: "I should like to see the German general who would fight on with the same stubborn resistance in a situation which seemed just as hopeless." December 26 was also a momentous day for him when his staff announced, with uncharacteristic bravery, that "we cannot force the Meuse River" (they never got closer than five miles). In an all-day conference Hitler acquiesced to fighting decisively east of the Meuse where the Bastogne salient constricted his supply lines like a finger poking into the trachea. Bastogne was to be taken with every resource in the Bulge. Overnight the 101st G-2's map sprouted with new symbols: 15th Panzer Division, Panzer Lehr, 1st SS Panzer, 3rd and 4th SS Panzer Grenadiers, *Kampfgruppe* Remer, and a bewildering array of lesser units, including two infantry divisions, pulling back now, contracting the Bulge to go into defense of the strategic penetration. They meant to stay—because Hitler wouldn't allow them to leave—and turned with a new intensity on Bastogne, what they called an abscess in their side.

Albers recalls: "They liked to attack just as it was getting dark. That was pretty early, maybe three-thirty or four. They'd shoot handheld flares in front of 'em. Without exposing themselves, flares illuminated where they wanted to go. We shot into the dark where the flares came from, shot right down at the ground, the snow. The flares started zooming in all directions like skyrockets on the Fourth of July. We were hitting the guys shooting the flares, and the krauts became confused about where they were headed."

The to-and-fro in bitter cold began to take a toll, even for veterans. There had been no resupply of grit. What they had was all they had, and even with the savvy and poise developed in Normandy and Holland, it was a finite quantity. In contrast with their senior commanders' confidence, troopers were coming down with "battle rattles," what was called shell shock in World War I, and post-traumatic stress disorder (PTSD) after Vietnam. A 10th Armored man came walking by after a German attack, his helmet dripping blood. "Where you going?" a trooper asked. "I gotta get a new tank. . . ." Barron Duber had acquitted himself well till after Christmas. Cagey, cunning, an accomplished sniper, Duber was never more happy than when he captured German "shoe" mines, explosives enclosed in wood to defy mine detectors. He found that freezing weather deactivated their detonators, so he collected them for the thawing day when he could go out on a patrol and strew them behind German lines. But after a freezing night in the woods around Foy, Duber never thawed out himself. He shook in his foxhole from battle rattle and had to be hauled out by his armpits, shuddering like an epileptic. Now that the 101st had an umbilical cord to Bradley's army, Duber was evacuated, gone forever. After V-E Day, someone in I Company saw him, no longer in the 101st, driving a truck in a convoy headed for Brest. "Hey, Barron!" the trooper called. Duber looked straight ahead as though he'd never heard his name.

During the siege, a certain defiant contempt for wounds developed. The division surgical hospital, with all its doctors, had been captured in toto on the road up from Mourmelon, so till after Christmas there was little but first aid for the wounded. Frostbite and trench foot were treated by changing to larger boots if there were any available from other wounded. The only way to prevent frostbite was burlap bags wrapped around your feet or taking the well-insulated boots of dead Germans. After four winters in Russia they had the best arctic gear in the world, including, of course, white camouflage.

What the 101st had were bedclothes, sheets worn like ponchos, pillowcases over helmets, all readily donated by Belgians. One gave up a bridal dress intended for her Christmas Eve wedding. McAuliffe was so touched by the gesture that on December 26 he had a white parachute delivered to her house. With it was a note expressing his hope that she could make a new wedding dress, this time with silk. She never had the chance. That day her house was destroyed by German shelling. The bride was found dead in the rubble.

No one faked a wound. No one in I Company doubted that Duber had indeed fallen to battle rattle and could fight no longer. He'd given his all for as long as he could, more than he had to give. Men with physical wounds took pride in refusing morphine, giving it to someone worse off. Such selflessness did not find expression, however, in sympathy. There had just been too many wounds inflicted on too many men. What numbed a wounded man's buddies was his loss: one less in the squad, a wider gap to cover, a longer period of night watch for the survivors. Often a casualty's main pain was the realization that his evacuation weakened the front so long defended at such cost. Disappointed in himself for being hit, he would need to be cheered by medics, reassured that no one held a wound against him. Medics were scarce. Men knew not to call for one just because they'd been hit. One would come running and perhaps get hit himself. Use your first-aid kit, veterans told rookies; that's what it's for. Call for a medic, if you have to, after the shooting stops.

Often it took more than one wound before a man went to the facsimile of a hospital, a basement in the ruins of Bastogne where patients lay in rows on the stone floor. The unofficial, unenviable division record for multiple wounds belonged to Charlie Eckman, a machine gunner in Second Battalion, 501st, who came to Bastogne by way of Toccoa, Normandy, and Holland. At five feet four and 120 pounds Eckman was a small target, but the Germans hit him seventeen times in six months. That was a rigorous count: several small fragments from one grenade counted as only one wound, though two bullet holes from a single Schmeisser burst were both counted. His seventeenth was a nine-millimeter slug in the ankle that drove a boot eyelet into his leg. This meant the boot had to be removed—it hadn't been for two weeks— something Eckman dreaded, and he heard from the medic, "My God, trooper, your leg's gotta come off! The foot's completely frozen!"

He went to the rear on a stretcher, the only time in seventeen he hadn't made it to an aid station on his own power. The surgeon was in the midst of amputations and had a less-than-perfect bedside manner. "You're next" was all he said to Eckman.

"No, I'm not, Doc!" he cried, and bolted out of the aid station. Medical aides tried to stop him. "Let him go," the surgeon grumbled. "He's going to die anyway."

Eckman was too weak to get back to his unit and Bastogne was no longer encircled, so he turned himself in at a tent hospital. He couldn't talk because of diphtheria in his throat, so he couldn't argue with a second opinion that gangrene had set in and that *both* legs had to come off. Eckman shook his head and whispered that all he needed was to warm up. The surgeon tried to convince him. "You don't understand, son." He ran a needle along the soles of Eckman's feet. "See? No feeling."

"Give me a chance."

"What do you want to do, die?" Then the surgeon was called away for another emergency. He was gone twenty minutes. Left alone, Eckman did push-ups, squat jumps, and rubbed his legs so hard the skin came off. He plunged back into bed when he heard the surgeon returning.

"Check my circulation now, Doc." Indeed it was noticeably improved. "Gimme a couple of more days. If I'm not better then, you can have my legs."

"You're battle-rattled, trooper. In a couple of days you'll have your dog tag between your teeth. But that's up to you. I've got plenty to do with guys who want to live."

Whenever no medical staff was around, Eckman resumed stationary but strenuous exercise, much of it all night. To do so he had to disconnect intravenous tubes, then stick them back in when doctors made their morning rounds. They were wide-eyed over his improvement:

"Eckman, this is almost a miracle. We were going to amputate your left leg above the knee and the right one below. Now we can cut off the left at the knee and the right at the ankle."

"Gimme another day, Doc." After another night of anaerobic calisthenics, the new prognosis was even better: "It must be because you're so damned young! [Eckman was nineteen.] Great circulation. Never seen anything like it. You're going to get out of this war with just four toes off the left foot and three on the right."

"Sir, can we talk about that tomorrow?"

But tomorrow Eckman was gone, AWOL from the hospital, and hitchhiking back to Bastogne. The division had departed for Alsace, but he joined them in Germany.

———

UPON FIRST ARRIVING AT division CP on the afternoon of December 27, General Taylor received the situation report from McAuliffe. "Sir, we're ready to attack" was the first sentence. Far from true, a statement of sangfroid like "nuts," but Eisenhower had ordered an attack to seize Houffalize, Patton was eager to get on with it, and the 101st was the nearest available division to spearhead it, notwithstanding its winnowing to less than 50 percent strength and the fact that many of them, like Eckman, were holding on from sheer will so as not to let their buddies down. *Stars & Stripes* and every stateside newspaper bannered their defense as a matchless feat of arms.* They'd done more than anyone, Allied or Axis, could ever have expected, and more than any other division in Ike's armies the Screaming Eagles deserved and needed relief and rest. What they got instead was fighting so vicious and unremitting that they would look back on the siege as their easier days in the Bulge.

During the week between Christmas and New Year's Currahees astride the Bastogne-Houffalize road attacked and defended on alternate days. Attacking was more difficult. The temperature was zero, the snow waist deep. They had to clear the wooded hills the Wehrmacht had occupied for weeks and fortified expertly, better than any other army in Europe could. There were log bunkers and slit-firing machine-gun nests, with overlapping fields of fire, registered on approaches by which the Germans knew the Americans would come—through dense stands of pine, with branches so low and the snow so high, a trooper couldn't help but rustle foliage as he wallowed forward; when he did the enemy saw him coming. The first action they took was to call for artillery, which they had in abundance and larger than any guns in the 101st. About thirty feet high, the forests were ideal for "tree bursts," explosions that added splinters to shrapnel blasted down on attackers who had to close within hand-grenade range before they could detect German infantry positions. The thin-trunked trees were no protection from their fire.

American tanks, and there were plenty after New Year's, were of

---

* Among the accolades that flowed into Bastogne by print and radio from Allied commanders, even some fighting in the Pacific, the most poignant was from another division that experienced a drastically different fate in a similar situation: Arnhem. The message: "Congratulations to all ranks of the 101 Airborne on their magnificent defense of Bastogne. We are full of admiration." It was signed by the CG of the British 1st Airborne Division.

scant help in the battle for forests. Because of thick ice, often blanketed in snow, tanks were roadbound, ducks in a shooting gallery for well-sited 88s. In Russia the Wehrmacht had developed antitank mines that worked in snow, so fields of mines awaited American armored forces that dared venture off the narrow roads. Only on the Siegfried Line were the Germans in better defensive positions. For the attack to cut off the base of the Bulge, the 101st were like Marines assaulting Japs in palm-tree bunkers on Tarawa—with deep fog, cold, and snow giving the defenders more advantage.

Model himself visited Houffalize to ensure that no matter how hard and heavily Patton attacked from Bastogne, he would not prevent extraction of the bulk of German forces from the shrinking Bulge. Model had accomplished similar feats, even more difficult ones, in Russia, and this time he had a shorter front manned by better and better-equipped divisions. He was said to have assured Hitler that as Bastogne had been for the Americans, so too would Houffalize be a vital hub held for as long as necessary by the Wehrmacht.

Spearheading Patton's drive, it was for the 101st to prove Model wrong, but with plenty of help. Their attacking zone was narrow, about five miles wide, pinched by the 17th Airborne and 11th Armored Divisions (though both were without combat experience) on the left, the 6th Armored on the right. It was the first time in the war that the Screaming Eagles' flanks were protected. Heavy-caliber artillery salvos of an entire corps supporting them made them flinch at first, much as the ground flinched as volley after outgoing volley seemed a redux of Bastogne in reverse.

On the Bastogne-Houffalize road, the 506th and 501st attacked in combination like left and right fists. The Currahees' first objective was to recover Foy and Noville, the hamlet and town from which they'd been ordered to retreat in the first days of Bastogne. Some of their dead were still there, frozen, it seemed, like the Snow Princess waiting for love to restore them. Foy was in a hollow; whoever controlled the hills could have it, and it changed hands innumerable times. To take those hills Blues set forth into the woods.

Albers recalls: "We hated to leave our foxholes. We'd been in 'em for a while, and it had been some job digging 'em deep in the frozen ground. Then we'd put down a layer of boughs, pine mattresses we called them. They'd get wet and we'd pile on another layer. Well, the layers got so high they were almost to ground level, so I guess it was time to leave.

"It was the most snafued attack I've ever been in. As soon as we started climbing through those woods we lost sight of each other. We couldn't make any noise or the krauts would hear us. All of I Company was following a compass azimuth. That's all we had to guide by, but no one except a couple of guys beside the compass man could see where he was going.

"We heard a Mauser. One round. The krauts are damn good snipers. One of 'em hit Harry Watson in the throat. He'd had his head shaved by a bullet in Normandy. He was still lucky, still alive, so two men dragged him back through the snow. It was ass deep. Captain Anderson chose the two strongest men because lugging anything extra, like a case of machine-gun ammo, made you stop and pant like somebody climbing Mount Everest. So the krauts got Harry but put three men out of action."

Sometimes shooting, sometimes being shot at, I Company was floundering, exhausted, and most of all lost. The worst of a bad situation was the cold, not so much now but what it would be later. During the wait to find direction and objectives they could squat down, their helmets dimples on the disturbed snow, wiggle their toes, and cup a cigarette, for it was still light, not much past noon. In three, definitely no more than four hours, I Company would have to find shelter before darkness, or else the cold would disable them more than a regiment of krauts.

Silently they removed snow from boughs and pushed it into canteens. After the melt from body heat, fifteen handfuls of snow would fill a canteen. There was time for that as they awaited a decision from the CO. In the thick forest Anderson had garbled radio contact with Third Battalion, but he knew that by heading east I Company would run into the Foy-Noville road. Better there than here, for sure. He asked for volunteers for a patrol, a few good men to go ahead and see what krauts might be on the road. Inspired by the grit of Sheeran, who had turned urine yellow and staggered from jaundice, Albers volunteered. If Sheeran could stay the course, everyone could.

"Yesterday we'd been watching 'em," Albers says. "Krauts were thick covering the road. I said, 'Sir, I'll go down that road whistling "The Star-Spangled Banner" if you want me to, but we know damn well they're there. They're there.' " Anderson was as spent as his men, more so for having their lives depend on his decisions. His decision this time was for I Company to swing over to the road. Fortuitously it arrived just in time to take part in a momentous push beyond Foy. That's what attacks had come to be called, pushes. The Americans would push for a while, then the Germans would push back and vice versa, back and forth in a Siberian landscape.

"We heard tanks coming from the right [south]. The sound scared us. Tanks moving always meant enemy. We parted the branches and looked at them. Shermans! Hell, says, Engelbrecht, let's get in on this."

His platoon wallowed through snow to parallel the tankers' flank. Turrets swiveled toward them, and luckily the tank commanders recognized the tatterdemalion, improvised white camouflage of the now famous "battered bastards of Bastogne." Artillery from both sides had destroyed Foy and cratered all the ground around it.

"We used the craters for cover. We yelled from one crater to another: 'You shoot, I'll move.' 'Okay.' We'd do that like leap-frogging. That's the way we advanced. Somewhere between Foy and Noville was this big barn. We wanted it real bad because it could be our shelter for the night."

The alternative was "tripods," a cluster of men putting arms around one another and leaning toward the center for mutual support. As profoundly exhausted as they were, they could sleep that way for minutes till their feet told them they had to move, which they would, regaining circulation, then re-forming tripods throughout the night.

"Tankers shot up the barn till we told them to stop. We didn't want it to catch fire and burn down. There were krauts in there, they said. Yeah, we know it, but we'll get 'em out. Engelbrecht had us shoot at the windows. Scare the hell out of 'em so they'll come out without a fight. Didn't know who was in there. If it was SS, they'd go down fighting. Under our covering fire a squad went up to the barn yelling and screaming. A kraut lieutenant dumps a sheet out. We're happy as hell, but Engelbrecht thinks it's a trick if they're SS. 'Who're we fighting?' he asks

Anderson. Latest intelligence is *Volksgrenadiers*—sort of the German national guard. They give up easy. Sure enough the lieutenant surrenders what's left of his platoon, three walking wounded and two 'mortals.' "

Now Engelbrecht's platoon, down to fifteen men, had the barn and ground around it, but he knew the Wehrmacht's S.O.P. was to counterattack as soon as they'd lost a position. So Dziepak set up his machine gun in the hayloft for a great field of fire. It was like the upstairs of the farmhouse in Holland but without thick stone walls. If an 88 hit at the level of the loft, it would fall and with it the squad's main weapon. Better put it at ground level. No, Albers argues, all he'll see is snow before he sees a potato masher. He prevails, and the machine gun stays in the loft.

As if by script the Germans came back in a counterattack, panzers supporting like artillery. The barn roof came off as if in a tornado. Damn, it's going to be colder without that roof, but no kraut is going to sleep here tonight. Tracers were added to Albers's machine-gun belts as a statement of strength: I Company owns this barn, and trespassers will be shot. The *Volksgrenadiers* backed off.

"The next morning we were feeling pretty good," Albers recalls. "Anderson had some pancakes sent up. They were frozen, felt like hubcaps. There wasn't any syrup, but some Belgian had soaked them with cognac. I've heard that's called crêpes suzette. What happened next is confused in my mind."

Albers was acting squad leader when G Company pulled out without notice on his flank. After leaving the barn, his squad was left hanging in no-man's-land, so short of men that single foxholes were more than twenty-five yards apart, within shouting distance but invisible from one another. German attack time was again twilight. There was much sudden shouting, grenades muffled by snow, a flurry of two-way fire, then silence except for the moaning wind.

The most dangerous approach in war, whether toward a friendly or enemy position, is at night. It was quiet over there, so either Albers's troopers, four of them, had held their own or krauts owned their foxholes. Albers investigated the next morning. The first thing he noticed was a bulge among the trees, a kraut silhouette. Easy to drill it, but it was so stationary, no condensed breath coming out of it. A frozen corpse from an earlier fight, Albers decided, and crept on. There was another snow-laden statue, this one American; it seemed his rifle pointed at him. No visible exhalations, so Albers continued silently.

One by one he found recently occupied foxholes, M-1 clips, expended shells in the snow, some blood around the foxholes and within grenade-range depressions in the snow, depressions containing krauts. Albers tore away white camouflage smocks; yes, there was the double lightning bolt of the SS on the collar. Forensically he looked for more evidence of what happened. The krauts hadn't removed their own corpses, so they certainly wouldn't have done so for American dead. Therefore Albers's four troopers, three of them rookies, must be prisoners. Indeed, there was an oval of tramped-down snow; easy to imagine it to be where the four had been herded together by the krauts and led away. A narrow trail through the snow led back toward German lines.

"I felt like a mother who'd lost my kids when the house burned down. A long time ago I could have been promoted to squad leader, but I liked being a machine gunner and didn't want to be responsible for other guys. Now I'd lost four . . . Jankoviac, Clever.

"I'd rather defend anytime, but I was glad when we started attacking again. The platoon was down to squad size. We were like the survivors of a shipwreck, sad and glad both. Sort of celebrating being alive because no one had a right to be, and because everything was moving forward. We could hear big outgoing shells headed for Houffalize. That was the divison objective, where we could stand down."

Where the artillery hit, lights went on like a pinball machine. Sink pressed his battalions to follow the glow. All the Currahees had to do was get up there and the game was over.

"The weather was clear, and P-47s were swarming like bees. They must have gotten new high-powered rockets. We'd see panzers flip into the air like toys. In Holland and up till then the 101st had been pretty much by itself. Now we felt the whole army and air corps with us. We had tanks alongside. We learned to work with 'em like a good basketball team. Troopers could see in all directions and pointed out targets. There was this 88 a tank commander couldn't pick out. We kept pointing, faster and faster because the 88 was turning toward his tank. We dove in the snow just as the tank gunner saw it and got off a round. He beat the kraut to the draw like in a Western movie. *Bang,* our shell goes out, *boom* on target. The 88's muzzle went down like a flat tire. We cheered and beat the side of the tank. But that was too close. One of our officers banged on the hatch and told the tank commander to get his #%*&^@! head out so he could see what we were spotting.

"The tankers liked the way we went out ahead of 'em with bazookas. They said no one else they'd worked with did that. Killing panzers was the tankers' main job, but with the end in sight we were going to get on to Houffalize with or without 'em. We were like rabid dogs. A tank battalion commander asked a 501st officer, 'Where do you get these men?' From a dog pound!

"Cyr, Sheeran, and I were leading, huffin' and puffin', heads down with 50-calibers outgoing overhead. Engelbrecht had just pulled some krauts out of their holes. He spoke German and was a great surrender maker. Germans are conditioned to take orders, and he'd yell orders at 'em as he charged. *'Raus! Raus!'* ['Out! Out!'], and up would come some krauts. Then he'd whack 'em in the ass with the stock of his tommy gun. *'Schnell! Schnell!'* ['Fast! Fast!'], and they run off to the rear with their hands up. Engelbrecht knew their ranks. If one of them knew something, he was on his back in the snow with a trooper knife at his throat. *Ja,* his battalion CP was over there! The three of us started that way. Cyr's knocked backwards. Sniper. The bullet hit his metal cigarette case. He's stunned but okay.

"The krauts were protecting that CP. We heard a big rumble. This Tiger Royal rolls out like a tyrannosaur. Our supporting tanks stop and take cover, but we took him on. I get a bazooka and hit him. Trouble is the Tiger Royal had chain-link fencing draped all over his hull. Someone else hits him with the same result. We peel off and wave our tanks up. Hell, their 90-millimeter don't do much more. The Tiger rules. Anderson must have been watching because in comes the air corps. That wasn't always good. With everything so mixed up it seemed we got plastered as often by air strikes as the krauts. This time a P-47 identifies the target and nicks it with rockets. The Tiger had enough. That whole action was like a video game. He pulled back and we moved into this CP bunker as big as my living room in Muskegon. It was hard to get us to attack anymore after the warmth of that bunker."

IN MARCH OF 1945 the 101st was back in Mourmelon. Word got around that some Currahees whose stalag had just been liberated were in a nearby hospital. Bullying the hospital staff, Albers's squad obtained the names. Among them were Jankoviac and Clever, whose capture had been recorded in the bloodied snow near Foy.

"We got their ward number, charged in there with muddy boots, told the head nurse to go to hell." They were going to see their buddies even if that meant the staff became patients in the hospital. "We looked around, went down the rows of beds. They all looked at us and we looked at them but didn't recognize anybody. Then one of them said, 'Ed!' "

Albers stared at him, but it still didn't register—Jankoviac, a buddy from Michigan. He was a skeleton, with hair like mutant crabgrass, lice bites that looked like smallpox. Next to him was Clever. He'd been a pretty big guy; now he was nothing. Their eyes were like goggles, bulging and watery. Albers could identify them only by their voices, raspy but still Currahee.

"I'd seen a lot of combat by then, but seeing them I knew I hadn't seen the worst of the war."

CHAPTER SEVENTEEN

GESTAPO VERSUS WEHRMACHT

THE CELL WAS ABOUT SIX FEET BY EIGHT, NO WINDOWS OR CAN, and it smelled like the last prisoner had died in there. Joe was shackled to the wall by a hasp, halfway between kneeling and standing, semiconscious and praying to die before they started in again. It was a prayer that reversed every value in his life, but he thinks God understood.

Overhead hung a grimy lightbulb that never went out; it reminded Joe of himself, weak and dim. At least once a day he was dragged upstairs, shackled in a chair, told to confess or be shot as a spy, then tortured till his screams became too hoarse to hear. The Germans doing this wore white shirts they managed to keep spotless despite spraying blood. Back in his cell, left without food or water, Joe would revive, hearing himself groan as if he were another person.

This went on for maybe four days. When he came to one time two men in Gestapo uniforms were bending over him. They gave him water and said they'd help do something for his dislocated shoulders.

"They picked me up. There was an almighty pain, then I passed out again. When I came to this time my arms were back in their sockets but the pain was out of control and I screamed and prayed out loud. They said in a couple of days it wouldn't hurt so much. I'm pretty sure they were Gestapo medics; their job was to keep me sane for the next session. They left me with scraps of black bread on the floor and a pan of water. I couldn't use my arms but crawled over and ate and drank just with my mouth."

Joe was not hoping or praying anymore, just cowering and shaking, trying not to think of the next time the cell door opened. There was nothing in his stomach, but he'd vomit bile whenever a guard walked by to peek in on him as part of a routine suicide watch. Intermittently between torture, memories came back like some substitute for hope: good memories like family gatherings in Muskegon, baseball and basketball games he'd done well in, the camaraderie at Toccoa and Camp Mackall, the good times with Bray and Vanderpool. It seemed Joe was reviewing his life, the best parts of it, in preparation to die. He was ready to go as if death would be his cherry jump and he was eager to get it over with; he would feel content if only he could die quickly.

In that state he was taken to a much bigger cell. It was like a hallucination. Quinn and Brewer, their faces the size of basketballs, were slumped in chairs, and a third one was for Joe. This was it, he was sure. They'd be given a last chance to confess, then, if lucky, get a bullet in the head. Okay, commence fire. He'd done his best, been true to his country, church, and family. He'd hold his head high when a Gestapo goon shot it. Joe had surrendered, surrendered everything, but only to God.

The hallucination continued. A Gestapo officer studied the three as he walked around smoking Joe's cigarettes while waiting for the goons who had originally captured them to arrive. Joe couldn't figure out why they needed to be present for the execution—German procedures and witness records, he supposed, or perhaps a mock trial.

The hallucination grew extreme when a German soldier stepped in, followed by a second, machine pistols across their chests, and stood at attention beside the door. Through swollen eyes Joe glanced at his buddies, tried to smile, and mumbled that they rated a firing squad.

The Gestapo group stepped back, pretending to ignore the soldiers. Joe became fascinated by the contrast in uniforms—black for the Gestapo, gray-green for the Wehrmacht—and gaped when they ended a brief conversation and started to look daggers at each other. In the tense silence he could hear Brewer wheezing through a broken nose. It seemed to Joe that there could only be a disagreement about who would execute the execution. He was thinking about some last words to tell them in German.

"Something like I regret having just one life to give for my country," Joe says. "A lot of Americans had already given theirs. I was ready to join their ranks on the other side of life.

"My German was pretty good in those days. Today I can't even order off a German menu. I understand the words, but they don't come out. But when you forced me back into that cell I understand what went on as if it had been in English."

A Wehrmacht lieutenant colonel strode in. He exchanged formal heel clicks and Heil Hitlers with the Gestapo officer. There was an unresolved point of protocol about who ranked whom. That struck Joe as very funny, and he started heaving in his chair. He looked over at Quinn and Brewer, but they didn't have any idea what was going on.

Essentially the colonel, with due respect, requested that the three prisoners be turned over to his custody. *Entschuldigung bitte aber nein,* said Gestapo ("Excuse me, please, but no"): they're admitted paratroopers, and where they were caught their mission could only be assassination and sabotage—typical jobs of spies—so, with equal respect, in the name of Himmler, the Wehrmacht's request must be denied and the spies retained.

Regretfully there is a contradiction, the colonel replied—these Amis have been confirmed as stalag escapees, so they could not be recent parachutists.

A clever Allied ruse, was Gestapo's answer; from the International Red Cross the OSS knew there were three paratrooper POWs named Beyrle, Brewer, and Quinn. It would be a simple matter to have IDs forged for their impersonators. Furthermore, Beyrle didn't even have Ami dog tags, so he will be executed first.

Unlikely, said Wehrmacht. From the Berliners they contacted you know that the three asked for nothing except help to escape. Does this sound like spies, assassins, or saboteurs trying to accomplish their mission? This brought a sniff from Gestapo—who indicated that he understood these matters much better—and assurance that further questioning would confirm the three to be dangerous spies. The colonel was invited to attend their interrogation.

Entschuldigung, but so far your thorough interrogation has resulted in little more than gradual execution. These men wore American uniforms. (They were presently stripped to their underwear.) Even if they had parachuted over Berlin, they are protected by the Geneva Conventions like the Allied bomber crews.

It surprised and disappointed Gestapo that his counterpart was unfamiliar with Der Führer's "Commando Order"—in effect since the

Dieppe raid in 1942—which required immediate execution of behind-the-lines combatants like these three, no matter how they came to be behind the lines. If the colonel was reluctant to accept Heinrich Himmler's jurisdiction, there certainly could be no disagreement about Adolf Hitler's edict.

The lieutenant colonel looked at his watch, perhaps estimating what time remained between the daylight American bombings and the nighttime bombing by the British. Both, at this point in the war, were as certain as a chronometer.

Enough, he said; jurisdictional questions can be reexamined later. You have my personal assurance that these three will be available for further interrogation by the Gestapo when we hold them in maximum security. Here is my receipt for them. Please unshackle the prisoners from their chairs. The two Wehrmacht guards produced handcuffs so that the Gestapo irons could be left with their owners.

Hallucination now became a scene fantastic for its reality. The prisoners were his property, said Gestapo. The steam of shit, said Wehrmacht, then cooled off enough to promise that the three would never set foot outside a stalag again. Joe couldn't tell who had the upper hand. It went on like this:

GESTAPO: They're mine! You were not invited here. I must ask you to leave now.

WEHRMACHT: With pleasure, and with our prisoners.

GESTAPO: You defy the highest authorities in the Fatherland! This will be reported.

WEHRMACHT: Show them my receipt . . . and transfer these three to me.

GESTAPO: What nerve. You say they're yours but admit you lost them! Such laxity. No one escapes from the Gestapo. [Indeed, kriege escapes became so frequent toward the end of the war that Hitler turned over jurisdiction of the stalags from the armed forces to Himmler, who ordered recaptured escapees to be summarily shot.]

WEHRMACHT: With authority of the Abwehr I'm prepared to use force.

GESTAPO: Use it against the Bolshi! What soldiers are you who cannot defend the Fatherland's frontiers?

The lieutenant colonel was a veteran of fighting against the Bolshi (Bolsheviks), as the Russians were called, and limped from a serious wound they had inflicted. Gestapo's remark about defending the Fatherland incensed him. He unholstered a Luger. His guards brought their machine pistols to horizontal. The Gestapo goons were unarmed except for truncheons.

"Shoot 'em!" Joe yelled like a drunk. "*Mal halten!*" the colonel shouted back, and Joe shut up as Quinn glared at him through the puffed slits of his eyes, a silent message that there could be no worse time for Joe to display his Most Obvious Temper. Because the Wehrmacht had won. A goon came over and unshackled Joe from the chair, then a soldier cuffed his hands in back. He, Quinn, and Brewer were on their feet but so shaky they had to be helped into convict clothes. The Wehrmacht shoved them out the door as roughly as the Gestapo had shoved them in.

They were in a staff car, three Americans in back, the lieutenant colonel next to the driver, who drove slowly with just cat's-eyes blackout lights. The colonel was smoldering.

"I could tell he was pissed," Joe recollects, "mostly at the Gestapo, but also at us for causing all this trouble. I thought it would be a good idea to approach him. He'd been our 'rescuer' and would probably have a lot to do with what happened to us.

"The only lieutenant colonel I'd ever addressed was Wolverton. I thought about him when I very respectfully asked, in German, from the backseat if he had been in combat. He turned and smiled and began talking a mile a minute, faster than I could understand, but yes, he'd seen plenty of action while invading Russia. He wanted to know about Normandy. I told him a little and how I'd been hit by friendly fire while a prisoner. He nodded and said he'd lost most of a shin near the town of Demyansk, and the foot was frostbitten in the winter of 1941–42."

The colonel related that he was now commanding garrison troops in Berlin. Joe could tell he didn't think much of the job but that it sure beat fighting Russians in the snow for the third winter in a row.

"Where were you trying to go?" the colonel asked casually, "if you'd gotten out of Berlin?" The question caught Joe short, and he immediately felt compromised when he answered, "East." The colonel nodded slowly as the staff car crept around bomb craters and rubble. "We soldiers must do what we must do." Joe felt great respect for him, almost as great as his gratitude.

Somewhere in Berlin they arrived at a garrison headquarters. Here the three were not enemy celebrities the way they were with the Gestapo; instead they were a problem. The old question of categorizing paratroopers came up again, and initially Joe's destination was to be Luft Stalag III at Sagan, in kriege circles reputed to be a country club. Wherever he was to go, the Wehrmacht cleaned him up first, reviving the eradicated pleasure of just being alive.

There was a perfunctory interrogation. The three confessed that their escape had been from III-C (known in Berlin as Kustrin). For some reason the Wehrmacht knew they had escaped but not from where. Perhaps the III-C commandant had not reported it. Anyway, tough luck, Joe was informed, his destination is changed—no Luft stalag—Kustrin was where they'd be returned. It was a long ride bound and blindfolded, but in a way it was going home.

It had been a terrible attempt, though it had started so well. Luck and judgment had not been good, but the only thing in Joe's mind was that he was still alive.

"We'd survived the Gestapo," he says. "As little as I knew about them then, I still realized that not many of their prisoners ever did survive. God had saved me in the strangest way. He'd never left me, even in Gestapo headquarters, so there was nowhere on earth outside His presence. I'd screamed for Him to take me. He hadn't because He knew better. That was like a personal assurance that God would forever watch over me, and watch what I did too."

Rolling through the gate at III-C made them forget their gratitude. They sat in the staff car for a long time while the Berlin Wehrmacht officer chewed out the commandant, who immediately sentenced the three to thirty days in solitary confinement on bread and water. That was mild treatment compared with the Gestapo, but extreme cold had settled in Poland, likely to be fatal for anyone in their weak and broken condition, and the treatment could become worse if they were closely interrogated about the escape.

On the grain train they had decided, if captured, to deny anything about the escape committee, the middlemen in the bribe. Actually the three didn't know the name of the bought guard, so they couldn't identify him no matter what was done to them. That fact worried Joe a lot because their whole cover story revolved around an exclusively three-man escape. A skilled interrogator would immediately see that if there were only three, which of them bribed a guard?

Quinn, Brewer, and Joe were dumped in separate cells so they couldn't coordinate their stories, but spontaneously they came up with the same one: no one was bribed; they just took a chance in cutting the wire. Joe's interrogator didn't believe that but tossed him back in the cell. It was a cagelike box about five by six feet with straw on the floor and lice in the straw. Cold lice that were glad to have a warm body to infest. The box was shaped so that a man could sit but not lie down or stand up. At night the temperature was below zero, so he had to keep moving or freeze. Joe's thrashing for warmth slowly subsided; he began to experience delirium and lose feeling in his extremities.

Concurrently the psychic impact of the Gestapo ordeal began to probe into his mind like deepening shadows, the forecast of imminent death. Logic confirmed it: he was dying, indeed should have already been dead. But he refused to let the Gestapo of Prinz Albrecht Strasse kill him after they had had their chance. Joe began a retreat to an internal place where they could not touch him, where he was inaccessible to their cruelty.

"There was a 'skylight' about the size of an envelope above my head," Joe recounts. "There was so little sun it was hard to tell day from night except for the temperature. It didn't seem I could get through thirty days of this. The pain I'd gone through in Berlin had weakened me more than five Atlanta marches. It was like ice forming around a candle. It kept flickering. I saw how it melted wax and the ice would back up, but with more water the ice got thicker. I was watching all this in a dream that kept coming back, watching in a detached sort of way, the way I had watched the fight between the Gestapo and the Wehrmacht.

"God stayed with me. After serving half my sentence the cell door opened as it did for Paul in the Acts of the Apostles and a guard rousted me out. He pointed to a pan of warm water and told me to wash up. I stripped and was shivering but didn't mind as I rubbed off the grime and filth. He tossed me a set of underwear and a wool GI uniform with no markings. I was marched out of the punishment block, shoved into the old American compound, and that was that. I was assigned to a hut. Quinn and Brewer were already in other huts, acting as if nothing had happened."

What had happened was a visit by the Red Cross, one of their semi-annual inspections allowed by the Geneva Conventions. Records of the stalag bureaucracy revealed that the three were being punished in solitary for the offense of escaping. The Red Cross representative pointed out that escape was not a crime but rather a duty of POWs, citing chapter and verse from the Geneva Conventions. The commandant reluctantly conceded the point, so the three were released. The Red Cross visit had been postponed from October.

"If it had occurred then, we'd have had to complete our sentence. God stepped in once again. Whenever I'd called to Him like Job, He responded as if to say, 'Believe it!'

"Back in the compound, back in a hut, was a very strange experience. My countrymen treated me like a leper: they gave me extra care but also isolated me. Word came down from Coleman to discuss the escape with no one. I received special rations from the PX, but a kriege would accompany me whenever I left the hut. It was like a quarantine. I could understand why the escape committee had to be protected. I was no longer on that committee and not allowed to talk with them at first. I had trouble understanding why because we should be debriefed for information that could help future escapes."

From his new hut mates Joe learned why the virgin escape from III-C had been resented in some quarters. The morning after there had been a lockdown of the American compound. No one could leave his hut except for the latrine, roll call, and to pick up meals. The three were gone about two weeks, and the lockdown had continued till recapture. Some krieges fumed at how Joe had changed their lives for the worse. In a way he understood why. They'd had no vote on the committees that had approved and supported the escape plan, which resulted in collective punishment. True enough, Joe concedes, but then tries to remember a saying attributed to Colonel Ewell of the 101st: Though the U.S. Army is that of a democracy, the army itself is not a democracy.

"What I really couldn't understand was Quinn's and Brewer's attitude. They kept very much to themselves and away from me. They'd been assigned to different huts. Maybe I had something to do with our separation. I'd been the only one of us who'd had his shoulders dislocated. American medics came around to put hot compresses on them and gave me some ointment, which helped relieve the pain and swelling. Maybe Quinn and Brewer had not suffered quite as much from the Gestapo. Maybe they'd told more than I did. I never asked them and never knew. It wasn't something to talk about, even with your wife after the war."

Maybe they were told how Schultz came around and took Joe aside. He put an arm around his shoulder—Joe winced because it was still filled with pain—and counseled him like a father: "Joseph, be a good boy now. The war will be over soon, and you can go home to your family."

Slowly recriminations and suspicions faded as stalag life returned to normal and the three were debriefed about the escape. They were not much help in describing the surrounding area because it had been late evening when they got away, and a lot of memory had been erased by torture.

"III-C began to improve as RC parcels came in every other week. I was paired with a mucker, Johnson, the kriege who had safeguarded the cache of cigarettes I'd left behind. My 'will' was that if I didn't return, he was to get half and the other half go to the escape committee for however they wanted to use it. Their honesty was guaranteed because none of them smoked! Cigarettes kill people these days, but back then they saved a lot of lives.

"I was having nightmares when hut mates had to grab me in my bunk, but I felt much better as Thanksgiving approached. Only Americans celebrate it, but Coleman convinced the commandant that it would be good for everyone if this was allowed to be a special day. We krieges had little to be thankful for, the Germans less, and the Russians least of all, but we all had our hopes, and hopes are helped along by gratitude."

There were some kriege artists who did pictures of turkeys and Pilgrims. Schultz granted an advance IRC allowance of evaporated milk, canned corn, and corned beef. "Before you take this be aware that you'll have less food for Christmas," he told Coleman.

Those ingredients went into a kettle, where they were stirred, seasoned with mustard, and steeped. The soup-stew that came out was the best-flavored food Joe had tasted since capture. He was much more thankful than in England a year before when the Screaming Eagles had plump turkey, cranberry, stuffing, and all the trimmings.

Between Thanksgiving and Christmas kriege morale was up, the Germans' down. There was now a clandestine crystal set in the American compound, tuned to the BBC. Coleman sent around couriers, like confidential town criers, who memorized the news and delivered it to every hut. The news was all good. The Russians were coming on like an avalanche, and the Allies had breached the Siegfried Line in some places. Nothing but the Rhine and the Oder looked like major obstacles from here on out. Krieges started talking about a stalag reunion at Times Square this time next year.

Joe's morale improved with his recovering health but had setbacks whenever he saw cords of freeze-dried corpses carried out of the Russian compound. With the spring thaw they'd become the reason for the wavy earth pointed out by the Polish farmer in 1992.

"Dear God, how can we give thanks when there is mass murder going on right across the fence? What if they're Communists, not Christians—what does that matter? They're humans, God's children. Having gone through some suffering like theirs, I felt close to them. Hardly anyone else did, though when we got extra of anything there was a way to get it over the fence and we shared it with the Russians. But to us they were a different species, people to be pitied but not too much because to relate to them was hard on the emotions. We wanted to preserve our emotions like a stash of cigarettes. The easiest way was to make the Russians separate, almost the way the krauts did."

Christmas was coming along, and everyone looked forward to it, something like the old-time feast days in England. Krieges knew they'd hardly feast, but Christmas was something they had in common with the Germans.

To general surprise the Germans became arrogant and turned up their noses. The commandant, with Schultz nodding beside him, reminded Coleman that Thanksgiving had been the Americans' luxury so there would be nothing extra for Christmas. The clandestine crystal set soon explained the change of German attitude. It was Hitler's surprise offensive, the kickoff of the Battle of the Bulge.

"Suddenly there were truckloads of new POWs coming in. They went to the 'new' American compound. Remember it was only Normandy POWs in the 'old' compound of III-C. Every American who came in after that went to the 'new.' Physically the compounds were the same. The krauts were smart to separate us. We could have given the new guys some confidence and tips on how to survive and endure."

Joe was shocked at how the new POWs looked, and he didn't shock easily. They were young but not strong, battle-rattled and forlorn, blitzed. Immediately Coleman worked to establish contact with them, identify their key people, bring them on board. Schultz was alert to this effort and doubled the guard to prevent it, but before long messages were exchanged with the new guys. When trucks unloaded new POWs, Joe went to the fence looking for 101st patches. There were few, and no faces he recognized.

"The cold in the Ardennes actually helped us in Poland. Piles of winter gear came in with the new POWs. Schultz liked us old guys. I was able to add a layer of wool shirts and pants and make a thick pair of mittens and a warm stocking cap. Actually a kriege who had been a tailor made them in exchange for my last stock of cigarettes.

"Johnson, my mucker, provided the packs for that trade. My pre-escape 'will' turned over half my stash to him and he had rights to keep it, but he didn't. He is another face, another of God's children I should but can't remember to the point of regaining contact with him. I'm too old now. Too much life has happened since then. This is my thanks and tribute to him."

Initial German success in the Bulge changed something in Joe's outlook. The krauts were crowing. Their propaganda was saying that the Allies would break up. The BBC was saying that Montgomery would have things under control, but the krieges weren't believing it, not after Market-Garden.

With things going badly in the west, the Western prisoners—so the rumor went—would reverse status with the Russian POWs, whose army was still coming on hard from the east. When there's not much information, people in confinement can believe speculation like that. What they knew was that no status could be worse than that of Russian POWs.

"So Christmas was a big deflation for us, a big inflation for the krauts. The *fest* food didn't taste nearly as good as at Thanksgiving. Over at stalag headquarters we could hear German drinking songs. Around midnight they ended with 'Stille Nacht, Heilige Nacht.' It's like Beethoven. How could a German have written such music?

"It was the day after Christmas, and all through the huts only the rats were stirring, but so was I. Over at the fence I saw Quinn. I looked around for krauts. Couldn't see any except in the guard towers, so I went over to him. We had to be careful because if any of the three escapees were seen together, Schultz would investigate. He had some good human qualities, but he also had a job, which was to prevent escapes, especially after ours."

Joe and Quinn acted like tourists who didn't know each other, watching Niagara Falls. Ten yards apart and looking in different directions, they talked out the sides of their mouths. Quinn didn't like to look at the Russian compound, so they reversed views. How's Brewer? Joe asked.

Getting along. He wants out.

So do I.

The Bulge had affected all three of them. They decided to investigate possibilities.

"That was how our second plan was hatched. We knew it would be unsupported because the escape committee couldn't take another chance with us, but what we came up with did require the help of other krieges. Just thinking about escape again made us feel better about ourselves—sort of like a rodeo rider who has to get right back on a horse after he's bucked off. What we'd learned was that if this time we failed, we also died. The first thing we bartered for was small sharp shivs. We wouldn't be taken alive and tortured again. Knowing that calmed us. We were much less nervous planning our second escape than we were before the first.

"We started off by approaching a few krieges we trusted, offered them cigarette rewards for cooperation but were turned down. Only one of them told me that if we were crazy enough to try again, he'd help just so we would hurry up and get away or get killed and stop upsetting stalag life! I thanked him because we'd need whatever help we could get for any reason."

Fights between krieges broke out now and then, not big fights, just a few fisticuffs between men irritated over little things that in other settings wouldn't have mattered. Such fights didn't bother the Germans much; in fact they would watch for a while—it was something to relieve monotony—before breaking them up. A fairly big fight was needed for Joe's plan, something significant enough to get the fighters punished. It took a while to identify a kriege who would take that risk. Worse than that, if the fight turned out to be a distraction for an escape, the punishment would be much worse, surely a month in solitary.

"Luckily there was one guy, the one who wanted us gone, who'd take that risk after we explained what might happen. His nickname was Weasel, not a very popular animal and not a very popular guy either. The more Weasel thought about our plan, the more he liked it because there were a couple of guys he hated who always went around together. They were a pair of bullies, and Weasel was their favorite target. He was willing to get in a fight with them, even though he'd get beat up, so long as they were also punished by the krauts."

Weasel's cooperation was the best aspect of the plan; however, Brewer was afraid that a staged fight would make the Germans suspicious, that they'd sense something was fishy. No, Joe argued. Just talk with Weasel and you'll know that this will be a *very* authentic fight. To reassure Brewer, Quinn made Weasel a blackjack for which he was grateful even though using a weapon in the fight would probably mean harsher punishment.

"From my sketch of III-C you can see there was a fence between the exercise area of the old American compound and the Germans' administrative complex, which included the infirmary. After the Red Cross visit that saved us, the guards kept a stretcher at the gate in that fence; maybe the Geneva Conventions called for something like 'immediate first aid must be available.' Anyway, that stretcher was a key to our plan."

The other key was a farmer's wagon that serviced the German mess hall every afternoon around the time krieges were walking laps and milling around the exercise area. On Tuesday and Friday the wagon came into the outside gate with three huge barrels full of cabbage, turnips, or beets. Brewer had observed that when the wagon departed the barrels tipped a little, showing they were empty. Whether or not they were empty made every difference for the go-or-no-go decision. They *had* to be empty or nearly so because one of the three would be in each barrel.

"It was on a Tuesday in January 1945 that we put it to the touch again. Quinn, Brewer, and I were the foolhardy boys. We were relying on Schultz, not on his cooperation but on the reactions we expected from him. He was a humane man in an inhumane army. If we escaped, he'd catch hell. His army had created hell on earth, so it was no problem for us to see him go to hell. He had his job, we had ours.

"This is what happened. Brewer, who usually walked around the exercise area, started jogging. He sounded gung-ho, upbeat, so people would notice how he was putting out. Then he staggered and clutched his chest. Quinn and I ran over to him. Quinn had been watching where Schultz was and then yelled for the stretcher. Schultz took notice and ordered the guards to open the first gate so we could carry Brewer to the infirmary. Quinn and I ran over, grabbed the stretcher, and rolled Brewer onto it. The main infirmary was on the German side of the interior fence. The guards let us through the gate, and we headed right for the infirmary. Between there and the exterior fence we dumped Brewer out and the three of us hid in a crawl space. Just then, just as we'd asked, Weasel started a fight. This turned Schultz's attention from the medical emergency to the brawl that was the biggest one ever in III-C. We couldn't see it but we heard it, and it was more than we'd hoped. This was in late afternoon, it was nearly dark, and the guards in the towers were focused on the ruckus in the compound. Timing of everything could not have been better."

And indeed the wagon was where they'd hoped, with nothing on it except the three barrels—and they were empty. Just before the wagon rolled away they scrambled into them. Many tense minutes waiting to clear the stalag. The horse started up. Joe heard the driver—who had been a big question mark in the plan—cluck to the horse. Fortunately he had been away watching the fight and they were able to slip into the barrels without his noticing. Joe's barrel had carried beets. There was something about the dark red stains on the wood that made him think some blood would spill. The wagon was also moving faster than it had during previous weeks. The driver evidently wanted to get away from the guard towers that might open fire at the brawl.

Leaving III-C on the stone road, the wagon went down a small incline and also made a right turn. At top speed the left front wheel hit a pretty big stone. Joe felt the jar, then his barrel started to rock. He crouched down lower to stabilize it, but it tipped. The driver reined in. The barrels went over and crashed into a ditch. The three spilled out. The driver saw them and yelled. Bullets started cracking from the gate watchtower.

They were up, running zigzag into scrub pines. The rifle fire was joined by a machine gun. Bullets struck Brewer on Joe's left, Quinn on his right. The sound was like a hard slap. They'd agreed beforehand that if anyone was hit, the others shouldn't stop to help. So Joe ran on. He had a feeling that they would survive their wounds and be treated back at the stalag. Joe was anaerobic and couldn't think any more about them except that if he got away, it would be escaping for them as well as himself—the way he'd thought about Bray and Vanderpool when learning they'd been killed.

The next few hours were the most intense of his life, as adrenaline fueled his flight, and mind and muscle worked together as never before. There was a goal ahead. What exactly it would be, how far or how hard, didn't matter for now, but it was out there, up to Joe alone to reach, and within his reach.

Dogs had been the main concern for this phase of the escape plan. They were soon on his trail, big ones like Heinz. He heard them. They barked and snarled and yowled when they came upon Quinn and Brewer.

"My high school training as a miler came in handy here," Joe recollects. "While the dogs were making the most noise I gained some distance, maybe a quarter mile.

"What I wanted to find was a stream, and I did. It had a sheet of thin ice with fast water underneath. Big question. Break the ice and get my feet soaked and freezing, or cross the stream on rocks? Throwing off the scent was more important, so I stumbled down the stream for a good ways before jumping off to the side into a smaller stream, which after a hundred yards I left for solid ground.

"I could no longer hear dogs or see lights behind me. My feet were numb. I knew they were the most important part of my body at this point, so I took off the brogans, dried them as best I could, and massaged my feet off and on for the rest of the night. The experience in solitary was valuable that night. I had a good sense of what my body had gone through so far and what needed to be done to keep it going. Fuel, food was most important if I didn't already have frostbite. I had no idea where I'd find food."

What he found in the next few days was almost as good—barns with grain for fuel and hay for some warmth. Joe holed up in hay with at least a foot of it over his face for concealment.

He was in Poland, but the part that had been repopulated by Germans. There was sure to be a local alert for an escaped prisoner, so he never went near the scattered farmhouses. During that week Joe probably covered no more than thirty miles. Then he started to hear artillery fire, big thundering volleys way to the east.

"For me it sounded like a welcome from God."

HATRED

See how efficient it is,
how it keeps itself in shape—
our century's hatreds.
How easily it vaults the tallest obstacles.
How rapidly it pounces, tracks us down.

It is not like other feelings.
At once both older and younger.
It gives birth itself to the reasons
that give it life.
When it sleeps, it's never eternal rest.
And sleeplessness won't sap its strength; it feeds it.

. . . .

Gifted, diligent, hard-working.
Need we mention all the songs it has composed?
All the pages it has added to our history books?
All the human carpets it has spread
over countless city squares and football fields?
Let's face it:
Hatred knows how to make beauty.
The splendid fire-glow in midnight skies.
Magnificent bursting bombs in rosy dawns.
You can't deny the inspiring pathos of ruins
and a certain bawdy humor to be found
in the sturdy column jutting from their midst.

Hatred is a master of contrast—
between explosions and dead quiet,
red blood and white snow.
Above all, it never tires

of its leitmotif—the impeccable executioner
towering over its soiled victim.

It's always ready for new challenges.
If it has to wait awhile, it will.
They say it's blind?
It has a sniper's keen sight
and gazes unflinchingly at the future
as only it can.

WISŁAWA SZYMBORSKA

CHAPTER EIGHTEEN

AMERICANSKI TOVARISH!

Joe KEPT MOVING EAST TO THE THUNDER OF BIG GUNS, WHICH rumbled several times a day like a distant storm. The terrain was open farmland with clumps of trees stripped of branches for firewood. In the big snowfields any moving figure stood out, so most of his progress was at night. By day he piled up boughs, crawled under them, and tried to sleep while the cold kept waking him, a reminder to massage his feet. He traveled the dirt roads only when the moon was down. A frigid wind blew constantly, numbing his face till it felt like a board.

Joe kept expecting to come across bivouacs of Wehrmacht rear units. In England he'd been taught what they looked like because the D Night jump was supposed to land on top of them. Though it had only been seven months since he'd been there, England seemed very long ago, and what had changed completely since then was his ideas about capture: he'd be KIA before being a POW again, the reverse of his attitude in Normandy. Joe feels his attitude was right both times. This time, even more than beefsteaks and blankets, he wanted a firearm; and there must be some kraut out there who wouldn't need his after Joe found him in the dark.

But there were scant signs of the Wehrmacht. For days he'd eaten nothing but cold grain and was desperate to find some of their garbage. Now and then there was a truck driving on blackout, during the day some horse-drawn ammo wagons. Once or twice he'd seen a formation of light bombers way off in the distance, but otherwise the Red air force wasn't around and neither was the Luftwaffe. Normandy had been densely concentrated fighting on the land and in the air. Joe was learning about a different war on the Eastern Front.

German troops didn't leave stuff lying around like GIs do. Joe found a few apple cores, potato peels, and chicken bones—all frozen, petrified— and some empty ammo boxes, but that's all. His energy fuel tank read empty, and the pain echoes from the Gestapo affected his mind. Crossing snowfields, he scuffed his tracks. That started him laughing—the last thing the Germans would recognize were footprints of American brogans on the Eastern Front. Or maybe they'd think that Eisenhower was attacking them from the rear! He had periods of silly thoughts like that. In his mind a song reprised maddeningly: "Move it over, move it over, move it over. . . ." He couldn't remember the rest but imagined Bray jitterbugging to it.

When Joe slipped too far into thoughts like that, something caught him up. He'd sit down, bring his rational mind over like a passenger taking the wheel from a tipsy driver. He remembers thinking there was a dragnet trolling behind him from III-C. Did that make sense? he'd ask himself. Do I really need to continue watching my rear? It took a long time to register again that III-C was now more than thirty miles distant. What's more, the commandant wouldn't put out a long-range alert for an escapee—an admission that there had been an escape, and by a second-timer at that. Thus confirming the irrationality of such fear, Joe got up and pushed on, only to have to review it again hours later. Over and over he had to bring two internal voices together like focusing binoculars.

On his journey to the east there were fewer buildings to be seen. All were silent, without a light or chimney smoke. By the fifth day Joe knew he'd have to enter one of those buildings, get out of the wind, and beg, steal, or kill for some food. He trudged through a wide stretch of woods and came up to the edge of a clearing that opened into fields. Fences were all down, but no recent tire tracks led up to his target, a small stone farmhouse.

There was a sagging barn on the edge of the woods where he could watch for activity from the hayloft. He did for half a day, munching straw till it liquefied enough to swallow. In late afternoon a candle was lit on the bottom floor of the farmhouse.

He climbed down, left the barn, and checked around for commo wires leading into the house. Not finding any, he went right up to the door and knocked hard. After a while an old Silesian German and his wife opened it a crack. A few chickens were cackling, and hogs grunted weakly inside.

As he had with Kamerad, Joe frankly introduced himself as an American soldier who needed help. Through the crack he could tell the farmer was looking him over and realized Joe was different from anyone he had ever seen before. From back in the room his wife called innocently, "Are the Amis here already?"

Joe began sobbing with laughter. The farmer closed the door on him. It later reopened, with an answer that respectfully conveyed that he couldn't help and please go away because if Joe were found here, the couple would be shot. No they wouldn't, Joe said—the Russians are coming. You could hear their artillery. When they come, I'll help you if you help me now.

The couple spoke together, then the farmer told Joe it was the SS *Einsatzgruppen* he was worried about. They roamed the area looking for deserters and hanged them. That or worse would be the farmer's fate.

"I didn't understand his German completely, and he had trouble with mine, so they may have thought I was a deserter from the Wehrmacht, someone with a strange accent from another part of Germany.

"I started to just push my way in and grab a couple of chickens, but this couple was probably armed—I would have been in their situation. I went back to the loft for the night, too hungry and cold to sleep, but maybe I did because there were these weird dreams about people and places that were fantastic and ridiculous at the same time. I'd wake up and realize the dreams were crazy, but when I dozed off they'd come back. My rational mind was saying go away, but the dreams kept returning."

The next morning a few Russian artillery shells fell on the woods. As fog lifted like a curtain, from the loft Joe could see into open fields. Out there tiny figures formed into clusters. The Red Army at last! Behind them, artillery flashes. The figures joined with vehicles, which came on over the snow till they were less than a mile away. Then Joe could tell they were scout jeeps and half-tracks mixed with an infantry platoon. They were greeted by a little antitank fire, then some machine guns and small arms that didn't do much except spread out the clusters. Though this fire originated only a few hundred yards in front of him, Joe couldn't tell from where because the German positions were so well concealed and camouflaged.

A Russian vehicle hit a mine and puffed gray smoke. Poorly aimed shells were fired at the Wehrmacht positions on the wood line. A German antitank gun scored on a half-track, then Joe heard a few engines start up and saw some kraut infantry drop back into the forest. Their fire had dispersed and held up the Russians, but the Wehrmacht had had enough fighting for the morning. Joe felt they were conserving ammo.

He could hear shouted commands as Germans assembled and boarded vehicles. They hurried when artillery sprayed them with tree bursts. Splinters were also hitting Joe's roof and he wanted out of that loft, but this was too good to miss—like watching a damn good war movie. Though he admired how the outnumbered defenders were putting up a good fight, it was the Russians who were coming, whom he would have loved to rush out and meet. But Joe could have been mistaken for a German, so he dug down in the hay and continued to watch the farmhouse, sure the Russians would occupy it.

Ground fog was suspended between lifting and drifting. The Germans had used it to get away—the sounds of their vehicles were gone. From the other direction Joe heard a few engines tentatively advance and perhaps a gun turret swiveling. Otherwise an anticipatory silence hung like the fog, as if to mark the exchange of control over a small, unremembered farmstead on the Eastern Front. He will remember forever the first armed Russians he ever saw, moving warily and quietly to surround the farmhouse. He recognized parts of their uniforms though the shadowy forms of the infantry were bulky with winter gear, in huge contrast to their emaciated comrades back at Stalag III-C.

The squad leader hung a demolition charge on the doorknob and set it off while his men covered the door with submachine guns. Joe heard the farm couple's voices. The squad leader yelled, *"Kum frau!"* ("Come out, woman!"), and out they came with their hands up. They were asked if anyone else was around. Joe sensed the opportunity to come down at that time, but he didn't.

The squad leader told three of his men to investigate the house. As they entered, other Russians came up and started talking to the squad leader. Pretty soon a few scrawny chickens flew out followed by the three men herding some thin hogs. That made all the Russians happy, but right away they pleaded with the squad leader. The scene reminded Joe of how Currahees distributed the lord's brandy in England. The problem in Poland seemed to be that higher-ranking Russians would be here soon, so the livestock should disappear right now.

The squad leader thought about it, and what he decided satisfied his men. One of them was wounded slightly, one badly. They took care of each other—there were no medics—and were very close buddies. Both of them were less concerned with their wounds than with the livestock. The slightly wounded one found an axe by the woodpile. That settled what to do. With a nod from the squad leader the farmer and his wife were blasted with submachine guns, which cut them through the middle like a chainsaw. They recoiled against the wall of their house. Some viscera stuck and froze.

"The Russians stood there till the bodies stopped twitching," Joe recounts. "Then the axe man started chopping them up while the rest of the squad went off to find wood and build lean-tos. I think the reason they didn't occupy the house was because officers were sure to boot them out.

"From my uncle I knew something about butchering, and this Russian was an expert. A dozen chops, and in no time the German couple was food for the hogs they'd fed yesterday." That changed his thoughts about rushing into the Russians' arms. Maybe they were too heated up by the recent skirmish; two were wounded, maybe some had been killed. "You don't want to surprise soldiers, soldiers of any army, right after they've had casualties. I stayed in the loft and got down in the hay. I was colder and hungrier than ever but knew that night would be my last as a fugitive!"

During the night Joe heard tanks in the farmyard. They sounded strangely familiar, and indeed they were Sherman tanks—the first ones he'd seen since England. A generator went on out in the darkness. Its throb was the last thing he remembered until the next morning, when the farmhouse had become the command post of an armored unit. Some headquarters troops stayed around while the rest of the outfit pushed west.

Joe watched them carefully to pick the right time and man to approach. That would be the senior NCO, whose first order of the day was to slaughter the hogs. Ghoulishly, Joe wondered if there would be any parts of the two Germans left. There were, but just the bones picked clean. He waited till the Russians had cooked up some pork and had a good breakfast of back fat and *kasca*.

"I didn't want to disturb them during chow. When they were finished I took out my last pack of cigarettes—Lucky Strikes, pretty wet—and came out of the barn with my hands way up.

" '*Americanski tovarish!*' ['American comrade!'] I yelled, and walked toward them, keeping a big friendly smile on my face.

"Someone told me that must have been like ET meeting Martians. Nobody knew what was happening. I'd counted five Russians. Two of them raised their weapons; the others, including the NCO, just stared at me. The Russians are great starers. If they're interested in you, they'll just keep staring."

These Russians were very interested in Joe. They let him walk up as far as he wanted to go, which was about two arm's lengths from the NCO. Joe halted and repeated, *"Americanski tovarish,"* then the NCO gestured for him to be frisked. Joe had the Luckies in his left glove as a welcoming present. They didn't notice it, and Joe was allowed to put his hands down. He extended his right hand, the NCO decided to shake it, and then all the Russians started talking.

They examined Joe's GI overcoat with its American Eagle buttons. That seemed to convince them that he might really be an American. Joe gestured to his mouth and made chewing motions. Oh, sure—have some *kasca,* the grain-and-pork soup simmering in the farmer's iron kettle.

"I used one of his big bowls and refilled it many times. Then I was full, very tired and pretty happy. They were happy too when I passed around my Luckies. While they went about their business, I curled up warm in a corner. My nap wasn't very long. Officers had been sent for, and soon they arrived to check me out. The battalion commander rode in on a Sherman accompanied by her commissar.

"I was still slumped in a corner and didn't get up. In winter uniform

I couldn't tell that the CO was a woman. It was the commissar who spoke some English. He asked me who I was, and I slowly got to my feet. It was a relief to tell him my name, rank, and serial number, tell someone other than a German interrogator. The commissar asked me my unit, where and when I was captured, my hometown, and lots of other personal data. I was glad to give him all the answers—they would help inform my family of what had become of me. I had never received a single postcard from them, though they had sent many."

Joe lay around, washed up, kept eating and napping for the rest of the day. There were so many visitors he stopped noticing them, but it wasn't till the next day that the CO came around again. She had a name five syllables long, so Joe just called her by her rank, Major. Major was a stocky, weather-beaten officer who had the complete respect of her troops. She announced that Joe was to go to higher headquarters for processing. She opened her arms, looked at him hard, and hugged him harder, then said, *Proshchai tovarish* (Good-bye, comrade), for now he must leave for the rear.

For her farewell Major had not just the commissar but a translator too. Joe asked him what was going on. Well, he thought some American POWs had been liberated back in eastern Poland, so Joe would join them.

" 'But I wasn't a liberated POW,' I said. 'I was an escaped POW.'

" 'So what?'

" 'So I want to stay with this outfit.'

" 'You *do*? Why?'

" 'To fight the Nazis, fight them with you.' "

JOE'S ANSWER BROUGHT HIM an invitation to a summit meeting at the White House fifty years later where President Yeltsin presented him, and him alone, with four decorations: the Order of the Red Star, the Order of the Great Patriotic War, the Medal for Valor (Armored Forces), and the Russian equivalent of the Purple Heart. In the Rose Garden, as his family watched, Joe reciprocated with D Day crickets for Yeltsin and Clinton.

About fifty other veterans, of both nationalities, took part in the

V-E Day commemoration. Two were American women who had ferried aircraft from Alaska to Siberia during the war; a dozen more were truckers who delivered supplies to Russia from the Persian Gulf. The other Americans had taken part in the famous linkup of Eisenhower's and Zhukov's forces at the Elbe River.

The Russian vets were all émigrés by way of Israel. One of the conditions of their release from the USSR had been that they surrender any decorations won during World War II. Yeltsin promised return of their medals and restoration of honors.

In the Rose Garden that day Joe was uniquely recognized as being the only vet on either side to have *fought* against the Germans on both the Western and Eastern Fronts, so his decorations were not only more numerous but different from any of the other honorees'. The difference was that the medals he received were for combat—and were scarred and previously owned. This recycling was perplexing till the Russian attaché explained the reason:

In Soviet times veterans of the Great Patriotic War were buried, or more often cremated, in uniform with all their ribbons; but these ribbons represented their medals, which remained government property and were thus reclaimed by the state upon the recipient's death, to be recycled. What Joe received could have first been worn on the chest of a tanker in the battle of Kursk, an infantryman at Stalingrad, or a partisan in the Pripet Marshes. What was no doubt the product of callous bureaucratic policy instead became a mystical legacy, for no one who received a handed-down medal was to know who had won it by earlier heroism. In Joe's case and Joe's alone the legacy would remain in his family, not with the state, a state now interred in history with the ideology of communism.

WHEN MAJOR UNDERSTOOD that Joe was volunteering to serve in her battalion, she broke out the vodka. The previous night he'd had a little but cut with grapefruit juice. In the Red Army the two always came together with the rations. Major decreed that for this occasion, this celebration, there would be no grapefruit juice: vodka was to be taken neat. There was more alcohol and emotion in the farmhouse than Joe could take in. He remembers only that his name was resolved. What should he be called, now that Joe was in her outfit, Major asked. Just by my first name, he answered groggily, easy to remember because it was the same as Stalin's. Her troops thought that was a good sign, and canteen cups were bashed all around. From then on he was known as Yo.

His new comrades wanted to know why, why if Yo had a free ride to the rear did he want to stay at the front—where the average life expectancy for a junior sergeant in the Red Army was less than a week. There was no way to explain, so Joe used a single word: Nazi. The commissar corrected him. *Nazi* wasn't politically correct, it was an acronym for National Socialists. The Soviet Union had the only true socialists, so the right term for Germans and everything German was Hitlerite: Hitlerite cows, Hitlerite woods—the Oder River was Hitlerite. To take or destroy everything Hitlerite was the best reason in the world to fight. Joe had no trouble using the term, and felt that every German who did not fight Hitler was a Hitlerite.

"Celebrating my induction into Major's tank battalion, many of my new comrades got sloshed. Because of my weak condition I had a low tolerance for their 120-proof vodka. I'd pretend to drink but keep it in my mouth, then go out as if I had to pee and spit it out. I did that so many times they must have thought I had a very small bladder.

"During my induction artillery was prepping the Hitlerites, but what the hell, World War II could wait, said the translator. The longer we waited the longer we'd live! That called for another round. The vodka was so strong it made my nose run. Major ordered attention and announced that if Yo was now a fellow soldier, what kind should he be? She really knew which buttons to push. The tank drivers said I should be a driver—of course, because the tanks were made in Michigan! The gunners shouted no, an American should shoot American shells! The recon sergeants shouted louder that I should be a scout because I'd already been behind Hitlerite lines. A scout is what I wanted to be, what I thought I'd do best. I knew something about the terrain to the west and what the Hitlerites had there—not much, from what I'd seen.

"What I started off as was an infantryman on Major's tank. That was okay. I'd be a few feet from the CO, and a battalion commander usually doesn't get killed—unless he's Bob Wolverton. Now I wanted a weapon and asked for a tommy gun like the one I'd jumped into Normandy with. There were plenty of Lend-Lease tommy guns in Major's battalion, but no one wanted to give his up. So I was armed with a PPSh-41, the Russian submachine gun they'd used on the farm couple. It held seventy slugs in a drum. With some grenades to stuff in my overcoat pockets, I was ready to get back into the war."

Joe asked for a steel helmet but was told *nyet*, we are a tank battalion and wear pile caps, not helmets. They gave him one, a furry wool cap with ear flaps and rayon padding. His new buddies weren't quite sober when he was taken out to test-fire the PPSh-41. It was one of the simplest automatic weapons in the world, "GI-proof" it would have been called in the U.S. Army—with nothing that could be screwed up— only the trigger to pull (no safety), two parts to separate for cleaning, and they could be put back together only one way. Bullets went in the drum and came out the barrel. That was all there was to the PPSh-41, but the men who pulled its trigger had sent the Wehrmacht retreating a thousand miles—at the loss of a thousand Russian soldiers' lives per mile.*

For Joe's second basic training he shot up some trees, reloaded, and then climbed on deck as Major hopped inside her tank and the Sherman revved up and headed off into the woods through which he'd escaped. Major shouted a battle cry. The infantry answered with the strangest and hugest sound Joe has ever heard from human voices, something like a lion with indigestion. *Ohh-AH!*—about two seconds for the *Oh*, a half second for the *AH*. The cry gave him a jolt, a shiver, and the conviction that he sure wouldn't want to be a Hitlerite in a foxhole hearing that coming toward him, for it seemed to be the voice of a wrathful God warning how the war would end.

---

* At least 7.5 million Red Army soldiers were killed by Germans, a staggering figure but one Stalin could better afford (with no loss of sleep) than Hitler, who lost three-quarters of his three million military KIA on the Eastern Front. By comparison (in all theaters), the British Commonwealth lost a half million, the United States about 300,000. Allied and Axis civilian deaths surpassed military by a factor of at least six, bringing the approximate total for World War II to 90 million, roughly a tenth of the world's population in 1937, if the war is considered to have begun with Japan's invasion of China.

Whenever the battalion attacked, Major bellowed out her battle cry, answered by the troops with *Ohh-AH*. Joe very much wanted to understand what inspirational words set and sent them off. After a successful assault he asked the commissar, who chuckled and said, "Follow my ass as if you can have it!"

ALL JOE REMEMBERS of her battalion's designation is that it was in the 6th Guards Tank Army, part of the First Belorussian Front. Major commanded about five hundred of the seven million soldiers who had been struggling their way west for two years since the war turned around at Stalingrad, now a thousand miles to the rear. Casualties had been so horrific that there were few veterans with more than four months' service in her unit. Manpower was so scarce that half the troops were teenage and the tank crews women. This made a virtue of necessity, as Joe saw it, because he found women to be more mechanically adept than Russian men, who treated a tank like a horse—put in fuel, then ride it till it dies.

The First Belorussian Front, under overall command of Marshal Georgi Zhukov, had been refitting and regrouping east of Warsaw during the fall of 1944 while other Russian armies spilled into the Balkans. Zhukov's well-prepared attack from the Vistula to the Oder kicked off about two weeks before Joe's second escape from III-C. Major's battalion was on the straightest line and in the forefront of Stalin's drive for Berlin and to annihilate the Third Reich.

Opposing him were two million Wehrmacht frontline troops. In the west another million were doggedly holding out in Italy and along the Rhine. On all fronts the Germans were being bludgeoned down to their death throes yet still viciously capable of fulfilling Hitler's last wish, which was to kill and kill till the last German who could kill was killed himself.

Joe's comrades well understood what the rules were in this last inning of the war. He himself began to understand when watching the German couple become hog fodder. That didn't bother him at the time because he was looking forward to a reunion with the Gestapo in Berlin. Though only two words, *Berlin* and *Hitlerite*, were enough of a common language to bond him with his new battalion ("I used to be a Blue; now I was a Red!").

It took him a week to get an idea of how they operated. That skirmish he'd witnessed out in the farm fields involved Russian reconnaissance troops and vehicles. They'd been sent ahead to probe the Wehrmacht positions and, without support except for artillery, had been able to push back the Hitlerites. The recon troops were the best he saw. They didn't belong to Major but came from her regiment. They were mostly Slavs from western Russia and the Ukraine and looked like pictures of Russians Joe had seen.

Her tankers were also Slavs, but her infantry were Siberians, actually Mongols. They weren't the finest, but they were surely the hardiest soldiers Joe ever saw in any army. The Mongols were cannon fodder; they knew it and didn't seem to mind. The tankers had tanks to keep them warm and carry rations and shelter. The Mongols had what they carried on their backs and only themselves huddled together for warmth. The rations they received were usually frozen. They'd scrounge wood and make little fires.

"Most of them didn't even speak Russian, so we had something in common. There was nothing called the Third World then, but that's what they were, from a third world used by a dictator from a second world, which was a world apart from the first world I was brought up in. I couldn't imagine how these third-worlders could be so tough and never complain."

The Slavs had long since understood the Mongols' place and shrugged when Joe mentioned it. There was not much sympathy in the Red Army, least of all for the cannon fodder.

"Operations went like this," Joe explains. "Recon elements went out and found Hitlerite positions. If they could penetrate, they did, as they had near the farmhouse. If not, Major sent up her Mongol infantry. They could move fast over the ground, a lot faster than I could. They closed in like Indians, using every bit of cover and concealment. They're little guys, most of them five-footers, so they could really hide and scoot.

"The Mongols had no radios, so they couldn't tell Major what was going on. She had to sense it from the amount of incoming and outgoing fire. Major hung back and moved her tank around till she got an idea of what the Mongols had run up against. Then she decided where to attack. She always attacked; there was never a question of whether, only where. That's what her men expected, and that's when they started slugging vodka."

On only one occasion while Joe was with Major did her initial attack fail. She had two radios—out of a total of five in the whole battalion. In Third Battalion 506th, there were about sixty radios of various types. Americans need to talk to one another a lot during battle in order to adjust plans, tactics, and support. The Russians had only one of each. They could only change what they were doing very slowly. It was the difference between a speedboat and an ocean liner. They steamed ahead till they overran objectives or their plans proved drastically wrong.

One time Major's attack stalled. Her first radio was to communicate with her three company commanders, who described the situation. Joe had picked up a bit of Russian by then, and it sounded like a telephone conversation, as if the Hitlerites couldn't overhear. But they did overhear, and often it cost the Russians dearly.

With her second radio Major called for artillery and Katyusha rockets, the famous "Stalin organs" that screamed like banshees and terrorized the Hitlerites. She had to really make a pitch on the radio for this support; other units were in hot fights and needed it too. She called the artilleryman by his first name, not a call sign. She persuaded him, so before long a dozen 1934-model Ford trucks drove up and parked behind her tank.

"On each chassis was a rack of six-foot rockets with forty-pound warheads," Joe recalls. "When they salvoed it sounded like jets taking off next to my ear. Major's crew knew this was my first experience with Katyushas and had a good laugh as I held my head.

"We got into action almost every day but usually not much. I saw no Hitlerites to shoot at, not with my short-range submachine gun, and Major's tank fired only a few times. What the Hitlerites were doing was setting us up for their artillery. They must have had spotters concealed in the woods. Suddenly we'd get a shower of shells. The tanks would stop and we'd get under them, then the tanks scattered when the shelling stopped. It never went on for very long; the Wehrmacht must have been short of ammo. But this harassing fire was effective in making us stop and restart. We'd usually cover only a few miles a day.

"About an hour before dark we'd coil up for the night. At that time it was crouch-over cold—subzero with wind, a small wind, but it went through your clothes as if they weren't there. The tank engines had to be kept running or else they'd freeze up. So the most important supply from the rear was gas and arctic lubes, followed by vodka and rations. Mechanics would work a little on the tanks, then everyone bedded down in any shelter they could find. I'd heard the Russians had a great reputation as night fighters, but you couldn't prove it by this outfit. They had combat habits that generally worked, so they stuck with them, even though to me it was like a mob fighting an army.

"They were pushing the Wehrmacht back, and that's all that mattered. Because I was sometimes close to the radio I could tell that Major's commander didn't call often and never chewed her out for advancing too slowly. One time the battalion on our left got ahead of us by a couple of miles and asked for her to protect their flank. She said relax, we'd gone far enough for the day.

"Once a day Major let me look at her map, which showed the front lines. It was printed in the Russian alphabet, so the names meant nothing to me, but I sure was impressed by the map's scale. It showed half of Poland! It was as if the 506th, in a small part of Normandy, had used just the map of France! With maps like that, how Russian artillery ever hit a specific target is still a mystery to me. I think the artillery commander had to go up and look at it, estimate the distance from his guns, go back and adjust fire by trial and error. It was even worse for the Katyushas, which could barely hit a given acre on the first volley. The krauts understood this weakness. They'd keep us under fire and wouldn't withdraw till either the Mongols closed in or the artillery finally found its target.

"Our tanks fired line of sight over the Mongols. The translator noticed how interested I was in the Mongols and told me a joke: Did I know why the Siberians were picked to assault in front of tanks? Because the Russians were so tall they'd be hit in the head by the tanks' fire.

"I was always glad when the translator was around," Joe remembers. "My Russian was so little, and there were many things I wanted to learn from the troops and they wanted to learn from me. They were very generous with everything I could use but not with each other. Sometimes the translator was pulled back to regiment to interrogate Hitlerites that had been captured. Then the only person who could understand me was the commissar. I wasn't a favorite with him the way I was with the troops.

"Obviously he had to keep an eye on me. Though I was an ally I was also a capitalist. When I'd ask him questions, even simple questions, he always answered in a roundabout way as if considering what ulterior motive might be behind my question. Then I'd get a long spiel about how the people this or the people that, and the Siberians were perfectly equal to everyone else and were proud to do their bit for the good of the proletariat, the Motherland, et cetera. Something I've never figured out: the krauts always referred to their country as the Fatherland, the Russians as their Motherland. After a while I just gave up with the commissar. He sounded a lot like Goebbels.

"But the tankers kept coming around asking him to ask me questions. He didn't like too much of that, and it took a long time before I got the gist of the questions, which were things like how much did I make in my civilian job, did my father own a horse or have use of a tractor, how many families lived in my house, had I ever been to school, how much did coal cost? Almost every question connected some way with standards of living."

The commissar's main job was to keep the troops pumped up to fight the war. His constant theme was how foul and cruel the Hitlerites were, how they'd scorched the earth of Russia and depopulated it. Joe was probably his most interested listener because the troops did not need to hear about the Hitlerites—they knew them firsthand, not only on the battlefield but at home—yet sometimes tears would trickle down and freeze in their mustaches as they listened.

Twenty-five years later John Beyrle was studying at Leningrad University with help from a Muskegon County grant. When Joe visited him and met some Russians he found that the attitude toward Hitlerites had hardly changed at all. They'd killed about one out of every ten Russians alive at the start of World War II and caused terrible loss and suffering for the rest. In America many people have trouble remembering World War II. In Russia they can't and never will forget it.

"Day by day we were fighting the war together and winning it," Joe says. "Just the same I began to feel that they were treating me in a way that meant I was not really one of them. Something beyond our difficulty in communicating and difference in nationality.

"When we'd hit some resistance I'd head off toward it, but there'd always be some Russians who'd get ahead of me, get between me and incoming fire. It got so I couldn't get in a fight if I wanted to—and I did! They were protecting me. I didn't like it, but I couldn't let on. I didn't want to be the battalion mascot or the CO's pet. The way I worked out of that status was by helping tune and repair radios, my subspecialty at Fort Benning. Things happen for a reason in life. What I'd learned in Panama produced results in Poland, of all places."

Joe gained much respect for that but not as much as for his secondary specialty, demolitions. One day scouts came upon a huge tree the Hitlerites had cut down to block a road. Major's troops went to work on it with axes till Joe saw that an antitank mine had been uncovered in front of the tree. He asked if it could be disarmed. Sure, said Major, her battalion had been clearing mines for months. Joe shaped the explosive in a goat bladder, set it off with firing pins, and the tree blew apart, saving them an hour. "Okay, Yo!" was his congratulation. He was no longer the exotic mascot but now the radio-demolitions specialist of the battalion.

CHAPTER NINETEEN

BACK TO III-C

JOE HAD ESCAPED TOWARD THE SOUTHEAST. MAJOR'S ADVANCE started in the opposite direction, part of Zhukov's mighty push to the Oder, Berlin being just fifty miles beyond the western bank. Now that Joe was fully integrated into her battalion she released him to ride on other tanks, which she rotated on point every day. While he was with them in Poland, nearly all the battalion's casualties were from artillery and snipers, not firefights. Almost daily some Hitlerite infantry were captured but in numbers too small for Major to report to regiment. One time eight were found holed up in a root cellar. They were brought out, stripped of their boots and overcoats; they were being herded to the rear when Major's tank came along. She asked the Mongols where the hell they were going.

The answer was pretty lame. Like grade-schoolers caught smoking, the Mongols hadn't expected to be seen by Major. Their story was that the prisoners were being taken back for interrogation. This brought a laugh from the tankers—no one was interested in interrogating any-more, especially the likes of these miserable Hitlerites. Half of them were teenage or younger; the others looked like grandfathers. We don't bother to question this type, Major indicated, so why hadn't they been sent to Valhalla on the spot? she demanded to know.

"I wish I'd understood the reason the three Mongols gave. They were teenage too. There was no doubt the Hitlerites would be executed, but the Mongols apparently had something extra in store for them. Major didn't approve, and I heard submachine-gun fire as soon as her tank moved out.

"Snipers were the main problem as resistance began to wilt. Instead of a morale lift, my comrades became gloomy because a river was ahead, the Oder. So what, I said. We haven't fought a single tank. That's because the tanks are on the *other* side, Yo—that's the way the Hitlerites always fight."

They knew Joe by then. They could confide that rivers were sumps, trenches for Russian blood that must be filled before crossing. Between slugs of vodka they spoke of the Desna, the Dnieper, the Bresina, the Vistula. No soldier in the battalion now had survived them all, but the rivers were legacies, the equivalent of four Normandies. Now ahead lay the Oder, the last river. The Hitlerites were concentrated to defend it, their last stand before Berlin. Drinking was harder when Major got her orders to move up to cross.

"Whatever I said through the translator got around quickly," Joe recalls. "Drunk Russians I'd never met came up and said, 'Hey, I heard you want to see panzers? They're over there, Yo, don't worry.' They'd name off the five best tanks on the Eastern Front. Fifth was the Sherman. The first three were Hitlerite.

"As we were moving up, a recon squadron was pulling back from the Oder. A squadron at full strength would have about seven hundred troops and a hundred vehicles. We had priority on the road, so when they made way for us I got an idea of how many were left—less than a hundred guys and ten shot-up scout cars. Major found their commander to ask him about the situation on the river. The senior man left in the squadron was a twenty-year-old lieutenant. He was in deep shell shock. Eighty-eights had blown every one of his amphibious vehicles out of the water with their crews. He put his head on Major's shoulder; she stroked it like a mother and crooned to him in a soft voice. At times the Russians were very open with emotions like that. She gave him two bottles of vodka before he climbed off our tank."

Major called her regimental commander to report what she'd learned from the lieutenant. The colonel told her to take anyone she needed from the recon squadron even though he didn't command it. Major said she didn't want anybody—the survivors were too shaken, they would lower her battalion's morale. That's the way things usually worked in the Red Army, though: a shattered unit wasn't re-formed and given replacements, its survivors were just absorbed by any outfit who could grab them. It was as if the 506th, after heavy casualties in Normandy, had been dissolved and whoever was left distributed around understrength units.

"With the help of John in Russia I've tried to find out what happened to Major's battalion, but I'm afraid it was one of those units that was worn down to nothing then dropped from the Soviet books," Joe says.

"After what had happened to the recon squadron I expected to see ambulances taking their casualties to the rear. There were no ambulances. Ammo trucks on return trips evacuated the wounded. The dead were buried in mounds, not temporarily as in Normandy but buried forever. Their families were informed that their son had died in Poland. That was it. After the war each village was presented with a scroll of names who had been killed."

While Major was talking with her commander on the radio he gave her a pep talk. First Ukrainian Front, about fifty miles south, had encircled Breslau and crossed the upper Oder, where it was not so wide. That sounded like good news, but it wasn't because First Ukrainian Front was commanded by Marshal Konev, Zhukov's rival to take Berlin. The good news was that the Hitlerites were reinforcing on the Neisse River and would hold Konev up. What Zhukov needed now was a bridgehead over the lower Oder. First Belorussian Front was to get it for him and fast.

During that conversation Joe overheard a familiar word: Kustrin. The stone-walled town had been heavily fortified by Hitlerites and was now their only stronghold on the east bank. Major started smiling. The colonel had given her a warning order to turn north toward Kustrin, where there was still a bridge up across the Oder. Wipe out "the pocket of resistance" and seize the bridge.

"We didn't know it, but she really had no reason to smile," Joe said. "Kustrin held out till the last month of the war. I was already back in the U.S. when it finally fell. I read Russian losses had been staggering, and I'm sure they included many of Major's—of my—battalion."

AT THIS POINT BEGINS a chaotic and sometimes contradictory chronology involving the German fortress at Kustrin, Major's battalion, Joe, and the POWs at Stalag III-C. The senior American there, the Man of

Confidence, was Sergeant Leroy Coleman. As the Russians closed in, the III-C commandant received orders from Berlin to evacuate Western prisoners across the only remaining bridge at Kustrin. His Russian POWs were to be exterminated.

The commandant ordered Coleman to prepare for this move. In the all-enlisted-men stalag, there were two American officers, Captains Niggerman and Hendricks, the chaplain and doctor respectively, as allowed by the Geneva Conventions. Coleman realized that a finale was approaching. As the man in charge and not knowing if he'd survive, Coleman felt an obligation to record the last days of III-C. He handwrote two copies and gave one to Sergeant William Wheeler. This copy found its way to Sergeant Henson of the 101st from the "new" American compound and by way of him reached Joe after the war.

Tech. Sgt. Leroy Coleman (MOC), Stalag 3-C.
As copied per his letter, 31 January 1945:

Strength in camp	1997
Commando [Coleman's staff housed outside the compound]	42
Canadians attached to camp but never seen	114
Total	2153

31 Jan. 1945. Awakened by Capt. Niggerman and told to be prepared to move everyone by 0730.

Delay ordered by Abwehr. 1045. Block III moved out after purposable [sic] delaying had been used. Block I followed. I with my staff was between the two blocks of prisoners. The direction we marched was north toward the east side of the Oder. Three kilometers up the road column was attacked by a Russian tank force.

Joe recalls: "I was on the seventh or eighth tank back. Major's was four in front of me. The two ahead of her opened fire with cannons and machine guns. It was the most sudden engagement I'd been in with the Russians. Usually the scouts started a fight. This time we had met some kraut vehicles and they shot back. We got the upper hand right away.

When my tank pulled up on line a kraut half-track and a scout vehicle were in flames. Behind them what looked like a mass of infantry had turned tail and fled. This wasn't like the krauts, and when I looked closer I could tell they weren't armed. I ran in front of the tanks, waved and shouted cease fire! Major yelled to get down. I yelled back, '*American-ski tovarish!*' "

COLEMAN:

We Americans were maybe mistaken for Hungarians (uniforms same color). Casualties conservative estimate 10 to 15 wounded. . . . Rest of POW column turned back to stalag. Ten minutes after arrival German officers demanded I move men out again in direction of Kustrin. I refused, saying we were safer in the stalag trenches.

Consultation held among a German major and two captains. They threatened to fire heavy artillery if we didn't move. I wouldn't do it. Asked for five minutes to talk this over with Cpt. Hendricks. His answer was the same as mine.

A German captain came up with more guards and forced us out of the compound. We were to go back toward Kustrin. This time we were cut off by Russians coming from another direction. Column returned in an orderly retreat to the stalag. No casualties this time. In the confusion about a quarter of the POW's escaped to the east.

With us six Germans re-entered the stalag minus weapons. I ordered Sgt. Fernechuck to separate them and be put in a room. When we were liberated they were turned over to the Russians who immediately killed them. The Russians put guards around the compounds to prevent looting. No food was issued but plenty of Red Cross parcels liberated.

1 FEB. 1945
Men continued to dig in and pile dirt against the barracks. German planes were strafing the roads. Russians promised to evacu-

ate us as soon as possible. Water is limited. Last German bomber of the day dropped butterfly bombs killing Sgt. Calhoun and Hall. Others were wounded. German snipers hit some Russian POW's who are kept in their compound just as we are.

2 FEB.

From 0100 till daylight heavy 88 fire from the Oder against Russian attack. Larger caliber artillery hit close to stalag. Everyone stayed in shelters. Roads dive bombed (Stukas) from 2 to 5 miles away as Russians build up to cross Oder. 120 cans of milk collected and given to Russian POW's. Men tried to dig up potatos in the fields but turned back by snipers. Wounded placed in stone barrack.

3 FEB.

A clear and sunny day. Food committee formed and collected 10 large barrels of sauerkraut, one complete cow, 600 lbs of turnips. 3 live cows held in reserve.

Cooking done at night because of planes overhead. Stukas out in force, 30 dive bombers for 2 hours. At some point 3 to 5 miles up the road a terrific concussion, probably Russian ammo dump. A great surprise—formation of flying forts overhead at noon. One was knocked down.

Received ½ hour notice from Russians that stalag was to be evacuated at 1700. Men unable to march are left in Russian Lazerett (Hospital). Two aid men and an interpreter left with them.

Auf wiedersehen 3-C!

Joe remembers: "So it was on 31 January that my battalion fired on the column of POWs. I begged Major to head in their direction. She was more than willing. The terrain began to look familiar. Pretty soon we came upon the railroad tracks from Breslau. I told her there would be a stone road pretty soon leading to the stalag. She decided to approach it from the woods and put Mongols out front to find the road for her tanks. The Russians were pumped up when they learned that this time they would hit a fixed position where the Hitlerites could not just fire some artillery and fade away. *Ohh-ah*, they started yelling as we went through the woods.

"We heard fire along the Mongol line up ahead. German small arms answered. I told Major this was probably from watchtowers. Then the Mongols were held up by barbed wire. They'd reached the outer fence of III-C.

"Major's tanks were now jammed on the stone road, just the way the Polish farmer told me he'd seen them when he was a boy. She asked me if the road led into the camp. Yes, I said, right to the main gate.

" 'Follow my ass!'

"I had to scramble back to a tank as Major roared off in the lead. I managed to tell her please don't use cannons, the camp guards don't have any antitank weapons and POWs could be killed. Major swore at me, said she'd use whatever was needed, but okay, she'd first try to batter her way in.

"That's just what happened. Four tanks back I made the turn that had dumped me out of the beet barrel a month ago. The main gate was down. Three tanks were churning around the kraut administrative area, machine-gunning every building. Their treads were full of barbed wire from crashing through the gate and fence. Other tanks were using their cannons to knock down the watchtowers. A few krauts tried to climb down and surrender, but Major's battalion was not taking any prisoners today.

"I jumped off my tank. The American compound looked abandoned, and the fence Brewer and Quinn had cut on our first escape was still up. Unless Major decided to knock down that fence, I'd just check out the Hitlerite part of the stalag. I remembered Schultz and where his little house was. He was there, on his back, eyes open, bloating from a stomach full of lead. I shed some tears for Schultz, did it alone because the Russians might misunderstand. If he hadn't been in Hitler's army, we could have been good friends. He'll be someone I'll look up when I soar."

Near Schultz was a woman facedown, no doubt his wife. At least she hadn't been raped, from what Joe could see. Later he mentioned this to a Russian buddy, who was offended: yes, rape was common but not with frontline troops like Major's battalion. It was the rear echelons who did that sort of thing. He'd seen too much of Hitlerite rapes and mutilations to do it himself.

As soon as the shooting let up Joe heard a long wail. It came from the Russian compound, a pitiful but joyful sound. Russian POWs began to come out of the ground. Major's men were frozen by the sight. Slowly then faster the risen POWs massed like a throng of stick figures. On Major's command a tank crashed down part of the fence.

"The POWs stumbled toward us like ghosts from hell. I was probably less stunned than anyone because I knew how they'd been suffering and dying. The commissar rushed over to Major. They had an argument, which he won. The POWs were pushed back through the hole in the fence. They obeyed that order, but Major's men rushed through to join them despite the commissar's protests."

Joe learned that all POWs were suspect in the Red Army. When the USSR was being overrun, soldiers surrendered by the hundreds of thousands, not knowing what Hitlerites were like. To discourage surrender, Stalin put out a policy to punish family members of POWs. "It took a brave man to be a coward," a Russian buddy told Joe. That was early in the war, but Major's commissar was still following policy. Her troops were not, at least not at III-C, from what Joe saw.

"All kraut rations were rounded up and taken into the POW compound. Belorussian troops found Belorussian POWs, Mongols found Mongols. They hugged like lovers and rolled around together for a long time. After that the POWs were lined up in ranks. A soldier gave a vodka bottle to the first POW. He took a slug and passed it to his left for the next man. Each POW sort of reeled back after his slug, but the discipline was perfect: one man, one slug, then pass the bottle on. The Russians had another name for vodka, which translated 'my friend.' It was as if each slug was an embrace from the closest friend the POW ever had."

Like everyone but the commissar, Joe was overcome by it all while he leaned against a fence post. It was like going from one vision to another when someone nudged him to look over at the American compound, which had seemed abandoned. Figures were starting to emerge there too, much stronger, many fewer, more cautiously.

What Joe saw corresponds to what Coleman recounts on the dates January 31–February 1, during which time the American krieges had been forced twice to march from III-C toward Kustrin, each attempt being turned back by the Red Army. Those present when the stalag was liberated were about half the number in camp on January 30.

"They'd look over at the Russians, then the Russian POWs. I rushed to the American fence and started yelling, 'Hey, it's me, Beyrle!' I took off my pile cap so they'd recognize me." They gawked and talked, then came over like they couldn't quite believe it.

" 'What are you doing over there, Joe?'

" 'I'm with the Russians!' I told them, holding up my PPSh-41.

" 'Can you get us out of here?'

" 'You're free! You're liberated!' They still didn't believe it. 'Is Brewer here? Quinn?'

" 'Yeah,' someone murmured, 'right over there.' " He pointed to the exercise yard. In the corner were two wooden crosses.

In shock, Joe asked about his mucker Johnson. No one knew, so he may have gotten away during one of the marches and countermarches yesterday. Yesterday. What a different day that was. Joe couldn't tell his compatriots when they'd be released. That was up to the Russians, who had their own priorities. He was pulled away by Major's first sergeant, who was greatly agitated.

Joe was taken by the hand and double-timed to stalag headquarters. Major, with some of her staff and company commanders, was pacing around the commandant's office. She had let two guards live long enough to show her where it was. The guards were now dead on the floor, their blood still flowing. Major looked at Joe impatiently, as if he had been playing hooky. Her order was, "Yo, open this vault!"

"What she was talking about was an iron wall safe the size of a walk-in closet. From where I'll never know she handed me eight pounds of nitro starch, American nitro starch the same as we'd used at Fort Benning. 'Enough?' I patted her hand and asked everyone to leave the room. The commissar didn't want to go. I said, Okay, you can light the fuse. He left.

"With the nitro starch were blasting caps and cords. All I had to do was prime the charges. 'Sergeant Lincewitz, be with me now,' I prayed, then set things up. I was conservative on the size of the charges, figuring to use more if the heavy door didn't blow open or hung up.

"I got behind the commandant's heavy desk and lit the fuses

bunched in my hand. As they burned down I could hear Russians stomping around like they couldn't wait to get in the room. 'Fire in the hole!' I yelled, though I'm sure they didn't know what that meant. *Boom.* Nothing very big, not too loud or shattering. 'Be clever in doing the Lord's work,' the sisters had taught me."

Through a cloud of smoke Joe saw the safe door hanging open like Ali Baba's cave.

After the explosion, shouting increased outside the office. Joe rushed to the door, said he was okay but had a little more to do, slammed it, entered the safe, and looked around. Papers and paper currency were scattered everywhere.

"Instead of the money—I'd be living in Monte Carlo now instead of Muskegon—I went for the papers first, papers and photos. The efficient krauts had every kriege's file listed alphabetically. So mine was near the top: my XII-A mug shot and the krauts' record of my POW life, including escapes."

Joe hardly noticed the Russians rushing in. Except for the commissar they cared nothing for records, only the watches, jewelry, and cameras that had once belonged to POWs, and money. Blowing around were reichsmarks, rubles, sterling, Swiss francs, greenback dollars, and many currencies Joe had never seen. He liberated two pocketsful of two-digit dollars.

Major grabbed his head, pulled it back, and planted a big wet kiss on his lips. Yo had come through, justified her faith in him. *Ohh-ah!* her first sergeant agreed. She ordered the currency shoved into a big mail satchel before the commissar could intervene.

Major radioed the regimental commander, said the situation at III-C was under control, so her battalion was ready for its next mission. That's the spirit, the colonel said, and gave her one—move on to Kustrin at once. They pulled out before Joe could say good-bye to the Americans, pulled out on Major's tank, which he guessed held about $200,000 in various denominations. Major threw out several cannon rounds to make room for the money satchel in her ammo rack.

As she rumbled away from III-C the second echelon of Russian troops took over and began evacuating the American POWs east. They ended up in Odessa, as Joe eventually did, but first they were used as hostages.

An army of Soviet defectors, mostly cossacks under General Vlasov, had been formed by the Germans when their own manpower ran short. Vlasov recruited in stalags where a huge number of Russians volunteered, first because nothing could be worse than being a Russian POW, and second because they hated Stalin more than Hitler. It's still debated today which dictator killed more Russians, but the nod should go to Stalin because he worked at it many more years, before and after the war.

As secrets of World War II have come out, one was that Stalin told the Allies that if they wanted their own POWs back, they'd have to turn over Vlasov's army, which had surrendered in the west. Eisenhower acquiesced in what must have been his most terrible choice.

FOR A FEW DAYS after liberating III-C the only resistance encountered by Major's battalion was from snipers. She hated snipers, probably because they didn't shoot the first Russian they saw—they waited patiently and bravely to pick off leaders. The Germans knew that without leaders the Russians floundered, especially when attacking. Except in a firefight Major always stood halfway out of the turret, so she was an obvious sniper target and knew it.

If a Mongol brought in the rifle of a sniper he'd killed—that was very rare—she rewarded him with a tank ride for the rest of the day. Joe saw one of those rifles, a Mauser, with a scope that had the best optics he's ever seen. The Japanese were famous for their snipers, but the Germans, on their record, were much better, the best snipers in the war.

It was "very unpublicized," Joe says, "but just a few could hold up a large number of Russians. Lord knows the Russians were brave, but they had to have a target to be brave against. Snipers never gave them a target.

"I haven't mentioned the weather, but it was our worst enemy. Not a lot of snow but very, very cold, below zero, and the wind felt like being sandblasted with ice. The doctors today consider my feet frostbitten, though I have all my toes. I know they're still with me because they become very painful at times. When there are cold snaps in Muskegon I elevate my feet on the La-Z-Boy; it has a vibrator, which helps. Frostbite didn't happen at one place; it was a combination of my time in solitary, the freezing during my escape across Poland, then with the Russians."

Joe guarded against the cold as they did, by wearing layers of cotton and wrapping strips of burlap around his brogans. Everyone's antifreeze was vodka. Alcohol draws blood to the center of the body, leaving the extremities more vulnerable to frostbite. That didn't matter. The Russian attitude was if you feel warmer, you are warmer. Joe had a drinking problem for a while after the war. It started with the Russians.

"On our way to the Oder we swept snipers aside and just accepted the casualties they caused. Berlin was just one more river away. Berlin was now the war cry. Hitlerite buildings were overrun with gusto because there was often something to scrounge inside—apples, beets, sometimes clothing. Anything wool or fur we could use, to stuff in our socks, pile on our head, or wrap around our ears. My buddies told me these were great pickings. When the Hitlerites were retreating across Russia and eastern Poland, they took or destroyed everything, completely scorched the earth. Now that we were in the part of Poland that had been repopulated by Germans, they must have persuaded the Wehrmacht to leave them with something, things we were happy to liberate."

This period after III-C was a calm before the storm on the Oder. At night before chow there were rounds of toasts, to the Motherland, to Stalin, Churchill, Roosevelt, Lend-Lease, to Sherman tanks, Dodge and Studebaker trucks. To Detroit, Michigan, too, because they thought that's where all American vehicles came from. Actually the Studebakers were manufactured in Indiana, but Joe never said so. He'd get up, urged to every night, and loudly sound off with the Notre Dame fight song.

Joe didn't know all the words, which didn't matter because the Russians didn't know any. What they wanted was for him to da-da-da the tune. Before long they could too, and much better. Many of them had wonderful voices and made tremendous harmonies. Polish forests filled with a stirringly wordless version of "Wake Up the Echoes."

"These things I remember," Joe says. "They are among the last of my memories with Major's battalion. I expected to be one of her casualties. It was like a premonition."

The Hitlerites were stiffening around Kustrin. The Luftwaffe made frequent appearances. Major knew this was serious because, before Joe joined her battalion, German planes had been committed only at crucial points when a large Wehrmacht force was in deep trouble. The Germans were not in such a tactical situation now. They had shortened their lines and were concentrated, reinforced, and well supplied to stop Zhukov at the Oder. The Luftwaffe overhead now meant the last hand of the war was being dealt and it was showdown.

"We started losing a tank and ten men per day. Through a snowfield the platoon I was with came up on a wood line where there was a nasty, well-prepared position with a machine gun and some *Panzerfausts*. The krauts had let us get pretty close; usually they used long-range fire to make us stop and disperse. This time it was more like an ambush. The Mongols got down and crawled up to grenade range, but the Germans concentrated on the tanks behind them. The one in front of me lost a tread to a *Panzerfaust*. The crew kept fighting with its machine gun till another antitank round hit the turret where it joined the hull.

"A damn good shot from about fifty yards, and it finished that tank. It was smoking and could blow up with all its ammo inside, but I felt that if I could get up behind it, it would give me good cover to spray the Hitlerite position. I crawled up along the tank's track in the snow. There was plenty of fire going back and forth, and I wasn't noticed.

"As I leaned on the hull to commence fire I heard the driver dying inside. That was horrible, and I shot off a whole drum in two bursts, screaming in English as I did. Maybe the krauts wondered which front they were on! They started sending fire at me, and that helped the Mongols close in on them. Then there were plenty of screams and yells on both sides. These were die-hard SS troops, and we made sure they died hard. Some flamethrowers came up from the rear. Their nickname was wiener roasters. They weren't needed this time—the Mongols had done the job without them—but the flamethrowers wanted to participate, so they finished off the wounded. For disease control it was normal to cremate the dead. So what if these Hitlerites weren't quite dead?

"My last morning with the battalion was clear, dry, cold but sunny. By normal rotation I was back on Major's tank. As usual we moved out at dawn. A Sherman makes a lot of noise. I couldn't hear anything but noticed the infantry scatter. Then there was a high whine. A flight of Stukas dove down from the east, out of the rising sun. I saw the bombs grow larger; that's the last thing I saw or remembered for a while."

A bomb blew Joe off the tank. He woke up in a ditch with a medic bending over him. Major was observing with her hands on hips. He'd taken a piece of shrapnel in the groin. The medic was packing the wound with snow. Joe had also been hit in the right knee but didn't realize it because the groin wound was so painful, the worst pain since Berlin. When the medic turned back Joe's overcoat, blood gushed out. When Major saw that she shaded her eyes. My God, he thought, she must have seen much worse than this, or else I'm about to die.

Major had lost her husband at Demyansk, in the same battle that the Wehrmacht lieutenant colonel who saved Joe from the Gestapo had lost most of his leg. Joe was in shock but also shocked that she was making a scene over him. She bent down and said something like Schultz had told him: go home now to your family; the war will be over. *Proshchai tovarish.*

Joe managed a salute, but she was jogging back to her tank. In the turret Major turned to look at him before yelling her war cry. It sounded different. Her eyes were also swimming.

"Our time together had been brief but like no other I've ever heard of. She felt it, I felt it, and we stared at each other as we both realized it. Of all the people who may have survived World War II, I wish I knew if she is still alive. And if she is, I'd go to Russia just to see her—my major, my CO, my second Wolverton—who was a woman.

"Her infantry was advancing as I was put on a stretcher. Some gave me the V for victory and shouted, 'Berlin!' They must have known I couldn't go with them but pretended I would. It was thirty-seven years before I reached Berlin, but at least I was alive to do it. Very few of them, I'm afraid, ever got there."

When presented forecasts of the cost to crush the heart of the Third Reich in its capital, Eisenhower set aside a plan to drop the 101st on the outskirts of the city, thereby giving over the honor and horror of capturing Berlin to Zhukov. Starting from their attack across the Oder, a quarter-million Russians died to take Berlin, about the same number the Germans lost at Stalingrad—and nearly the total of American dead in World War II.

"SO I'D NOW LIKE to salute and say, *Proshchai tovarish.* You took it to the end. More than anyone else you won the war."

And with it, Joe's heart.

CHAPTER TWENTY

EVERYONE IN HELL IS GRINNING

I'D HAD MY SHARE OF PAIN IN THIS WAR. I WAS RUNNING OUT OF whatever it takes to deal with pain. You have to take it because there's nothing to do about it, but on top of that you feel the reserve tank going dry. Then you have to accept that too. Accepting that is accepting death, whether you're ready or not. Now I didn't feel I was ready anymore—not like Berlin when I was ready to take a bullet in the head. The difference was being free again, a soldier with a weapon and a lot to live for, including revenge. My battalion took revenge the way they took vodka. It was something like compensation. It had kept my new buddies going, right out there where death was facing them across the Oder."

It was infuriating that he could no longer take revenge, the vodka of a soldier's soul. Now wounded worse than ever before, Joe watched himself slipping toward a final weakness and nadir of the psyche. What he saw was his young but much tried body going to the rear: in one of myriad trickles of casualties that became streams, then a river, filtering through eddies, many men dying, fewer continuing, all stopping here or there with Halloween masks of pain, body parts grotesquely mutilated, gasping voices heralding premature death for boys sucked down by the whirlpool of pitiless war between two pitiless tyrants. Like an oddly colored leaf, he was being caught in that vortex, but unlike the Russians he was not prepared to go gentle. And he didn't feel justified to go. As back at the prison farmhouse at St. Côme-du-Mont, there were so many other wounded worse off than he.

Somewhere behind the front, Joe was pulled out of the flow when his medics indicated there were certain Russians nearby who wanted to speak with him. They were a unique group of about a hundred technical officers and NCOs who had been following the advance but hadn't done any fighting. To Joe that sounded like a good outfit to be with.

He asked them who they were, and after a little hesitation they didn't mind revealing it was a rocket research unit. Some of them spoke English because they were scientists in uniform.

To Joe, rockets meant Katyushas, but the scientists just smiled when he said so. Their goal was not Berlin but a town about a hundred miles north of there, Peenemünde, on the Baltic Sea, where V-2 guided missiles were tested before being launched against England. Peenemünde was second only to Berlin in Stalin's priorities. This unit lived well and bragged how they could order generals around. Much later Joe learned that they succeeded in their mission of capturing most of the top German rocket scientists—Wernher von Braun was the exception—thus beginning the Soviet space and ICBM program, which became the biggest threat to the West in the cold war. Back in the States Joe's debriefers were most interested in this unit. He was the only American who ever had any contact with it.

"They were a threat to my health at the time!" Joe said. "I had bomb fragments in my groin and knee and should have been moved back immediately in medical channels. The rocket scientists must have known that I needed treatment, but they had this rare opportunity to talk to an American, so they detained me though I could tell they didn't feel really good about doing it. They compensated by giving me plenty of the all-purpose medicine: vodka. I had a ton of fever from infection and barely recall anything we talked about except American industry in general.

"They weren't interrogating me, they were just very curious about how things worked in a democracy. One scientist was pretty outspoken; he said minds couldn't do their best when they were under government control. I don't think the research unit had a commissar, but this guy's colleagues told him to keep such opinions to himself. Shut up, in other words, because there was no telling where 'Sergeant Yosef'—that's what they called me—would go or who I would speak to. They were right to be suspicious. My debriefers in the States were very anxious to know this officer's name and were frustrated that I'd forgotten it. They showed me some photos, but he wasn't among them."

Upon his return to the United States, Joe, still in uniform, was offered to a press conference because of his unique experiences. The officer in charge abruptly terminated the interview when Joe reached this point in his time with the Russians. A secondary reason for sending the reporters away was that Joe was insinuating "political" views about the USSR. He'd expressed that he liked Hitlerism only slightly less than Stalinism. At this point in 1945 it was not yet politically correct to make such a comparison.

"I was released by the rocket scientists to the care of a woman doctor they knew. She took a liking to me and treated me with everything she had. So I arrived at a field hospital as a special patient, as much as an enlisted man could be. There wasn't much medically, but the food was better than anything on the front lines. There was not only *kasca* but also thick soup with bread, sausage, and scalding hot tea."

He was told this field hospital was near an unpronounceable Polish town the Germans had renamed Landsberg in what they called Silesia.* The hospital was formerly a schoolhouse. There were blackboards that still had German writing on them. In Joe's small ward were a dozen beds and four dozen mattresses on the floor. It was as much a morgue as a recovery/emergency room. There was not even a stove, so covers were piled on the wounded, layers up to a foot thick, a tapestry of sheets, blankets, throws, spreads, and rugs confiscated from German houses.

"We still shivered with cold," Joe remembers. "I've often wondered why under such unsanitary conditions our wounds didn't become infected enough to kill us, though many died every day. Maybe the cold kept infection from spreading.

"The ward was purgatory. I've read a lot about the Civil War, how wounds were judged. If you were hit in a limb, you could hope to survive an amputation. Hit in the body and you'd better forget about this world and get ready for the next. It was just that way in Landsberg. Soldiers hit in the chest or gut were just trying to find peace and die. They all seemed to be communicating with their mother. Trouble was they were in the most pain and had no painkiller except vodka. The medics,

---

* A few months later the 506th liberated a concentration camp, previously a prewar prison, near Landsberg in Bavaria, where Hitler wrote *Mein Kampf.*

triaging, didn't pay much attention to them. I couldn't help but pay attention. Theirs were like the cries I'd heard in my mind in Berlin. Only God knows how much suffering it takes to fight a war."

Joe was still pretty much his own and only doctor with a grim prognosis: he had a new extremity wound but also a much more significant one in the body that had received no treatment except snow, vodka, and sulfa powder. Nevertheless he felt that if someone would just take the metal out of his knee and groin, he'd have a fighting chance.

In an American field hospital a guy would bitch and yell till a doctor came along and removed the bomb fragments in a proper operation. Russians in the beds beside Joe made no such demands, though they were at least as bad off. But he was an American and made his feelings known. A woman doctor came along and said she'd heard what he wanted. Joe nodded. Okay—she took out forceps, threw back the sheets, and pulled out the fragments on the spot.

"I screamed louder than any of my fellow patients ever had. It was like pulling wisdom teeth, appendix, and tonsils one after another— without even a shot of vodka for anesthetic. She seemed to be saying, hey, soldier, this is the Eastern Front—get used to it. I felt I'd done all I could do for myself at that point. If only I could have a little painkiller, I was ready to die again.

"I wanted to. Where there had been bomb fragments there were now big holes. A medic packed them with sulfa, or something like it, that burned like hell. I could feel myself growing weaker as I thrashed around in pain. The wounds kept draining. Usually the medics were too busy to change the dressings, so I'd turn them over till both sides were soaked, then ask for more. The new ones were taken from Wehrmacht casualties. They didn't get any.

"I'd reached another low in my young life. I'd been praying, but the purpose had changed. Before I'd prayed to get away and be a credit to my family and country. I felt I'd done that with God's help; now I was free but dying among people who cared about me. So what was I to pray for? I needed to get away from the caregivers, into the hands of American doctors. I was sure they could bring me back to life."

God stepped in once more. One afternoon there was the biggest commotion Joe had witnessed since Rommel's visit back in France. Doctors and medics came around to check all the patients, changing dressings, laying on new blankets, plumping pillows, and generally straightening up. From nearby wards Joe faintly heard something like *Ohh-ah* among the wounded. A VIP was coming through the hospital—that was the word spread around the ward. A Russian word Joe knew was *who?* A nurse looked at him proudly and announced it was none other than Marshal Georgi Zhukov. As good generals do, he was visiting unfortunate men to whom he owed his fortunes.

Zhukov came in at the opposite end of the ward from where Joe's bed was, so Joe could view the marshal's progress down the slew of beds and mattresses. The patients looked at him like he was the pope rather than a general. They praised him to his face before he could say a word. He didn't have to. Zhukov was the most impressive general Joe ever saw, including Ike, Montgomery, and Rommel. The first two were sort of slouchy and casual, qualities that appealed to soldiers of a democracy. Rommel was all business, coldly yet charismatically professional. Zhukov had a bearing, a presence resembling Churchill's but more victoriously erect. He carried himself the way Russia was carrying out the war: with much pride, and understanding of the suffering necessary for victory. He was a great captain. On the one hundredth anniversary of Zhukov's birth, the U.S. Army held a symposium about him at Fort McNair, which Joe attended.

His most noticeable feature was a large dimple in his chin. It would have almost been cute had not his chiseled face commanded instant and sober respect. He was accompanied by an English-speaking officer, who came to Joe's bed and identified him as the American casualty. Zhukov reached out with a crushing handshake. It was painful to bend forward, but Joe was proud to do so.

Russia's premier marshal looked him over as if "Yo" were a kid who'd done all right in school, nothing great but adequate. The interpreter whispered that Joe was a paratrooper. Zhukov brightened, flashing a smile of bemusement and amusement. He'd heard that D Day drops were widely dispersed but

"Did Yo drift all the way to Poland?"

Everyone within earshot broke into laughter, a venting laughter when there had been little humorous in their lives. In quick, clipped tones Zhukov expressed the wish that he could have more time to hear about the American Airborne. He ordered his chief of staff that when Joe recovered he was to report to Zhukov's headquarters for a debriefing.

"He asked how was my family? I couldn't say because I hadn't received any mail in the stalags."

Zhukov winced, for he had a most personal connection to stalags. His son had been captured in 1941 and resisted Gestapo coercion for two years before his fear of succumbing caused him to charge the barbed wire, where he was shot to death in an act of suicide.

"How was I being treated now? Very kindly, I answered. He gave a little speech to everyone in the room, which was so cold you could see his breath. The interpreter told me the gist of it later, that Zhukov said the Allies would finish the war shoulder to shoulder, and if Hitler thought otherwise, he should see this young American comrade who bravely chose to fight with us."

Zhukov then raised his fist like a toast and said in English, "Sherman tanks!" Joe chuckle-chortled, in his characteristic way, and said the same thing back. Zhukov shook his hand again, as only soldiers who understand each other can do, and moved on to other beds, as only commanders of soldiers must do.

When the VIPs left the ward the interpreter came back to Joe and asked if there was anything Zhukov could do for him. A light went on in his head. Yes, if the marshal would be so kind as to put something in writing that stated Joe was an escaped American POW, that would be a big help to get through the Soviet system and assure return to America. The interpreter said something like "No problem."

The next day he came back and handed over an envelope of heavy paper with a red hammer and sickle surrounded by a wreath embossed on it and a lot of stars underneath. It was the most beautiful stationery Joe has ever seen. He asked permission to open the envelope. Inside was the same elegantly raised letterhead and a few sentences written in Russian. He asked for a translation, and the interpreter said proudly that it was written by Zhukov himself and was a sort of passport, directing anyone to provide Joe with every assistance when moving through Soviet-controlled territory.

"I thanked the interpreter profoundly and shook his hand with both of mine. He then said about the same thing that Schultz and Major had: the war will soon be over, and I could go home to my family.

"You know how much I followed Schultz's advice. Now, with Zhukov's letter, I started planning my last escape. Actually there would be one more after that—from the U.S. Marines!"

Casualties were pouring in now from the Oder, terrible cases whose screams and moans never abated. There were even worse sounds during operations without anesthetic. Bodies were being carried out as fast as wounded were carried in. Joe couldn't take it any longer. He really didn't escape from that field hospital, merely went AWOL. His bed was probably occupied within the hour. He left by putting on his brogans and uniform, complete with overcoat and pile cap, as if to go to the frigid latrine outside.

"Without all your clothes there was a good chance for frostbite if you stayed on a crapper very long," Joe remembers. "The first phase of my plan had been to complain to a nurse that I felt diarrhea coming on, though my real problem was exactly the opposite. So when I dressed and went out no one noticed. The staff was much too busy with incoming casualties, and the patients around me were deep in personal pain."

Joe started walking in the direction where there was the most military traffic. About a half mile from the hospital he came to a headquarters, greeted the guards with *"Tovarish,"* and handed them his passport from Zhukov. If this didn't work, he planned to ride the rails toward Warsaw, where he assumed there was an American embassy.

The sergeant of the guard came back with the passport and indicated that there was no one in his headquarters who spoke English but he would drive Joe over to a bigger headquarters. The way he eyed Joe and tried to make conversation demonstrated that the passport had made an impression. At the second HQ an English-speaking captain took charge of him, saying there was a convoy leaving for Warsaw that afternoon. Let's go over there now, he suggested, and you can get out of the cold in the cab of a truck. It was a Studebaker. Joe sprawled out on the seat till the driver showed up and the convoy got under way.

They drove for hours and hours. The groin wound was draining and bothered Joe badly. He figured Warsaw was about three hundred miles east, but first the convoy made a big swing south to Cracow. There it broke up, apparently unplanned, but the driver indicated that if Joe wanted to go to Warsaw, that wasn't this truck's destination. He pointed toward the rail yard. They both took a slug of his vodka.

"He asked to see my passport again. I handed it to him. I don't think he could read, but he shook his head with awe as he fingered the embossed letterhead. He did recognize the name Zhukov and said it out loud like it was the name of a saint. We shook hands warmly, said, *Proshchai*, and he pointed once more to the rail yard, where there were only two trains, both very long, and both steaming up."

The way the engines pointed it seemed both trains would head east. Joe hurried to the nearest one and clambered on the closest car. His bad luck with trains continued. As the locomotive slowly chugged off, he realized it wasn't a passenger or freight car but a gondola for hauling coal. Joe wasn't agile enough to move up along the cars, so he painfully climbed the metal ladder welded to the sloping side of the gondola. It was empty. To get out of the cold wind he slid down the inside slope. The metal was rough cast iron. Immediately Joe realized that it was carrying away his body heat.

"I prayed as hard as I ever have for a way to get out of that gondola. At some point I stupidly took off a glove, maybe to sit on my hand to warm it. My skin stuck to the cast iron. The pain to pull it up was terrible, and if I did, I'd leave most of my palm. For the next hour I blew breath hard on my hand. Little by little, with awful pain, the skin released."

After a couple of hours the train came to a halt. Joe started yelling. There was no way to climb the side of the gondola, so if someone didn't help, he'd end up another frozen corpse in Poland. His only hope was that someone would come along and pull him up. A Polish yard worker did happen by—God had decided to save Joe once more.

"I sure put God to a lot of work," Joe says, "with all He had to do during World War II!"

Someone yelled back, and a stocking cap peeked over the ladder. A chain rattled down the gondola, and Joe was hauled to the top. Helped down the ladder, he stood shaking with cold and pointed to his groin wound. The yard worker nodded and walked him up the train. After a quarter mile he gestured to get on a car. It was a hospital train. When Joe realized that he looked back for the yard worker.

"He'd saved my life," Joe says. "I had a wad of rubles from the III-C safe and wanted to give them all to him, but he was gone. I still commend him to Mary in my prayers.

"My passport put me in first class on the hospital train. The staff couldn't do much for my wounds but were experts in cold injuries and took care of my scorched hand with some wonderful salve that deadened the pain while increasing circulation. I wish I knew what that stuff was; I could sure use it in Michigan winters."

Next stop was Lodz, where patients bound for Warsaw were to get off and then board a medical convoy. The train was continuing to Lublin for everyone else. Joe's train luck again. If he'd stayed on to Lublin, he'd have probably reached American control. But he thought the Americans were in Warsaw, so he got off the train and onto the convoy.

His journey to the east so far had been mostly during darkness and he'd hardly noticed the flat, featureless countryside. Now he traveled in daylight to Warsaw. Even with all he'd seen of the war and its effects, the route from Lodz to Warsaw showed that he'd seen little. The landscape was from World War I no-man's-land: craters, dead trees, destroyed cottages, farms, whole villages with little left except toppled chimneys and blackened foundations. This is what Hitler and Stalin meant by scorched earth. They invented it, tried it out on poor Poland. There were many more wandering people than livestock.

What Joe finds closest to describing those people is a movie about the aftermath of nuclear war. Bands, small groups, and scattered individuals drifting back and forth like trash blown by winds. They had a name in those days, DPs, displaced persons. Some were concentration-camp survivors—Auschwitz was only about thirty miles from Cracow. More were Polish peasants uprooted when the Soviets overran their half of Poland. Others were city dwellers whose cities had been reduced to cold rubble. Joe had no idea of the composition of the DPs till he studied the history of the war's end. What he saw of them was a staggering scattered rabble—begging, falling, dying during Europe's coldest winter of the century.

The Russians he was among did not impress him as callous, but instead unreachably resigned to the stupefying consequences of their war, as if such suffering was little different from killing cold and blizzards. War against the Hitlerites meant stark facts to reckon with, realities to protect against, or else enter the ghastly whirlpool of the dying. A concatenation to end only when Hitler's Germany was destroyed. Joe was with them on that, his main regret that he could not be part of the final destruction—and a reunion with the Gestapo goons on Prinz Albrecht Strasse.

Hate can be a tremendous stimulus, but by the time Joe reached Warsaw he couldn't draw on that kind of energy. He'd seen too much killing and even enough Hitlerite bodies. They were as plentiful as road signs in the countryside, identified by what was left of their uniforms. The Poles had stacked them like cords of logs in a frozen woodpile, ten feet high and a hundred feet long, speckled by frosted eyes, pop-eyed as if shocked that death had reached them. There was such a stack at each crossroad; they became fertilizer after the spring thaw.

This was the Wehrmacht, its collective corpse, the echoing remains of its curse. Except within Germany, all that Hitler did had been enabled by the Wehrmacht. They were the school of sharks upon whose jaws the Gestapo and *Einsatzgruppen* attached like pilot fish. Extraordinary soldiers the Wehrmacht, but animated only by a hateful superiority, finally disproven, finally cold and stiff in discreditation of values their enemies fought and died for. The Wehrmacht was good, usually very good, as the word relates to competence, efficiency, and proficiency.* However, what they fought and died for was not their country but to subjugate. And that applied not only to the SS.

AT LAST JOE ARRIVED in Warsaw. Though a stretcher case, he left the hospital train with the ambulatory patients so it would be easier to get away. That wasn't hard, but there was no city to walk into, only rubble and rubbish, craters and devastation. He could make out where the

---

* But not, in the last three years of the war, the military beau ideal as represented by its stunning successes in the first three years. In postwar interrogations, the principal Wehrmacht generals admitted to serious blunders at Bastogne for which American counterparts would have been relieved of command. After blitzkrieg failed to win the war early, the Wehrmacht's opponents learned how to both foil and imitate German tactics. Strategically the Wehrmacht was hamstrung by Hitler's micromanagement.

streets were, but to walk down one meant weaving between buildings collapsed into the street. The only human activity was a few old people pulling scraps of wood from the rubble. Joe had learned the Polish words for American embassy, and he asked these people. They just shook their heads and didn't look up from their scavenging. Off in the distance was what was left of a big church or cathedral. It looked like the center of town, so he headed that way.

The *Warsaw* Concerto affects Joe deeply. Warsaw was one of the most fought-over cities in World War II. First came the Hitlerites' invasion in 1939, followed by their obliteration of the Jewish ghetto, then the Polish uprising in 1944, then the Russian conquest in 1945. The only place Joe had seen so leveled and totally destroyed was St.-Lô, and that was a town, not the capital of a great and ancient nation. As he trudged toward the cathedral it began to dawn on him that if there weren't any whole buildings, how could there be an American embassy in Warsaw?

He kept looking for buildings in use. The only ones standing were gutted and roofless. What had been windows were jagged holes where daylight came in one side of a skeleton building and out the other. His boots kept crunching on broken glass. He had seen not one vehicle and only a single horse cart. He approached the ruins of the cathedral in despair, very much regretting going AWOL from that hospital train. The Russians would have sent him *somewhere,* not into the deadly cold of a lifeless city.

He was right, though, that the cathedral was at the center of what life existed. In what had been, he guessed, the cathedral square there was a small group of men trying to keep warm around a small fire of rubbish and scrap wood. The wood scavengers he'd spoken to before had dressed in scarves and piles of wraps like peasants. Maybe they were peasants from the country, scrounging stuff from the remains of the city.

The group of men by the fire weren't dressed like peasants; they wore heavy overcoats. Joe approached them. When he tried German, his best foreign language, they stiffened. A little Russian, and they relaxed some. When he said *Americanski,* they lightened up a lot and beckoned him over to the fire. One of them went to get an English-speaking Pole.

"He was the very old uncle of a boy in Milwaukee who was probably an American soldier like me. I said there was a daily ferry from near

Muskegon to Milwaukee. Some of the others in that group had relatives in the U.S. They all wanted to know what they could do for me.

"In the cold I showed them my wounds. They knew just what I needed and led me there. The uncle said it was a convent, but I didn't see anything but rubble and a low bunker. That's right, he said, the convent was largely destroyed during the uprising, but the sisters were in the basement. If there was anything that could help me, they'd have it. Before we reached the entrance to the basement I saw a bullet-scarred statue of Saint Joseph outside. This seemed like a good sign. It sure was—the sisters were from the Order of Saint Joseph, a healing order."

CHAPTER TWENTY-ONE

TO MOSCOW

THE SAME STATUE OF SAINT JOSEPH, OVER A HUNDRED YEARS OLD, is still where Joe found it on his first revisit to Poland in 1988. Only one of the twelve sisters from 1945 was still alive, but his story remained part of the convent's history, and he was welcomed like a living legend.

"I've given the convent some money because I owe them so much. The mother superior, who was also a nurse, spoke some English, heard my story, looked at my wounds, and assured me I'd receive care—and added that it was a small miracle I'd found the convent because it had the only medical skill in Warsaw that could help me. The miracle wasn't small at all. When I look back it was as large as any of the miracles that preserved me in World War II."

The sisters praised God that Joe belonged to Saint Joseph parish in Muskegon, for it could have been only the hand of God that guided him to the convent of his patron saint and namesake. As a healing order they were swamped with people to care for in wasted Warsaw. Though the sisters were openly religious, the Soviet occupation hadn't bothered them at all, probably because the experiences of these women had been so horrific even in comparison with that of the Russians. The sisters didn't want to talk about it; they were still grieving, but perhaps an American could help tell the world about the wartime of Warsaw.

Most of all they wanted Joe to know how beautiful the city had been before the Germans. The worst of the destruction occurred during the August–September 1944 uprising when guerrillas, called the Polish Home Army, seized strong points, holding them for two months against

Wehrmacht forces stunned by their strength and determination. Many streets were still cut by antitank ditches they had dug. The sisters said the entire city had been aflame, with smoke hanging over it like a giant parachute canopy. Rains finally put out the fires.

The convent of course had been mobbed with casualties. The Germans might have spared it because their wounded, even SS, were treated by the sisters—who were then raped by some of the patients when they recovered.

Warsaw was once home for a half million Poles. During the uprising Hitler sent in two panzer divisions and one SS division under General Bach, plus swarms of bombers. Most of the Polish dead were crushed by bombs in their cellars. Those who escaped did so through sewers. General Bach stopped this by throwing in poison-gas grenades. He was hanged as a war criminal. The sisters thought there were fewer than a hundred thousand inhabitants left in Warsaw. There appeared to be many fewer.

The Polish Home Army had been betrayed by Stalin, who stopped his advance on the east bank of the Vistula, as close as Arlington is to Washington, D.C. The uprising received no support except from British bombers who flew all the way from Italy to drop in supplies. The Americans offered a hundred B-17s, but Stalin refused to allow them to land on Soviet airstrips. That's what Roosevelt got in return for Sherman tanks delivered at great peril and price in lives by American merchant mariners. What Stalin wanted was for the Polish non-Communist resistance to be exterminated by the Hitlerites; he got what he wanted. When he decided it was time to take Warsaw (about six weeks before Joe arrived) it cost him fifty thousand casualties, but what did he care?

Yet the Poles Joe spoke with didn't hold a grudge against the Red Army, which was dutifully following Stalin's orders not to help the uprising. Major had said something about waiting on the Vistula, and knowing her, Joe is sure, if ordered, she would have charged across to help anyone fighting the Hitlerites. In his presence Russian troops had never bitched about bad commanders—Stalin being the worst—some of whom were as incompetent as the World War I generals whose troops were slaughtered by the tens of thousands. Probably Joe's buddies in Major's battalion just didn't want to air their feelings in front of a foreigner—certainly not within earshot of the commissar—but Joe thinks they just felt that any commander who gave them the opportunity to kill Hitlerites was good enough.

The Red Army made amends to the Poles by paying back the Hitlerites in kind. Across from the convent was the shell of a burnt-out four-story building where dozens of bodies protruded from windows. SS prisoners had been herded and locked in. Fuel oil was poured till it saturated the roof, lit by flamethrowers. Joe was staring at this huge crematorium when an emaciated Pole sidled up. He had been some kind of scientist at one time, then an inmate of Auschwitz. In a cackly voice, he began to speak like a docent:

"Body fat turns liquid at high temperature, then the skeleton comes apart like a boiled chicken. They were writhing, you see, and that helped separate the bones." Some had jumped and many had fallen as they burned. Their scorched limbs strewed the street like offal dumped from a slaughterhouse, but left there, for there was no odor from the scorched jumble of remains. "The skulls—look closely—they're all cracked. That was from the heat too. That plastic is their brains. But no eyes. They all popped out. See those big smiles? High heat does that. Everyone in hell is grinning."

Machine guns took care of anyone trying to get out. Thus the forces of Hitler and Stalin imitated each other. That had troubled the sisters, but they expresssed no sense of equivalence because it had been the Germans who had set the scales of immorality on the Eastern Front.

As soon as Mother Superior examined his wounds Joe was taken to the infirmary, a structure half above ground, half below. The lower half had been for protection against bombs and shelling. There he was given a cot among many elderly Poles and a few children, all malnourished. There was no doctor, but a nursing sister treated everyone expertly, better than anything Joe had seen with the Russians. She didn't speak English, didn't need to, as she cleaned and packed Joe's groin and knee, manipulated his shoulders, salved his hand, and even checked his head. It surprised him that she indicated the head wound was more serious than the groin; indeed, in the long run it was.

"After a few days of treatment another sister told me that I could now have a hot bath," Joe recalls. "Oh, happy day! Upstairs was a big iron kettle heated by a scrap-wood fire. My dressings were waterproofed, and another patient helped me into a four-leg tub that had once been in a house. You can't imagine how warm and comfortable I felt after months of deep bitter cold. After a good wash I soaked till the water cooled. There was only burlap from sandbag casings to dry off with, but I was given clean underwear and my clothes. They'd not been washed, but the sisters must have done something to them because they smelled fresh."

While Joe got better a number of old Polish men visited, told him about their relatives in the States, and brought his ambitions up to date. The former American embassy was rubble; it had been for years. The American consulate in Lublin had been taken over by the Soviets, who set up a rump Communist government. It was not recognized by the United States, so if it was medical help Joe needed, he should stay here with the sisters.

He'd have gladly stayed until Americans eventually found him, but he felt he could only stabilize his health at the convent, not improve it. Joe was also aware of taking up space and resources that could be used by more needy patients. He talked this over with Mother Superior, who said, "Then you must rejoin the Russians. They have transportation from here to Moscow. There is surely a big American embassy there."

"I'll be very sad to leave," Joe told her.

"We will be glad, not to see you leave but because you will go where you should and can regain what you have lost. We wish that for everyone who comes here."

Joe says, "I promised to pray for her convent, she blessed me, and we parted in tears. Mother Superior died in the 1970s before I got back to Poland. She is surely in heaven because she'd done so much for people suffering in hell."

The only sister still living when Joe returned forty years later was so old herself that she didn't remember much at all. He presented himself and told her his story. Yes, she recalled the story but looked Joe up and down and said she didn't recognize him. Nevertheless they enjoyed a long embrace. She felt as fragile as a bird in his arms.

IN 1945 THERE WAS a big Soviet headquarters right across the frozen Vistula. Joe was driven there in a horse cart. All the permanent bridges had been destroyed, so the crossing was on Russian pontoons. The man who delivered him was old and gaunt; he worked at the convent for food. The sisters had provided Joe with black bread, jam, and some sawdust sausage; he gave it to the driver for his help. They embraced, Joe painfully got off the cart, and the driver clucked to his horse and turned back to Warsaw.

"I gave him my picnic but still had what was most valuable from the convent—the sisters' promise to pray for me each morning at mass. They'd done their part for my salvation, now it was up to me to complete the last leg of my journey from Normandy to freedom."

The Soviet headquarters was in a medieval building with a courtyard. As Joe was in a combination Russian-American uniform the guard looked at him curiously and assumed he was a veteran of the Polish Home Army. There were very few of them left. Joe presented Zhukov's passport and was ushered right into the HQ. An English-speaking officer invited him to sit down and offered assistance. This was a logistical base, he said, and most of the activity was to push supplies up to the front. Joe told him he needed to get to Moscow as fast as possible for medical treatment. The officer asked to see his wounds, then said the only transportation to Moscow was trains.

Any chance of a flight back there? Joe asked. The officer went off to some office to check. A Red air force major returned with him and informed Joe that the planes were not pressurized. That might not be good for a head wound. Joe hadn't thought of that. The two officers left and came back with a high-ranking doctor, who looked Joe over, heard his medical history, and seconded the advice against trying to fly to Moscow. The planes hopscotched all over, the air force officer added, and were often diverted in flight as higher priorities came up. There was no telling when it would get there. The consensus was, Better take the train. With luck he'd reach Moscow in two weeks.

"I figured out that meant the train would average about sixty miles per day. We'd almost *marched* that fast to Fort Benning! Two weeks in a rolling field hospital didn't sound like it would be good for my health, but what choice did I have? I just hoped there wouldn't be too much screaming and dying, the kind that drove me out of Landsberg, but I didn't want to offend the Russians by showing what I thought of their medical system. It would be insulting, as lightly wounded as I was, to object to riding with comrades who were worse off.

"I said it would be a privilege to be on a train with such men. The officers congratulated me, and we shook hands all around. They asked how I'd obtained the letter from Zhukov. Every Russian who looked at the letter asked me the same question."

Joe was put on a train that night. It was worse than he'd feared. His car was for ambulatory patients, about sixty feet long with about seventy passengers, including officers up to captain and enlisted men of all ranks. The officers took more than their share of space, the choice space next to the two woodstoves. They took the seats and left the benches for the enlisted men. NCOs didn't have much status either.

"This surprised me because communism was supposed to make everyone equal. On an American train like that the worst wounded would get the choice space. That's what we'd done on the forty-or-eight after the terrible strafing of the train to Stalag XII-A. The Russian military caste system was worse than the British. I've heard that was because it started with the Czarist army, when the officers were nobility, the soldiers serfs. But it carries over even today. When I attended a Russian veterans' reunion in 1992, almost all the members were former officers. Maybe the enlisted vets had their own organization, or maybe not enough of them survived to form one.

"Looking back I see that the American Airborne was very democratic; very disciplined but also very democratic. That may have been because, though we were all volunteers for the Airborne, many of us had been drafted (or barely escaped the draft like me) from all walks of life, so just being an officer didn't mean everything.

"I remember a Bing Crosby song after the war, 'I've Got My Captain Working for Me Now.' That must have been a dream for many GIs, that a typical CO was nothing special, and under peacetime conditions he'd need something from GIs who no longer needed him. Can't argue with that, or agree with it either. The truth was a mix.

"Off-duty we'd sometimes socialize in the 506th (that is, drink) with officers, but that didn't lessen the respect for rank when everybody started training the next morning. In the 101st Airborne Division Association there is no officer-enlisted divide at all."

Against his democratic principles Joe accepted special status as an ally and took a seat near a stove. All the officers wanted to hear his story and see the Zhukov letter. In return Joe asked if anyone knew Major. The answer was shrugs—there were so many women commanders toward the end of the war. In this way, his fellow passengers pointed out, the Red Army was more democratic than the American.

The train to Moscow made innumerable stops. The Russian rail gauge was wider than in the rest of Europe, so during the Germans' conquest of the USSR they had to tear up all the Russian track and replace it with their own. They did this of course with POW and slave labor. During the German retreat the track was destroyed again. Most of Joe's stops were for track repair and replacement of the original gauge. That was now being done by German POWs from what he could tell.

Joe mentioned to an officer on the train that, uh, it didn't seem the Red Army was taking a lot of prisoners anymore. That's right, was the reply, because so many had been captured previously there were enough to work on the railroad—like the lucky ones Joe had seen in summer uniforms toiling in subzero cold. No more than one in ten POWs of the Russians ever got back to Germany, and that wasn't until the 1950s.

The hours rocked by slowly, reminding Joe of the forty-or-eight from Paris, so he rose and moved around, reassuring himself that this train was not headed for Germany but instead leaving it far behind. Memories and impressions merged as he scrubbed hoarfrost from a tiny slat of glass. Out there were nicks of distant light from the algid countryside, scraps of stiff paper twitching on railroad markers, pinioned there by the wind. The by-product of combat was as much trash as blood. Colonel Sink wouldn't have tolerated such tatters. "Police up the area" was his dictum—what you control controls your mind. But that was on another front, amounting to another war. Here those scraps of paper twitching in an arctic gale were ghosts. Thousands, tens of thousands, hundreds of thousands of specters, uncountable as the snowflakes wailing against the wobbling train. The sounds of the railroad tracks became those of tanks. Buffets of wind felt like concussions of artillery. The heat of bygone battles—whether Carentan or Kustrin—was blanketed by a cold even more violent.

What sleep Joe got was sitting up. Food on the train was as bad as the worst days in III-C: black bread so hard it cracked one of his teeth, washed down by scalding tea that produced a heat rush when it hit bottom and spread through the middle of the body like an internal sauna.

"There was no water on board, so we melted snow scooped up at stops. It wasn't very clean. Many trainloads had stopped here and pissed. One time I scooped down into a drift and uncovered a hand. The skin was almost gone, so the body must have been there longer than the start of that winter. I still think about him sometimes. When and why did he die, what was his nationality? He had an untold story, like how many million others? It makes me feel very small.

"One of the awful smells on that train was from frostbite wounds that had turned green. The Russian treatment of frostbite was very effective, but it didn't involve removing dead skin, though sometimes maggots were used to do the job. I was told they generated some heat, which was good for the lower tissue."

Under those conditions Joe's wounds became reinfected and began draining again. He perceived that the men on this train were a much lower medical priority than the casualties at Landsberg. There the system had been triage in order to send as many of the wounded back into action as soon as possible. No one on the train was in that "recoverable" category. The war was over for them, so they weren't as important to Stalin. None of the passengers seemed to resent that; they were just grateful to be returning to homes they had never expected to see again.

The sisters had known Joe was in for a long cold trip and had wrapped cotton strips around his body for warmth. On the train he unwrapped some strips, asked a one-legged corporal to tear them, then used the strips as dressings to soak up drainage. After two to three weeks, about the time Joe ran out of strips, the passengers became excited. There were two small windows in the car. Joe was invited to take a look, and condensation was wiped off the glass to reveal windswept desolation. Look again, Yo—the outskirts of our destination! Snow had drifted into deep, wide trenches. These, he was told proudly, were anti-tank ditches dug by Muscovites in the winter of 1941.

The mile-long train ground to a halt at a station that was large but had no city around it. Nonetheless, this was it, New York and Times Square for his fellow passengers. In their tunics they had hoarded flasks of vodka. Now was the time to break them out in gratitude and also break out in song. Joe accompanied when he knew a tune like

"Meadowlands," but his thankfulness was nothing like theirs. He'd come a long way from Normandy but still felt he'd struggled up to just an upper ring of hell.

Arrivals of hospital trains were not publicized, so there were no families to meet the returning wounded. Only when the soldiers limped into their homes—often after hitchhiking hundreds of miles—did their families know they had survived the war.

"I wish I could have been at one of those reunions," Joe says. "It would have been overpowering beyond any level of emotion I can imagine, even my own homecoming."

Joe was with the ambulatory patients who had plans to get home. They were released with a month's leave paid in advance—Stalin's generosity—about three dollars for most of them. A stretcher case could only get news out to his family through word of mouth. Then it was for them to find him in an army hospital and bring food, dressings, whatever he needed, lest he die.

When Joe hobbled off that hospital train a snowstorm was building. In Michigan it would have been called the start of a blizzard.

"Our snow and cold rolls in off the lake," Joe says. "Whenever it does I'm back in Eastern Europe and feeling glad to be inside on my La-Z-Boy. The snow at the Moscow station made a ghostly scene. It seemed like the dead were coming back to life, given a second chance without expecting much more than before. The singing stopped."

Joe was wearing everything he owned, so outside the train the temperature seemed even colder than it was. The other debarking patients felt the snowfall was good because they knew from long experience that the worst cold came alone. He looked around at shapes eerily vague in the gliding snow. There was steam exhaling from parked army trucks, not nearly enough of them to transport all the patients. A few medics were helping with stretcher cases. Between them and the trucks was a huddled group of soldiers around a trash fire. Joe went up and saluted the only officer there, a major, and handed him Zhukov's letter. He had to bend away from the snowfall to read it, worrying Joe that the passport would become wet and illegible. The major brightened, returned Joe's salute, then told a subordinate he was leaving and to take charge of the debarkation.

He pointed Joe to a car, and they drove off. The major put the letter on his lap and kept glancing at it in a pleased way. It was about an hour before they reached a headquarters. Joe's wounds were draining again, and he didn't feel good at all. It seemed bureaucracy would kill him after the Germans couldn't. He was sat down by a stove; that was welcome but built up his intermittent fever. He was barely coherent in answering questions by various officers.

"I was ready to pass out, just hoping someone would get me to the embassy before I faded completely. In a way it was like listening to the Gestapo and Wehrmacht argue about what would happen to me.

"The Russians made some phone calls. I got the feeling that Zhukov's name hadn't quite the clout it did back in Poland. But it was enough. Eventually a colonel who spoke very good English took charge of me and commandeered a Dodge truck with its driver. In good spirits (I was groggy) they drove me into town to a subway station."

The colonel ordered a train held while he pointed out the tile and murals of the station. They were remarkable, much more attractive than anything Joe had seen in New York. The colonel noticed his admiration: "We have the only subway system in the world, but with our help someday America may catch up." Joe let that go.

At the subway's destination were many steps to reach street level. The colonel said proudly that the depth was for bomb protection and had worked very well. Joe had trouble climbing; his breath was short when they emerged into a luminously bleak snowscape. The state-of-the-art subway seemed to represent the future of the USSR, while the absence of streetlights was their present. Joe has come to believe he was taken on the subway as sort of a tour; the colonel's truck could have driven to the American embassy faster.

They trudged through compacted snow for about a half mile. Whenever Joe staggered the colonel supported him, muttering in English and Russian, mostly about how Hitler had caused so many terrible things.

"I was running a fever, and it made me start thinking about Hitler, not that I hadn't before, but in a new way. Here I was just one of millions of people, most suffering much more than I, who were Hitler's victims. How had God allowed him, what would He do with him?

"I recognized Red Square. It was lit up, though there was very little electricity in Moscow. The colonel steered me toward the entrance of a compound."

They were stopped by two armed Americans, the first Joe had seen since Normandy, Marine guards in overcoats. Apparently the Russians hadn't told the embassy he was coming, so the Marines didn't quite know what to do with him. The Russian colonel stayed to explain the arrival to a U.S. Army major who was called to the gate. The colonel showed the major Joe's passport and stood with hands clasped behind his back while it was read. The major nodded approval and thanked the colonel, whose task was now completed.

"He bear-hugged me. I was pretty weak and could hardly squeeze back but shook his hand and thanked him. The major thanked him again, we all saluted, and the colonel marched off into the snow. I didn't think to ask him for my passport—it had served its purpose. My head was swimming, for now I'd made it, made it back, reached the end of my stalag dreams and fulfilled my obligations."

For many years Joe's son John has been inquiring with Russian military historians about recovering Zhukov's letter. It hasn't turned up, probably because it was used as evidence against Zhukov that he was too palsy with Westerners. When he became so popular during the war Stalin saw him as a threat. Zhukov was the foremost national hero, so he wasn't purged; Stalin just retired him.

The major took Joe into the embassy, formerly the National Hotel. The lobby was high-ceilinged and ornate but cold enough to require an overcoat. Joe was ushered to an office to be interviewed by a man who introduced himself as a member of the U.S. Military Mission to Moscow. He was the first American civilian Joe had seen since the USO shows in England.

"He said he'd check out my story with the Soviets, then asked if I was feeling all right. My appearance must have shown him before I answered. He made a phone call, and in a few minutes two men in U.S. Army uniforms came in and asked if I'd like to have a shower and some good hot American food. Would I! My bath in the Warsaw convent had been great, but this shower was like heaven. I felt I had fever but not a care in the world. After drying off with fluffy towels I was given new underwear, socks, shoes, uniform trousers, and shirt. Someone took my temperature. When it was read I was told to take all that off, put on pajamas, and climb into a bunk. I must have slept for at least ten hours. It was full daylight when I awoke. At some point I remember orange juice beside my bed left by a doctor who had examined me, but I didn't remember him at all. I sucked it down like an alcoholic. Anything citrus was ultimate luxury. I could almost hear my body say, 'Hey, this is vitamin C!' "

When Joe was back in uniform again the major informed him there had been a glitch. In his possessions was a kriege dog tag but no GI tag. How did that happen? Joe explained how the GI tags had been taken during his first interrogation in Normandy. The major indicated this was unusual—Joe certainly agreed with him but didn't say anything about Greta—so some more things would have to be checked out. After that Ambassador Harriman wanted to see Joe. The wait was fine, and he went back to bed.

"The major gently woke me and said he was just checking to see if I was still alive—I'd been out cold for another ten hours. Maybe it was because I was coming back to my senses, but I had a feeling he was looking at me differently."

IN THE FALL of 1944, when Joe's parents had been informed that contrary to previous telegrams he had not been KIA but was instead a POW, this information somehow did not reach a certain branch of the War Department, which continued to carry Joe as dead, with a notation that a body had been found with his dog tags but also with uncertainty if the corpse was actually Joe's. Someone in G-2 had added a flag to the file requiring that information about anyone purporting to be Joe should be sent by the fastest possible means to the Pentagon.

The major in the Moscow embassy complied with this instruction. The fastest means of transmission at that time was telegram. While Joe was asleep, the answer came back from the Pentagon to regard him as suspect, possibly a Nazi assassin targeted on Ambassador Harriman.

"I WELL REMEMBER my first Moscow breakfast. An orderly asked what I wanted and was surprised that I said just oatmeal with milk and sugar plus some hot toast from real bread. I explained that I hadn't had much food and I was afraid that anything rich or fried would be too much for my stomach. I was offered American cigarettes but said I only used them for trading and gambling.

"The embassy doctor came by again, and this time he was concerned about my shoulders, which he said were in very bad shape, as if I didn't know. He was working on them when the major came in and said something about a problem about my identity. Officially I'd been KIA in Normandy and my parents so informed. This was an awful shock because I couldn't imagine them thinking I was dead. And something was wrong, I realized, when remembering that Schultz had checked on my mail that had been held up at XII-A. If someone had written me late in the summer, they must have known I was alive. I was confused, feverish, and then really disturbed when the major said I'd have to be moved to the Metropole Hotel until my identity was confirmed. This was because of a diplomatic agreement, according to him, which allowed only bona fide Americans to stay at the embassy. I became angry and said if my identity was in doubt, why not fingerprint me and send the prints to Washington? I knew I'd been fingerprinted when I joined the army, so there must be a set on file. The major said that was a good idea. An intelligence NCO was brought in, and I was fingerprinted before being taken to the Metropole."

It irked Joe to be driven there by a Marine guard who said he was along only for protection. Joe replied he was a veteran of the Red Army with nothing to fear from Russians. The next morning the Marine took him over to the military attaché's compound, where the food was much better than at the Metropole.

"He was sure right about that. I remember my first meal at the compound: roast chicken, mashed potatoes, white bread, rice pudding, and chocolate cake. It was too much for me, and I got sick. Before we returned to the Metropole, I was interviewed by two intelligence officers, who seemed doubtful about my story. One got in back of me and said something loud and fast in German. I didn't react. I guess they expected me to, if I were a kraut. Then they started in on my German background, asked if I'd ever visited Germany before the war or if any of my family was there. The questions sounded a lot like our interrogation of Websky, the mole we executed in III-C."

Back at the Metropole Joe gazed out a small window at dark, drab

Moscow. There was very little sunlight, only a few hours a day during the Russian winter. It was depressing and he was depressed. This situation was impossible, for all he'd done to get here—to be suspected of being some Hitlerite plant. Even worse was thinking about his parents and the grief they must have gone through. That night he went out in the hall to go to the latrine and was confronted by two armed Marine guards.

"I'm afraid I cursed them.

"My fever grew higher, I could feel it, and had periods of wooziness. I was going bonkers and began planning an escape from the hotel. Of all my escape plans, this was the wildest and dumbest of all!

"I'd noticed that around midafternoon there was only one guard on my door, till a second one arrived about a half hour later. My plan was to jump the single guard and lock him in my room. What I'd do then was rejoin the Red Army and get home by way of Berlin.

"I very quietly opened the door a crack and peeked out into the hall. The guard's profile was toward me, about three feet away as he read an American magazine, his chair tipped back against the wall. He didn't look as big as I had been (before losing seventy pounds) and of course couldn't be as tough as a paratrooper, he being a mere Marine. I grabbed him around the chest, pinning his shoulders, and with a lunge pulled him off the chair and toward the door. With his forearm he flipped me back and flat on my ass. Beyrle, I thought, you've really slipped a long way from Toccoa!"

The Marine looked at Joe sympathetically, handled him easily, and put him back in the room. The second Marine arrived to say, sorry, but Joe would have to be locked in. That afternoon the major came to reason with him: confidentially, *he* believed Joe's story, but that couldn't be the embassy's official position till his prints were confirmed in Washington. Joe was still ranting betrayal but after a sedative fell asleep while still talking with the major.

"I had a pent-up need to talk, and did about everything—my experiences at home and during the war. After that I clammed up for many years. I remember the major sitting there like a psychiatrist, not taking any notes, though, and that calmed me. Gradually he darkened into a silhouette and was gone."

The embassy doctor came the next morning to see if Joe had been reinjured during his scuffle with the Marine. Nothing had been hurt except pride. Joe asked what happened next if his identity was confirmed. The doctor said he'd be put on the first means of transportation to begin the trip home. That was good news, unless it meant another Russian hospital train. No, the doctor assured him, the embassy had U.S. aircraft at its disposal, pressurized transports, and he'd recommend that Joe fly out. From that point Joe's morale and health began an upward trajectory.

Still he was a prisoner at the Metropole, the same hotel where he was to stay in 1979 while visiting John, who was a guide for the American Agriculture Exhibit. Joe's previous room had become a suite when he and his wife were guests of the Russians for commemoration of the Great Patriotic War.

Incarcerated at the Metropole in 1945, Joe spent the days catching up on news from the Marines. They brought him magazines with every guard shift. The one who'd decked him said there could be a rematch when Joe got back into shape but he'd have to find the Marine in Florida, where he would be a civilian as soon as the war was over.

In a few days the major appeared with the first secretary of the embassy. Sorry for the delay, he began, but mix-ups happen in war. Anyway, Washington has confirmed the fingerprints and had received word from the International Red Cross that Joe had been a POW whose last record was at Stalag III-C, now in Russian hands.

"I started laughing like a maniac. Yeah, those records had been at III-C, but I'd liberated them! The other great news was my parents had been informed that my death report had been false and I was now under U.S. control in Moscow. 'Now let's go back to the embassy and celebrate,' the first secretary said. He opened the door, and the Marine guards were dismissed and congratulated me. I was still laughing and crying while they hugged me as if we'd been lifelong buddies. The sergeant of the guard had been wounded in the Pacific and had an idea of what I was feeling.

"From there on there is nothing unfortunate to tell in my story. Life didn't become perfect, but it sure beat anything I'd known before.

"There were two wonderful events before I left Russia. The second was when the plane flew us to Odessa, where there was a U.S. Navy ship waiting to take us to Egypt. There were maybe a thousand of us on the dock, all liberated POWs, air corps and army, many from III-C. We were formed up, called to attention, and marched in file up the gangplank. It is navy tradition to salute the American flag on the fantail when you board. The file was very slow moving up that gangplank."

When Joe reached the top he knew why. Men were holding their salute, then bending over and crying. Sailors helped them go aboard. When Joe reached the saluting position he could hardly bring his hand up. There was a light, cool breeze. The flag seemed to be in fluorescent colors, red, white, and blue from another world.

"I made my salute slowly, the way it's done now at military funerals. I hadn't planned to salute that way, it just happened."

The first event was the night after his "confirmation." Joe was Ambassador Harriman's guest of honor, though he was the only enlisted man among several officers who had been krieges at Oflag 64 in Poland. After hearing his story, they insisted that he sit on the ambassador's right.

Harriman was a most gracious host and began a round of vodka toasts after recounting how he'd sacrificed his liver for the sake of Allied cooperation.

"I knew what he meant. The Russians never started eating before everyone was drunk. The ambassador asked me to say grace. The last time I'd done so out loud was with the sisters. They had understood what I was saying but not the language I was speaking.

"A waiter came around and asked how I'd like my steak. 'Soon!' I said."

It was a meal from his dreams: filet mignon, au gratin potatos, puréed squash, lemon cake, Caucasian wine, and Turkish coffee. All the krieges were slower to finish the main course than any of their hosts. Joe's filet was so wonderful that he whispered to the waiter, please wrap this up so I can take it to my room. Harriman overheard the request, announced it to the guests, who all chuckled, then applauded when he said the kitchen was open twenty-four hours a day.

"The other krieges agreed that the habit of saving something for later was hard to break. I'm still an icebox hoarder.

"That dinner at the embassy was the finest I've ever had, though I've become sort of a gourmet and tried to top it many times. That's fun to try, but I know I never will. You understand, don't you?"

EPILOGUE

IT HAD ALL HAPPENED SO FAST, A CAVALCADE OF HISTORY SPEED-ing away like a stupendous comet to become smaller and smaller in memory, yet as vivid as when it filled the sky. Three years, two months, one week, six days: that was Joe's stint in the army, a sum that trips off his lips with a ready smile. The ten months at war were like a convex mirror, enlarging and distorting in its violence but also because ten months constituted a much larger percentage of his life in his twenties than in his seventies.

Joe's final journey began with passage through the Dardanelles to Port Said, in Egypt, where he transferred to a ship of irony, the HMS *Samaria,* which had carried him over the Atlantic and U-boats to En-gland, where he'd arrived on September 17, 1943, exactly one year after being inducted. This time the destination was Naples, where doctors re-moved the last of his war souvenirs in exchange for two Purple Hearts and GI dog tags.

"Hey, what happened to your other ones?" asked the sergeant who issued them.

"You really want to know?"

For ten days Joe enjoyed Neapolitan cuisine and evidence that the war, though not over, had become almost casual in southern Italy. Daily a German plane flew hundreds of miles to drop propaganda leaflets over Naples. The message was for Americans to surrender now before the Wehrmacht reconquered Italy. Rather than shoot the plane down as they easily could have, the Allies welcomed its visits for their comic effect.

On March 31, 1945, Joe began a long-awaited westward voyage. The next day was at sea and Sunday, the most beautiful Easter of his life. It was celebrated by mass on decks crammed with GIs. The priest asked if anyone had been an altar boy; Joe volunteered and is proud that he could recite every response in Latin.

Naturally during the boring days ahead dice rolled constantly for troops flush with back pay. With three hundred dollars in his pocket Joe started hot. By mid-Atlantic his winnings had reached thirty thousand, so vast a sum that he paid two bodyguards a thousand dollars each to protect it, not just from theft but from himself. "Throw me in the brig if I touch the last ten grand." They almost had to. Joe lost the other twenty thousand.

From the Statler Hotel in Boston Joe called home, heard the voices of his parents and their emotion for nearly an hour. Their every other sentence was "You sure you're all right?" I soon will be, was his answer, because the next day he'd be on a train for Chicago.

There at Fort Sheridan occurred the last macabre event of Joe's war. As the homebound GIs were processed for leave and discharge, they were fed in a mess hall where German POWs were the KPs. Dinner one night was steak, baked potatoes, and all the trimmings. Several ex-krieges went back for seconds but were refused by the Germans. Mêlée and mayhem broke out when someone noticed SS tattoos. Before MPs arrived, a number of Germans were beaten to death with cafeteria trays or stabbed with steak knives. The incident never got into the papers. The war was not yet over, and censorship was still in effect.

Homecoming in Muskegon was in May 1945, the same month as V-E Day. Joe's train arrived at 11:30 A.M., to be met by a score of family, friends, and more kisses than he'd received in his previous twenty-one years. The welcomers proceeded to his parents' house, where dozens of neighbors came by with congratulations, affection, and so many long hugs that Joe had to announce that his shoulders were still a medical problem. The phone never stopped ringing during the reception.

A huge dinner followed. He ate to the point of gorging but secreted some of the leftovers in his bedroom. Untouched during his absence, the room looked just as he'd left it at the end of his last stateside furlough, less than two years ago but a chasm in the past. Yet at that time in 1943 he had premonitionally known that his room would never be the same, and it wasn't. He'd left his youth there. Its symbols were now artifacts.

Concurrent with the hero worship bestowed upon him (which lasted for months), Joe started to point the course for the rest of his life. The postwar period had just begun while the personal consequences of the war, now overwhelmingly pleasant, lingered. Joe was not discharged till November 1945, a medical discharge with a percentage disability, from a hospital in Maywood, Illinois. The army made a pitch to retain him with a commission and assignment to Soviet counterintelligence. His posting would be in Berlin. Joe thought it over seriously but declined because "I didn't think I had any more luck left in Germany."

During those months while hospitalized in Illinois he was invited to homes several times a week, feted on Chicago's Gold Coast, a guest at plays, operas, and even the World Series between Detroit and Chicago, the last time the Cubs were in it.

Postwar reality set in with his courtship of JoAnne Hollowell, who worked at Continental Motors. Hero was a status, not an occupation, and an occupation was the first building block he needed when he married in September 1946. Presiding at his wedding was the priest, Father Stratz, who had conducted Joe's funeral mass in September 1944.

Soon the Beyrles became parents in what would be called the baby boom. A major question was what to do with the GI Bill in which all veterans were eligible to participate. Notre Dame was still a possibility, though with a shattered knee Joe's track scholarship was off the table. Mortician's school seemed to promise a more direct payoff. Security was Joe's need now, never a necessity in his past.

Joe immersed himself in peacetime challenges for which his wartime attributes had little apparent application. His experience receded into a reflection of a Steinbeck title, *Once There Was a War*. Indeed there had been. It was in everyone's immediate memory but rarely evident as the U.S. economy boomed, absorbing the attention and pent-up constructive energy of the veterans.

Gradually and incidentally, further recognition seeped out of war records. It was not till 1953 that Michigan senator Arthur Vandenberg successfully petitioned the army to award Joe the Bronze Star for valor. On V-E Day, however, Joe had his own ceremony of closure.

Muskegon had erected a flagpole with a tablet at the base engraved with the names of some fifty local sons who had lost their lives in World War II. Joe's name was near the top alphabetically. He called up the local Veterans Council and announced his intention to go down to the memorial and remove his name. Regardless of what the city government might think—they'd probably only delay the ceremony bureaucratically—the veterans thought this was a great idea and attended in large numbers for the unpublicized, unauthorized ceremony.

Kriege George Rosie reflects on the Joe who emerged from that ceremony:

"He and I have been friends for many years. At times I wonder why because Joe sure has a mind of his own and no one's going to change it. I've gone head to head with him so I'm confident no one has ever backed him down.

"Last year on the phone he told me one of my best friends in the 101st was an SOB. I said if he said that again I'd hang up. He chuckled and said I had a right to my half-ass opinion. That's Joe—he gives and receives a lot of respect."

The last word goes to Joe as he reflected on removing his name from the tablet of the war dead.

"I had the feeling—it was similar to the near-death experience after my heart bypass—that the occasion had something to say and to listen to. Quiet civilians were all around as I spoke. The long terrible war had just ended in Europe. That we all knew. What I knew which they didn't was how terrible it had been, and I'd seen only samples of the worst.

"Waiting at home the war had been slow for them, but for me it was like a combat jump. Those who were killed disappeared with so many others there was little time to think about them. They are probably greater in death than they were in life, but also many KIAs were better soldiers than many who became vets. It was God's call. What we were doing when I removed my name was remembering without understanding.

"Many people at that ceremony were living with the slow part of remembering. I didn't want that part, didn't feel it was something for me because I'd put it to the touch as the KIAs had. I was living. That's why we were there at the flagpole, to recover my name from those of the dead. I was living and ready to go.

"So I went out fast into the postwar world because I was young, had new responsibilities, and was able to push monsters down into caves. Never went into them till many years later when I felt I could and should."

I thank Joe for taking me there with him, and for what he did.

"Okay," Joe concedes, "I showed some courage in World War II. To tell you my story I needed to see if all these years later I could show it again. That's it."

NOT QUITE. Earlier there had been an unforeseen reunion at the Hubb Recreation Center, where someone asked Joe if he remembered Ed Albers. No, though the name sounded familiar from somewhere. Well, you played against him in basketball, then he went into the Airborne like you. That's him over there shooting pool.

Joe's story joins those of other screaming eagles, recounted in films such as *Saving Private Ryan* and *Band of Brothers*. Presently the 101st is embattled in Afghanistan, as it was in Vietnam and the Gulf War. Readers inspired by this singular fighting force for freedom are invited to contribute to the erection of a monument at Fort Campbell, Kentucky. Tax-deductible donations may be sent to

101ST AIRBORNE DIVISION ASSOCIATION

FT. CAMPBELL MEMORIAL MONUMENT FUND

P.O. BOX 101

BENTONVILLE, OH 45105

PHONE: 937-549-4326

E-MAIL: assn101abn@aol.com

There is a 101st website with this address:

http://www.screamingeagle.org

THOMAS H. TAYLOR, a veteran of the 101st Airborne Division, was awarded the Silver Star, two Bronze Stars for valor, the Purple Heart, and five other decorations for his service in Vietnam. A graduate of St. Albans School and West Point, he left the army in 1968 to take a master's degree in sociology and a Juris Doctor from the University of California, where he won the Carothers Prize for literary composition; in the same year, he was designated a Bread Loaf Fellow at Middlebury College, Vermont. He lives in Washington, D.C.

ABOUT THE TYPE

This book was set in Sabon, a typeface designed by the well-known German typographer Jan Tschichold (1902–74). Sabon's design is based upon the original letter forms of Claude Garamond, and was created specifically to be used for three sources: foundry type for hand composition, Linotype, and Monotype. Tschichold named his typeface for the famous Frankfurt type founder Jacques Sabon, who died in 1585.